HORSE TRIALS

Donated by

Lindsey Johnson

HORSE TRIALS

Guy Wathen

PARTRIDGE PRESS

LONDON · NEW YORK · TORONTO · SYDNEY · AUCKLAND

TRANSWORLD PUBLISHERS LTD
61–63 Uxbridge Road, London W5 5SA

TRANSWORLD PUBLISHERS (AUSTRALIA) PTY LTD
15–23 Helles Avenue, Moorebank, NSW 2170

TRANSWORLD PUBLISHERS (NZ) LTD
Cnr Moselle and Waipareira Aves,
Henderson, Auckland

Published 1989 by Partridge Press
a division of Transworld Publishers Ltd
Copyright © Col. G. L. Wathen 1989

British Library Cataloguing in Publication Data

Wathen, Guy
Horse trials: a complete guide to the world of eventing.
1. Eventing
I. Title
798.2′4

ISBN 1–85225–059–3

Printed in Great Britain by
Butler & Tanner Ltd, Frome and London

CONTENTS

PREFACE

On being asked to write this book my reaction was that there were many people better qualified than I to do so. However, some have already written books with a different aim, while others are still so busy competing that we shall have to wait a while before they can find the time to give us the benefit of their experience.

In the meantime, I hope that this book will help those who are attracted to the idea of taking part in horse trials, and that those who are involved in other ways, whether actively or as spectators, will find something of interest within these covers. It is not intended to be a manual of instruction, but rather to explain the requirements and to point the reader in the right direction. And in any case, no book can replace the services of an instructor, who alone can offer the advice and criticism without which progress is difficult, and the serious competitor should make use of the wealth of talent that is available both from specialist instructors and from past and present riders.

In acknowledging those who have helped me to write this book, I must first mention some of those, some of whom are no longer with us, from whom I learned something about the training of horses and competitive riding. First, I was fortunate to belong to a Regiment which produced horsemen of the calibre of Major General Perry Harding, champion amateur National Hunt rider, Colonel Sir Michael Ansell, father of modern British show jumping, Colonel Alec Scott and Brigadier Arthur Carr, both members of British Olympic teams, and General Sir Cecil ('Monkey') Blacker, outstandingly successful National Hunt rider and past President of the British Equestrian Federation. I learned much, too, from Colonel Paul Rodzianko, a trainer in a class of his own

(as was his language!), but perhaps most of all from Captain Edy Goldman, who came from Switzerland to settle in Cheshire, and who helped so many of us in the days when the sport of horse trials was beginning to develop in this country.

Among those who have put up with my requests for information or photographs, or who have helped in other ways, I must record my thanks to Major Derek Allhusen, Brigadier Lyndon Bolton, Lorna Clarke, Peter Doresa, the late Lt-Col. Stephen Eve, the late Major R. G. Fanshawe, Jane Holderness-Roddam, Bill Henson, Elizabeth Inman and the staff of Burghley Horse Trials, Mandy Jeakins, Robin Leyland, Lt-Col. Bill Lithgow, Captain Mark Phillips, Major Laurence Rook, Nigel Taylor, Major Tim Taylor, Sarah Bligh and the staff of the Horse Trials office at Stoneleigh, Hugh Thomas of British Equestrian Promotions, Bill Thomson, Major Malcolm Wallace, Director General of the British Equestrian Federation, Messrs Weatherbys, and Lt-Col. Frank Weldon, Director of Badminton.

My special thanks are due to Brian Hill, Executive Editor and founder of *Eventing*, who gave me the opportunity to write this book, and who has supplied most of the excellent photographs, and to Janet Hill and the staff of *Eventing* who have put up with endless requests for information.

Finally, I must acknowledge the part played by my wife, Sarah, who, with Mandy Jeakins, agreed to act as a 'guinea pig' for the training photographs, and who informs me that she is not sure whether it is more difficult to live with an author or a horse trials organiser, but has managed to put up with both!

Burley, October 1988   Guy Wathen

FOREWORD

There have been many books on the subject of Horse Trials and Three Day Events, but most of them have dealt with particular aspects of the competition – dressage or cross country for example. Few have covered the subject as comprehensively as this.

It starts by tracing the history and development of the sport from its origins on the continent of Europe and its introduction to the Olympic Games, with special reference to the extraordinary story of the 1936 Olympics in Berlin. Having paid tribute to the influence of foxhunting in Great Britain, both on the success of British riders and on the overseas demand for British horses, the author traces the development of the sport in this country up to the present day.

The core of the book aims to assist those riders who, having perhaps seen the thrills of Badminton or Burghley on television, would like to have a crack at this most demanding and satisfying of equestrian sports. The reader is taken step by step through the process of finding and buying a suitable horse, his elementary training in dressage, show jumping and cross country, his first official Horse Trial, and on to participation in Three Day Events. As the author himself points out, the aim is not so much to instruct as to point the ambitious rider in the right direction, and to encourage him to seek assistance from a knowledgeable helper or trainer.

Finally there is a look at the Horse Trials scene as it is today, together with a record of British success in international competition.

From the active participant, whether as rider, helper or official, to the armchair television viewer, there should be something here of interest to everyone.

R J H MEADE OBE
President, British Equestrian Federation

Part

1

THE SPORT OF HORSE TRIALS

CHAPTER 1

The background and history of the sport

Today's champion ● 'Eventing', getting the name right ● The origins of cross-country riding in England ● The hunting field ● The Army ● Early efforts ● The continent of Europe ● Schooling as an end in itself ● The requirements of the cavalry charger ● A competition to test him ● Early Olympics Berlin 1936 ● 1946: a new start ● London 1948 ● The Three Day Event at Aldershot ● The German influence ● Enter the 10th Duke of Beaufort

It is December 1986, and the evening television audience eagerly awaits the announcement of the Sports Personality of the Year. Among the contenders is Virginia Leng, and to many of those watching, and to a few of those in the studio audience, both the name and the sport, Horse Trials, are unfamiliar. In the equestrian world, racing they know about as a major television sport; show jumping is familiar through the televising of Wembley, Birmingham and Olympia, as well as the big outdoor arena at Hickstead. But 'Horse Trials', popularly known as 'Eventing' – what are they, and what has Ginnie Leng done to achieve this recognition?

Well, in 1986, amongst other successes, she had won the Individual and Team Gold Medals at the World Championships at Gawlor in Australia in May, the International Three Day Event at Le Touquet, France, in June, the British National Horse Trials Championships at Gatcombe Park in August, the Burghley Three Day Event (for the fourth successive time) in September, and, to round off the season, the International Three Day Event at Bialy Bor in Poland. Not a bad year's work!

And previously she had won Team Silver and Individual Bronze Medals at the 1984 Olympic Games in Los Angeles, and in 1985 Team and Individual Gold Medals at the European Championships at Burghley, and the trophy that many top riders consider more important than anything else apart from the Olympic Games – Badminton.

Ah! Badminton. At least most people know that, besides referring to the game played on a sort of tennis court with racquets and a shuttlecock, Badminton features on our television screens during a couple of days in May each year, when horses and riders hurtle round a course of terrifying obstacles, and with any luck they will see some spectacular falls, almost certainly a certain amount of splashing about in the lake, and possibly a glimpse of the Royal Family as well.

So what is this most demanding of all equestrian sports all about? What is it that attracts the owners and riders of five thousand horses, that persuades hordes of voluntary workers to devote their time to organising events throughout the country, and that can draw over 160,000 people to Badminton on the Cross-

Country day alone? Certainly the owners and riders cannot be in it for the prize money, for the ratio of prize money to expenses is far too low, and the risks of injury to horse and rider too great for that to be a draw. Not only is it expensive to compete, it is also costly to organise, and probably requires a higher ratio of officials to competitors than most other sports.

Even the name of the sport is confusing. The official name is 'Horse Trials', but this gives no clue to the standard or duration of the competition, which may last for one, two, or three days. The term 'Three Day Event' has since the earliest days of the sport in this country been used to describe competitions of that length, but in fact a Three Day Event can last four days, and the six Three Day Events held in 1986 were equally divided between those that called themselves Three Day Events and those that preferred the term 'Horse Trials'. Those in the know, which includes riders, owners, camp followers, organisers and representatives of the media, seldom use either expression and universally refer to the sport as 'Eventing'. This is all somewhat confusing to the outsider.

There are several sports being played around the world today, both by teams and by individuals, that originated in the United Kingdom or in what used to be the British Empire, and which we introduced to other countries. In many cases our erstwhile pupils now outplay us, but in two of the major equestrian sports the reverse is true. Both Show Jumping and the Three Day Event were imported into this country from the continent of Europe, yet we have in recent years more than held our own in both sports.

The origins of equestrian sport in this country lay in the hunting field. The hunting of four-footed game by packs of hounds controlled by men on horseback and viewed by mounted followers goes far back into history.

Foxhunting in England dates back to the seventeenth century, but the so-called Golden Age of foxhunting dawned in the 1750s, when the legendary Hugo Meynell began to exploit the possibilities of the sport to be had from galloping across the rolling grasslands of the Midland shires, and especially Leicestershire. It continued through the nineteenth century and on, with the interruption of the First World War, to the outbreak of the Second World War in 1939. So it was that in the 1930s the height of most English riders' ambition was to gallop across the grass of Leicestershire, jumping its formidable fences and ditches. For those with a more competitive streak, the sport of steeplechasing had seen its origins in the nineteenth century, when success in those early races owed as much to a man's eye for the country as to the speed and jumping ability of his horse. Eventually that sport evolved into National Hunt racing as we know it today, while for the true amateur – another term that has had to be redefined in the light of modern sporting practice – there were the Point-to-Point races held by each hunt at the end of the hunting season.

Thus, the tradition of cross country riding became firmly entrenched in England as in no other country other than Ireland, where it was introduced from this country. For no other countries could offer the three essentials for cross country sport – rolling grasslands, relatively small enclosures with imposing natural hedges, and coverts of manageable size. The English were generally taught to ride either by their fathers, or by members of their fathers' establishments. The only organised instruction was provided by the Army, at the Cavalry School at Weedon in Northamptonshire. But formal instruction at Weedon, though based on the concept of 'a firm seat', was dictated by the requirements of cavalry tactics, and was otherwise heavily slanted towards cross country riding. Indeed, not only were officers encouraged to hunt, but it was virtually mandatory, since it improved an officer's horsemanship, tested his courage, and developed that essential in an active-service cavalry officer, an eye for the country. Thus the hunts adjacent to Weedon, notably the Pytchley and the Grafton, became extensions to the Weedon training areas, while those on leave ventured further afield to the Fernie, the Quorn, the Cottesmore and the Belvoir.

Competitive riding did not feature highly in the School's programme, though British officers did venture abroad occasionally to compete against the officers of other nations. Thus, in the 1924 Olympic Games in Paris, Major (later Brigadier) P. E. Bowden-Smith was fourth in the Show Jumping, while Captain (later Major-General) B. de Fontblanque came sixth in the Three Day Event. On the Continent, on the other hand, things were very different. Without the impetus or the relaxation of hunting, equitation developed along different lines. The training of the horse, which in England was regarded as the means to the end of riding it across country or on the parade ground, became an end in itself. Moreover, especially in Central and Eastern Europe, where the winters were generally more severe than in England, such training could for much of the year only be carried out indoors.

The basic concept and methods of training the young horse may not have been very different here in England or on the Continent. 'Schooling', as it was called here, and 'Dressage', which the French dictionary defines as, among other things, 'Training (of animals); breaking (of horses)', both had the object of making the horse an obedient and pleasurable ride. But whereas the British officer, and even more so his civilian counterpart, progressed as soon as possible to the hunting field, the continental rider continued his horse's schooling for much longer, and eventually dressage became an end in itself.

As with any sporting activity, standards improved, the horse was schooled to new heights, new movements were developed, and at the highest level horses progressed beyond the realms of mere 'Dressage' or 'Schooling' to what became known as 'Haute Ecole'. The literal translation of this term is 'High School', but it is not one that passes easily into British equestrian vocabulary, and in any case it is generally accepted that 'Haute Ecole' includes artificial movements which the horse will not perform naturally, so it does not feature in the training of the competition horse. This development of classical riding to its highest level can be seen today at the Spanish Riding School in Vienna and in the Cadre Noir at Saumur, France, and both these schools have shown their skills to audiences throughout the world, including those at the London international shows.

Similarly, whereas in England the main object of teaching the horse to jump was to enable it to carry its rider safely across the hunting field, in Europe, since there was little hunting, it was natural that jumping also should have become an end in itself. Hence show jumping flourished as a sport on the Continent long before it became accepted in this country; it is easy to understand how after several months spent in the indoor manege the officers of the European cavalry schools began to devise a form of competition that reflected the requirements of the cavalry charger, as the officer's mount was called.

What then was required of the cavalry charger? In order to understand the original concept of the Three Day Event it is necessary (and interesting) to reflect upon the various roles of the cavalry before the advent of mechanisation. First there was the ceremonial role; the officer's charger must be steady on parade, calm, obedient and sufficiently well schooled to perform the various parade-ground manoeuvres. Then, as far as active service was concerned, the cavalry had four main roles. They had to be fit enough to undertake the long marches that the European armies carried out – and some of the distances covered were prodigious. Having arrived in the area of operations, the next task was to acquire information as to the exact whereabouts and dispositions of the enemy; this required swift movement whilst avoiding decisive engagement. Once battle had been joined by the main force, the particular contribution of the cavalry was to deliver the final blow in the form of the cavalry charge; then, with the enemy in disarray, came the pursuit. But that was far from the end of the matter, for a battle won was but one phase in a campaign, and so the horse had still to be fit enough to continue in service without respite.

Olympic Games, Berlin, 1936

Bowie Knife	Bob Clive	Blue Steel
Capt. R. G. Fanshawe	Capt. A. B. J. Scott	Lt. E. D. Howard-Vyse
(16/5th Lancers)	(5th Royal Inniskilling Dragoon Guards)	(Royal Artillery)

Thus, cavalry officers in Europe devised a form of competition to test both the rider and his horse, and to provide some diversion when years of peace provided no other challenge. In England, cavalry officers were finding this in the hunting field. As Jorrocks was to proclaim, 'Hunting is the image of war, without the guilt and only twenty-five per cent of the danger.' The early competitions on the Continent varied considerably, but the first test usually consisted of a demonstration of basic schooling – dressage. The second sought to test the horse's speed, stamina and endurance, together with his cross country ability. And the third sought

to show that after his exertions the horse was still sound and fit enough to continue in service and to respond to whatever demands might be placed upon him. So there emerged a competition which took place over three days: dressage on the first, cross country, speed and endurance on the second, and a relatively simple jumping test on the third. It is then interesting to note that our European cousins of those days seemed as uncertain as we ourselves as to how this new form of competition might best be described, for they resorted to

Berlin 1936. On the Cross Country course was the infamous Pond, with the surface of the water covered in green slime

an English term and called it 'The Military'.

In 1912 the first equestrian events were included in the Olympic Games in Stockholm, and a British team took part, but since they failed to complete the competition the archives are noticeably reticent about what actually happened. 1924 proved more encouraging, and in 1936, by which time the format of the Three Day Event had been more or less settled, the British team won their first medal in Berlin. It is interesting to recall what happened.

The British team, all members of the staff of the Cavalry School at Weedon, consisted of Captain Dick Fanshawe, Captain Alec Scott and Captain Ted Howard-Vyse, with Major Bowden-Smith as *Chef d'Equipe* (Team Captain). Fanshawe was the third rider to start, and on the second day's Cross Country course there was the infamous Pond, with the surface of the water covered in green slime, so that the early horses could not see the water. Jumping boldly into it, Fanshawe and his horse were completely submerged, and on resurfacing Bowie Knife galloped off into the distance, leaving his rider covered in slime and with his boots full of water.

Berlin 1936. The early horses cannot see the water of the slime-covered Pond

Now in those days there were two significant differences in the rules as compared with today. First, no outside assistance of any kind was permitted, not even the catching of a loose horse or help with remounting; second, there was no time limit. Since all three team members had to finish, Fanshawe set off after his horse, which he eventually found in a farmyard a couple of miles away. Returning to the Pond, he then completed the course, no mean feat, as anyone who has had the misfortune to suffer submersion in the lake at Badminton will testify.

Bowden-Smith then went to the Pond, and he observed that, though the majority of foreign competitors also fell, owing to the depth of the water, the home team all jumped it on the extreme left, and with the exception of one member who veered to the right on landing, negotiated it successfully. He then discovered that in the left-hand corner there was a ramp about a couple of metres wide where the water was quite shallow! He also observed that the spectators were now helping to catch loose horses. A protest was duly made, but it was overruled on the grounds that it had been incorrectly lodged. None the less, Fanshawe's determination to finish had brought us the Bronze Medal, since only three teams managed to complete the competition, the others being the Germans and the Poles, who took the Gold and Silver Medals respectively.

Today, of course, not only is the depth of the water restricted by the rules, but a Technical Delegate is appointed to ensure that the obstacles are constructed in accordance with the regulations, the Ground Jury will check everything before the course is opened for inspection by the competitors, and most riders, and certainly one from each team, will don suitable footwear in order to wade into the water and thoroughly test the landing. Moreover, assistance is now allowed with catching a loose horse and helping a rider to remount,

Berlin 1936. Only three teams managed to complete the competition. Capt. Scott and Bob Clive in the Show Jumping

while there is also a time limit for the completion of each phase of the Cross Country.

This same year that saw the first British equestrian medal at the Olympic Games also saw the beginning of the end of the British cavalry, for it was in 1936 that the nettle of mechanisation was finally grasped by that most conservative arm of the British Army. In World War II horsed units managed to retain a mounted role in the Middle East until 1942, but henceforth there would no longer be a reservoir of horses and riders from which competitors could be drawn. 1945 saw a Europe in devastation and a situation that was hardly conducive to the resumption of equestrian sport. But the Olympic Games that had originally been scheduled to take place in London in 1940 were rescheduled for 1948, and just before the closing ceremony in Wembley Stadium the British Show Jumping Team initiated a long list of British post-war equestrian successes by taking the Bronze Medal.

At Aldershot, venue for the Three Day Event, we fared less well. With no similar competitions in this country upon which to base the selection of a team, and no cavalry school or national equestrian centre on which to base the training, it was a wonder that we could produce a team at all. That we could do so, in both the Show Jumping and the Three Day Event, was largely due to the Army. Of the six team members, all of whom had to count towards the team score, five were serving Army officers, and the sixth was someone who had come second in the 1929 Grand National and who was to dominate the Show Jumping scene for most of the next decade – Lt-Col. (now Sir) Harry Llewellyn. But another reason for our ability to produce teams was the help that we received from a most unlikely quarter – Germany.

Although the horse played very little part in the British Army in the Second World War, he continued to have a significant role in the

German Army right to the end. Partly because of the acute shortage of oil, considerable use was made of horse transport, a fact that amazed the British and U.S. armies as they swept through northern France in the summer of 1944. In Germany the breeding of horses had been well organised, with each region having its official stud, and when hostilities ended it was in these studs that the occupying forces found not only the products of the breeding programme but also the remaining horses of the national equestrian teams that had been preserved at these centres. British officers took over these German horses and later started to use them for competitions, and these formed the basis of our Show Jumping

teams for the first few years after the War. Not only that, but they also employed German instructors, and indeed the chief Dressage instructor for the Three Day Event team in training at Aldershot was a German general whom Lt-Col. Alec Scott of our 1936 Berlin team had rehabilitated on his release from a prisoner-of-war camp.

In the Aldershot Three Day Event our team of Brig. Lyndon Bolton, Lt-Col. Duggie Stewart and Maj. Peter Borwick failed to complete the competition owing to the lameness of Col. Stewart's horse after the Steeplechase, but their performance, and the concept of the whole event, had fired the imagination and the ambition of those connected with British equestrian sport. Among these was the 10th Duke of Beaufort.

Olympic Games, London, 1948

Dark Seal			Sylvester		The Abbott
Lt-Col. D. N. Stewart			Brig. L. Bolton		Maj. P. Borwick
(Royal Scots Greys)					(Royal Scots Greys)

CHAPTER 2

The development of the sport in Great Britain

The Duke of Beaufort • The first Badminton • The Combined Training Committee
• 1952 Helsinki Olympics • The Golden Age of British Eventing
• International successes to 1988 • The development of Horse Trials at home
• The Horse Trials Committee • The Horse Trials Group • The Rule Book
• Spring and Autumn seasons • One Day Horse Trials • Classes;
Novice, Intermediate and Advanced • Championships • Two Day Horse Trials
• The Three Day Event • The F.E.I. and the B.E.F. • The International
calendar • Badminton

The 10th Duke of Beaufort was the very epitome of the British Master of Foxhounds. He had hunted his own pack of beagles from an early age and was now Master of a six-days-a-week pack of hounds; in addition he held the post of Master of the Horse to His Majesty King George VI, whose mother, Queen Mary, had spent much of the War at Badminton. Inspired by what he saw at Aldershot, and recognising the lack of competitive experience and training facilities that had handicapped the British team, he offered to run a Three Day Event at Badminton, mainly with a view to producing a better prepared team for the next Olympic Games at Helsinki in 1952.

So in April 1949, the sport of Eventing was launched in this country, with twenty-two competitors, a handful of helpful volunteers, and spectators who were able to wander freely round the course and picnic beside the obstacles more or less where they chose. Today, nearly forty years later, Badminton remains the one event in the world that most riders would like to win. But Badminton on its own was not going to promote successful British participation in international events. Of those twenty-two competitors, only Brigadier Lyndon Bolton, who had competed in the Olympic event at Aldershot, had had any previous experience of this type of competition, and clearly there was a need for a stepping-stone towards this most demanding test. In 1951 the first One Day Event was held, and in 1952 the Combined Training Committee of the British Horse Society was formed in order to control these new competitions, which consisted of a Dressage test, followed by a Show Jumping test, and a Cross Country course of between $1\frac{1}{2}$ and 2 miles.

The interest of British riders had been aroused, and here it seemed was a competition admirably suited to the talents of those riders and horses whose education and experience had been acquired in the hunting field. The Dressage was regarded as a drawback, but since the rules of the Three Day Event stipulated that the second day's Cross Country test should exert an influence on the whole compeition equal to 75% of the whole, this was not thought to be too great a handicap. By 1952, sufficient progress had been made for the British team at the Helsinki Olympics to have hopes of improving on the Bronze Medal won in Berlin. The 'Old Guard' of Weedon-trained military riders had been succeeded by a new breed, and although the Army was to continue for several years to produce its quota of team members, their success was mainly due to their own dedication and effort.

The British Team in Helsinki consisted of Reg Hindley, whose equestrian background lay in hunting and point-to-pointing, Bertie Hill, another recruit from racing and point-to-pointing, and Maj. Laurence Rook of the Royal Horse Guards, who had benefited from four years of jumping in Germany before turning to eventing. The team having done better than anyone expected in the first day's Dressage, a Silver Medal looked a distinct possibility; as Laurence Rook, our last rider to

Team Gold Medal at the European Championships, Windsor, 1955

Kilbarry	Countryman	Starlight
Lt-Col. F. W. C. Weldon	A. E. Hill	Maj. A. L. Rook
		(Mrs. J. R. Baker)

start, neared the end of the Cross Country even a Gold Medal was not out of the question. But as he and Starlight approached the end of the course and sped round a bend on a track skirting a cornfield, a foot slipped into a small drainage ditch and they were on the ground. No penalties were incurred, and they were quickly reunited, but Laurence had been concussed in the fall, a turning flag was missed, and with only three riders in the team, once again we were eliminated.

1953, however, saw the start of what might justly be termed the Golden Age of British Eventing. At Badminton, Laurence Rook and Starlight won the Individual European Championship and our team took the team title, thanks in no small way to the efforts of a newcomer, Maj. Frank Weldon of the King's Troop, Royal Horse Artillery, who finished second on Kilbarry. The combination of Hill, Rook and Weldon went on to take a clean sweep of the European Championships in

Team Gold Medal at the Olympic Games, Stockholm, 1956

Wild Venture	Countryman	Kilbarry
Maj. A. L. Rook	A. E. Hill	Lt-Col. F. W. C. Weldon
(Royal Horse Guards)	(H.M. the Queen)	(Royal Horse Artillery)
(E. E. Marsh)		

Basle, Switzerland, in 1954, to retain the title again at Windsor in 1955, and to win the Olympic Team Gold Medal in Stockholm in 1956, where Frank Weldon won the Bronze. (In 1955 H.M. the Queen had invited the European Championships to be held at Windsor, and because of quarantine regulations for horses the 1956 Olympic equestrian events were held in Stockholm instead of Melbourne, Australia.)

Meanwhile a second Three Day Event had been added to the Horse Trials calendar. Harewood in Yorkshire, home of the Earl of Harewood and H.R.H. the Princess Royal, daughter of H.M. King George V and aunt of our present Queen, became the site of the Autumn Three Day Event from 1953 until the European Championships of 1959, when after a year's gap the autumn event was moved to its present home at Burghley. In 1959 Frank Weldon took the Silver Medal on Samuel Johnson, with Derek Allhusen third on Lochinvar, and the British Team was only deprived of the Gold Medal by the disastrously slow round in the final day's Show Jumping by the third member of the team, the fourth having been forced to retire after a fall on the Cross Country.

The catalogue of British successes continued. In the Olympic Games, there were Team Gold medals in Mexico (1968) and Munich (1972), and Silver Medals in Los Angeles (1984) and in Seoul (1988). The Individual Gold went to Richard Meade in Munich, the Bronze to Virginia Holgate (now Leng) in Los Angeles and Silver and Bronze to Ian Stark and Virginia Leng respectively in Seoul. In World Championships, the British Team won at Punchestown (1970), Luhmuhlen, Germany, (1982), and Gawlor, Australia, (1986), and there were Individual Gold Medals for Mary Gordon-Watson in 1970, for Lucinda Green in 1982 and for Virginia Leng in 1986. In the European Championships, Team Gold

Medals were won in Copenhagen (1957), Punchestown (1967), Haras du Pin, France (1969), Burghley (1971, 1977 and 1985), Horsens, Denmark (1981), and Luhmuhlen (1987). Individual Gold Medals went to Rachel Bayliss at Frauenfeld, Germany, in 1983, and to Virginia Leng at Burghley in 1985 and at Luhmuhlen in 1987. A fairly impressive record!

But international success does not come without a firm competitive base at home. In the 1988 Horse Trials fixture list there were 8 Three Day Events, 7 Two Day Events and 135 One Day Horse Trials. But since one day events, in which a horse completes all three tests in one day, normally hold sufficient classes to run on two or even three days, there were in fact 226 days of competition in the calendar. Taking part in these events were just under 5,000 horses. No other country can match this base, and those other nations that are successful achieve their success largely through a more highly organised national training system in which a 'squad' is developed into a team for international events and championships.

We have already referred to the confusion that exists in the minds of the public with regard to the name by which the sport is known. Officially the name of the sport is 'Horse Trials'; it is governed and regulated in this country by the Horse Trials Committee of the British Horse Society, and in order to compete in Horse Trials, all riders and owners of horses must be members of the Society and of the Horse Trials Group. In the offices at the British Equestrian Centre at Stoneleigh, Warwickshire, a Director of Horse Trials and a permanent staff administer the sport in accordance with the directives of the Committee. This Committee consists of twelve members, half elected by the membership and half appointed by the Committee itself. This apparently undemocratic procedure in fact enables the membership to elect those whom they wish to represent them – usually senior current competitors – while the Committee can appoint people of experience (and, hopefully, wisdom!), who tend to represent the organisational side or to have knowledge of the international scene. There are then seven sub-committees which deal with Finance, Rules, Events (and fixture lists), Publicity, and the three selection committees for Seniors, Young Riders and Juniors.

The Horse Trials year really ends and begins with the annual Group Conference which is normally held at the end of October. Here the past season is summarised, the awards for leading riders and horses are presented, the provisional fixture list for the next season is issued, changes to the rules are notified, and members have a chance to raise matters which they would like the Committee to consider. There are also several regional meetings during the year in various parts of the country to enable members to discuss matters in greater detail. The 'bible' of the sport is the Official Rule Book which is republished each year, together with the Omnibus Schedule, which contains the schedules for all events and is published three times a year. Group bulletins

Team Gold Medal at the Olympic Games, Mexico, 1968

Lochinvar		Cornishman V	The Poacher
Maj. D. Allhusen	Our Nobby	Richard Meade	Sgt Ben Jones
(Silver Medal)	Jane Bullen	(Miss M. Gordon-Watson)	(M. J. Whiteley)

are issued to members three times a year in order to keep them up-to-date with news and developments.

The official Horse Trials year is divided into Spring and Autumn seasons, and there used to be a break in mid-summer for a couple of months or so between the two. But the demand by competitors for events has been so great that there is now a break of only a couple of weeks in June between the two seasons, which are now only really relevant for qualification purposes. The Omnibus Schedules, which used to be published twice a year, are now produced three times a year, covering the Spring, Summer and Autumn events. Thus one great advantage that Horse Trials participants have over their Show Jumping counterparts is that they do not have to write for individual schedules. The Spring season usually opens in the first week in March, though often the winter weather does its best to have a final fling. It continues through to the middle of June, and the Autumn season opens two weeks later and closes in the middle of October.

The term 'Horse Trials' covers One, Two and Three Day Events, but to add to the confusion of the uninitiated, One Day Events often cover two, sometimes even three, days, and a Three Day Event usually involves four days of competition and will actually involve the competitors for five days at the competition site. The title of a Three Day Event refers to the fact that the competition consists of three tests which are held on three separate days – Dressage on the first, Cross Country on the second, and Show Jumping on the third. But the Dressage test takes approximately ten minutes for each horse, so that if there is a large entry, some competitors will have to do their Dressage on one day and the remainder on the second, with all doing their Cross Country on the third and their Show Jumping on the fourth and final day.

At a One Day Horse Trial, competitors are required to do a Dressage test, a Show Jumping test, and Cross Country course of between 1 and $2\frac{1}{2}$ miles, normally in that order. Classes are divided into Novice, Intermediate and Advanced, and the rules lay down the standard of each separate test. A One Day Horse Trial may, however, run Novice classes on one day and Intermediate and Advanced on the second. Sometimes, in order to accommodate a large entry, some competitors, normally those living near the event, will have to do their Dressage, and perhaps their Show Jumping, on the day before the advertised first day, mainly so that the Cross Country test can be started in the morning without having to wait for the early competitors to complete their Dressage and Show Jumping. It still remains a One Day Horse Trial – all a bit confusing until one gets used to it.

The expressions 'Novice', 'Intermediate' and 'Advanced' refer to the classes, and each class will normally be divided into a number of sections of up to forty starters. Horses, on the other hand, are graded III, II or I according to the number of points that they have accumulated for winning or being placed in competitions, and the schedule will show which grades are allowed to enter in each class. But since not all events can satisfy the requirements for an Advanced Cross Country course, and since riders may not always want to test their best horses at Advanced level, there is also an Open Intermediate class, run over the Intermediate course and open to all grades of horse. There are also classes for Young Riders (aged 19 to 21) and Juniors (15 to 18).

The first step on the Eventing ladder is therefore the Novice One Day Horse Trial. (1987 saw the introduction of Pre-Novice classes for unregistered horses and those who have not earned any points, but there are as yet few of them and most will have to start their careers in Novice classes.) The Dressage test is very simple, takes only four minutes to execute, and includes nothing that should not be part of the preliminary schooling of any riding horse, whether it is to be used for hacking, hunting or for competitions. This is followed by a not very difficult Show Jumping course of up to ten obstacles, which again should not prove too demanding for anyone who has taken the trouble to teach his horse to jump and has introduced him to jumping at small local shows. Then comes the Cross Country with between sixteen and twenty obstacles over a distance of between 1 and $1\frac{1}{4}$ miles, and it is here that the variety between events is found.

The rules govern clearly the dimensions of the obstacles, and the maximum height is only 1.05 metres. But the degree of difficulty of an obstacle lies as much in its setting and in the way in which it is built as in its actual size. Obstacles with a difficult approach, those sited on uphill or downhill slopes, and those requiring accuracy in jumping, for example, are more difficult than straightforward fences set on level ground. All courses have to be passed as fair and complying with the rules by a British Horse Society Steward appointed by the Horse Trials Committee. But some Novice courses include hills which make the whole test considerably stiffer, while others have water obstacles and ditches. Some consist mainly of obstacles set in natural hedgerows, which are easier to jump than those 'island' fences set in the middle of a park or field where a horse can see a way round them. So competitors learn from experience which are the easier and which the more testing courses, and will enter according to the capabilities and experience of their horses.

Intermediate classes take the competitor a stage further forward, with a more demanding Dressage test, a slightly stiffer Show Jumping course, and a longer and more difficult Cross Country. The ultimate test at a One Day Event is the Advanced class, an altogether more serious test for horse and rider, which also constitutes an important part of the quali-

fications that are required before horse or rider can take part in the highest grade of Three Day Event such as Badminton or Burghley. All three classes have their own championships in the autumn, and in the case of Novice and Intermediate there are Regional Finals as an additional stepping-stone to the championships. For the Advanced class there are the British Open Championships, held since 1986 at Gatcombe Park near Stroud in Gloucestershire, home of H.R.H. the Princess Royal and Captain Mark Phillips. Though still a One Day Horse Trial, the Open Championships differ from most other One Day Events in that the Dressage is normally held on the first day, the Show Jumping on the morning of the second, and the Cross Country in the afternoon. This enables competitors in the Show Jumping to run in the reverse order of merit according to their scores in the Dressage, and in the Cross Country in the reverse order of merit after the first two tests. This can lead to a most exciting climax for spectators, though it does also place before the leading riders the temptation to drive their horses round the Cross Country harder than they would in a Three Day Event, where they have to conserve the horse's energy for the third day's jumping test.

The next step towards the ultimate goal of the Three Day Event is the Two Day Horse Trial at Novice or Intermediate level, whose object is to introduce riders to the added complications of the second day, which includes two stretches of roads and tracks, a short steeplechase, and a slightly longer Cross Country course. It differs from the Three Day Event in that the Show Jumping follows the Dressage on the first day, with the Cross Country, now called the Speed, Endurance and Cross Country test, on the second. Lastly, before moving on to the Three Day Event, Scotland and Wales have their own championships, Scotland with Open and Novice classes and Wales with a Two Day Event.

The ultimate goal, then, is the Three Day Event. If it is a National event it will be run under the Rules for Official Horse Trials issued by the Horse Trials Committee and the Rules for Three Day Events produced by the F.E.I. (Fédération Equestre Internationale), the governing body for world equestrian sport. Between the F.E.I. and the British Horse Society is another body, the British Equestrian Federation, whose task is to co-ordinate the activities of the British Horse Society (and its competitive committees such as the Horse Trials Committee) and the British Show Jumping Association, and to deal with the F.E.I. on all international aspects of equestrian sport, excluding racing and polo.

Three Day Events are held at all levels from Novice to Advanced, while Badminton and Burghley are graded as Championship events. These last two, together with Bramham, are International events, which are now graded by the F.E.I. on a star system according to their degree of difficulty; thus, in 1987 Badminton and Burghley rated three stars, and Bramham and Chatsworth two (Chatsworth has now been removed from the calendar). These are individual events, shown in the F.E.I. calendar as a C.C.I. (Concours Complet International). There is also each year one C.C.I.O (Concours Complet International Officiel) which is a team event with both team and individual classification. Every four years come the Olympic Games, and in the middle year of the four-year Olympic cycle the World Championships are held; in the other two years there are Continental, in our case European, Championships.

The highlight of the British Eventing year is Badminton, which is generally acknowledged to be the world's most prestigious event. It is perhaps unfortunate, therefore, that it comes so early in the calendar, normally in mid-April, since this often makes it difficult for competitors to prepare their horses, and it precludes the holding at Badminton of World or European Championships. But, as any visitor will appreciate, the effect upon the agricultural operations of the estate of running an event of that size is considerable even when blessed by good weather; in a wet year, the parking of coaches and cars, and the many thousands of pedestrians, can leave the park looking like the battlefields of the Somme, and to hold the event later in the year would seriously damage the estate's primary function of producing hay crops and providing grazing. In fact, in 1988 Badminton was held in May, and if this proves successful it will go some way towards alleviating the problem. But whatever the weather, Badminton remains the 'Mecca' of world eventing.

European Champions, 1987.

Virginia Leng   (Night Cap)
Rachel Hunt   (Aloaf)
Lucinda Green   (Shannagh)
Ian Stark   (Sir Wattie)

PREPARING TO TAKE PART

CHAPTER 3

Finding a horse

The Three Day Event type • The requirements • Temperament • Presence • Movement • Conformation • Stamina • Jumping ability • Courage • Riders' views • 'An eye for a horse' • Where to look • Advertisements • Geldings or mares • Thoroughbreds or less • Telephone enquiries • A preliminary selection

There is probably no other equestrian sport for which it is so important to choose the right type of horse, nor one for which it is so difficult to make the right choice. Nor does examination of the successful horses of the past prove particularly helpful. At one end of the scale Lt-Col. Frank Weldon's Kilbarry, for example, was 17 hands, a true thoroughbred who would not have looked out of place in the paddock at Cheltenham, and the mainstay of our teams in the golden days of the mid-1950s, when he helped Great Britain to win an Olympic Gold medal and three European Championships. A real Three Day Event type if ever there was one.

At the other end of the scale, there was Our Nobby, a mere 15 hands, who started life in the hands of the R.S.P.C.A. and was then fortunate enough to come into the possession of Jane Bullen, who rode him in Beaufort Pony Club teams, went on to win Badminton in 1967, and helped the British team to win a Gold Medal in the Mexico Olympics in 1968. But perhaps the strangest-looking Three Day Event winner was Lorna Clarke's Popadom. As Lorna Sutherland, she bought this 15.3 skewbald, who was causing his owner insoluble problems, won Burghley with him in 1969 and finished 12th in the World Championships of 1970 over the (then) notorious Punchestown course in Ireland.

So just what sort of horse are we looking for? Let us remember first of all just what we are going to ask our Three Day Eventer to do, for it is the real Three Day Event horse that we are trying to find, not just the horse that can be successful in the less demanding area of One Day Horse Trials. On the first day he must perform the Dressage test, and although according to the rules the relative importance of the three tests of the Three Day Event should ensure that the true Cross Country horse will normally come through to win, in practice today's top riders are finding more and more that unless they can achieve a high placing in the Dressage, they have little hope of retrieving the situation on the Cross Country. Only if the weather conditions make the Cross Country course significantly more difficult than the organisers intended can a rider do what Rachel Hunt did with Piglet in the almost disastrously wet Badminton of 1986; lying 47th after the Dressage, they pulled themselves up into 2nd place after the Cross Country, and maintained this position to the end.

Lt-Col. Frank Weldon's Kilbarry would not have looked out of place in the paddock at Cheltenham

The Three Day Event Dressage test is not particularly demanding, but apart from the basic paces it does require circles at the medium trot, half-passes, extended trot, serpentines at the canter, extended canter, a rein-back, and three periods of immobility at the halt. It is designed specifically for the Three Day Event horse, but does contain certain movements that the super-fit thoroughbred, ready to gallop and jump for his life on the second day, may find quite difficult to perform smoothly and without fuss. It is also quite long; it takes about eight minutes to complete – rather a long time in which to maintain his attention. Most of our leading riders have memories of a horse which has ruined an otherwise excellent chance by 'boiling over' in the Dressage test. (Starlight XV, who had won the European Championships at Badminton in 1953 with Major Laurence Rook, and went on to take Team Gold Medals in the 1954 and 1955 Championships, 'exploded' and jumped out of the Dressage arena at Badminton in 1956!) An important requirement for the Dressage test is therefore temperament.

Now in theory this test is a test of schooling as exemplified by performance, and therefore it should not matter greatly whether the horse is particularly good-looking or rather ordinary, or whether he has brilliant natural paces or those that are merely satisfactory. But Dressage judges are only human (in spite of what some competitors think!), and they tend to enjoy a pleasing performance by a good-looking horse more than a technically correct test performed by an ugly horse, and the movements of the test will be more pleasing to watch and will therefore probably gain higher marks if the horse naturally moves well. But care should be taken not to fall into the trap of selecting the horse with 'flashy' movement; the horse with an extravagant action is not likely to cover the ground economically on the Steeplechase and the Cross Country, and the

horse that flashes his toe in the extended movements may look impressive to the uninitiated, but is unlikely to impress the Dressage judges, who are looking for impulsion marked by engagement of the hind legs; the 'daisy cutter' may look impressive in the show ring, but is not the type that we should be looking for as a three day eventer.

So the next two qualities that we are looking for are 'presence', rather than sheer good looks, and good, but not extravagant movement. By 'presence' we mean that difficult-to-define air of superiority on the part of the horse that gains our attention and draws our gaze to him rather than to others.

For the second day's Speed, Endurance and Cross Country test, which at the highest level may extend to a total of 31,230 metres, or nearly 20 miles, and which includes a Steeplechase and a course of fairly severe Cross Country obstacles, a number of qualities are required, and it is not easy to place them in strict order of importance. Starting at the bottom – of the horse, not the list of priorities – he must have the feet and limbs to enable him to stand up to the stresses and strains of this test and to remain sound thereafter – and to continue to do this for several seasons. He must have stamina, which requires adequate room for heart and lungs, and clearly he must have the ability to jump. How much ability we expect will depend upon the age and experience of the horse, but even in the young unbroken three-year-old it is possible to see him jumping loose over a few low poles and to judge whether or not he has the inclination and the natural ability. Jumping ability can be developed by schooling and experience, but although many unpromising starters have turned out well in the end, it is better to start the long road forward on an animal that shows some aptitude, however minimal, at the start.

The final indispensable quality is courage. This is difficult to assess until he is put to the

test, and there are some successful riders – Nigel Taylor is one – who believe that, given the other qualities, courage can be developed

At one end of the scale there is Our Nobby, a mere 15 hands, and fortunate enough to come into the possession of Jane Bullen through proper training. Nevertheless, a fair idea can be had from the general attitude of the horse and the way in which he tackles what we ask him to do, and also from the look of his head, especially his eyes.

The requirements of the third day's Show Jumping test do not demand any qualities that we have not already considered. So the list of qualities that we would like to see in our young horse, not in any particular order, are an even temperament, presence, good movement, sound limbs, stamina, natural jumping ability, and courage. It is worth noting at this stage what some of our leading riders consider when selecting young horses. But first a quotation from a well-known horseman who has found and sent out from his small stable in Yorkshire a large number of successful National Hunt and competition horses over a period of many years – Archie Thomlinson: 'I start with the feet and work upwards,' he said. 'You can usually improve the rest but not the feet. My father used to say: "Legs, feet and feather; top may come, but bottom never."'

Capt. Mark Phillips, four times a winner of Badminton, also emphasises the importance of good feet, and his second priority is temperament. 'You can usually make a success of the less talented but ridable horse, whereas the brilliant but difficult horse will seldom be reliable.' Next he looks for movement, and then for Cross Country ability, with the interesting observation, 'I always choose the horse that shows Cross Country ability and work on his Dressage, never the reverse.'

Lorna Clarke, twice winner of Burghley and a member of our victorious team and individual Bronze Medallist at the 1986 World Championships, has always preferred the smaller horse. 'They seem to be less prone to leg injuries and tougher than the larger ones. They are generally more agile and find it easier to put in a short stride when necessary to get out of difficulty. Any well made small horse can carry 75 kg [11 st. 11 lb] and a small horse can still have a big stride. I find, for example, that short combinations still ride short on a small horse. The lovely big horses seem to spend more time off the road than the small ones. But I wouldn't turn down a big horse if he was good in other ways. I always look at the head and eyes – the outlook. Of course he must be sound, and it is no good having a bad mover. But Cross Country ability is all-important.'

Even a very tall rider such as Nigel Taylor, 6' 4" in his socks and short-listed for the 1985 European Championships, does not go for the very large horse: 'I regard the 16.1 to 16.3 as the ideal. First I look at the conformation, especially below the knee; next, for jumping ability, then movement – without it you just can't get the Dressage marks, and without a decent Dressage score you can't get anywhere today. Next, I look at the temperament and then for courage, though I find that if a horse has natural jumping ability, then boldness comes with training. Finally I look for quality, at least 7/8 if not thoroughbred.'

We should now have a fair idea of what sort of horse we are going to look for. Finding him is another matter. There are those who say that 'an eye for a horse' is something that a person is born with, something he either has or has not. Like most generalisations it may be only partly true, and it may be more accurate to say that it is something that is developed by background, upbringing and experience rather than inherited. Although there are probably more people riding today than at any time since the arrival of the motor car, unfortunately there are relatively few good judges of a horse. The parents of many of today's riders did not themselves ride seriously, and there are few substitutes for knowledge that is handed down from father to son – or from mother to daughter – starting at an early age.

The Pony Club does a good job of educating

the young, but reaches too few of the children who ride. The British Horse Society, too, does its best, but again only a fraction of the adults who ride are numbered among its membership. The National Light Horse Breeding Society, formerly known as the Hunters Improvement Society, whose main object is to improve the breeding of hunters and competition horses, and which controls the showing of young horses and hunters in the show ring, finds it very difficult to get enough good and knowledgeable judges. Probably the best judge is the person whose livelihood depends upon his judgement, the successful dealer in horses. He will know what sort of conformation in a horse will stand up to hard work, particularly if he himself has been an active participant in the hunting field or in racing. But of course his main aim is to sell a horse, and though a satisfied customer is important to him, he may not appreciate the particular demands of Eventing.

So in the end it is the rider himself who must make up his own mind as to whether to buy a horse to which he has taken a liking. The novice should, however, always ask the help and advice of someone more experienced than himself. Not only are two pairs of eyes better than one, but a vendor whose main aim is to sell his horse is less likely to try to 'put one over' on a purchaser of obviously limited experience if he is accompanied by a third person who, if nothing else, can see all that happens and hear most of what is said.

Let us assume that we are now trying to find a potential Three Day Event horse, one that has been broken and has received some basic schooling on the flat and that has at least been introduced to jumping over small obstacles, and is probably four or five years old. Potential eventers can be found from many different sources. The classified advertisements section of the weekly *Horse and Hound* probably contains the largest selection of horses for sale, but the choice can be bewildering to the inex-

perienced first-time buyer. Every advertisement is couched in glowing terms in order to tempt at least a telephone enquiry and, with luck, a visit. We cannot afford, and do not want, a horse that already has competition experience in Horse Trials, so this will rule out 'Intermediate Eventer'. 'Novice Eventer' sometimes means 'Potential Eventer', and so is worth a closer look. Headings such as 'Hunt/Pt-to-Pt/Event' and 'Pot Dressage/ Event/SJ' must all be looked into, but often the most promising entry is to be found under a more general heading. 'Promising 4 yr old', 'Quality Middle Weight', 'Brilliant Prospect' are examples of entries that may repay closer study. Many a potentially good horse is advertised under the name of his sire: 'Bay gelding by Noname', Noname being a well known and fashionable sire of steeplechasers or competition horses. Some headings are more a cause for mirth than for serious consideration: 'Proven Potential' is not unknown.

The small print of the entry will then give an indication as to whether a telephone call is worth while. The advertiser is only going to mention the horse's good points in print, but the information given should include sex, age, colour, breeding, stage of training and any achievements or experience to date. Other expressions such as 'good natural paces', 'big bold stylish jump', or 'likely to go to the top' should not raise our hopes unduly at this stage. Sometimes a price is mentioned, sometimes not. Before answering an advertisement that looks promising, we should be clear in our own minds about two important points.

The first is sex. The majority of successful competition horses are geldings, which are generally regarded as tougher, easier to train, and more reliable than mares. On the other hand a really good mare will give everything she has, and will for that reason be an outstanding ride. There is also the possibility of breeding from her when her Eventing days are over, especially

33

if she should have to retire early from competitive work owing to some unlucky accident or injury – but not if her retirement is due to her inability to stay sound for other reasons. Normally mares, as competition horses, will command a lower price than geldings, a factor which may turn out to be to our advantage.

The second point is the question of 'blood'. 'An ounce of blood is worth an inch of bone' is an old adage that still holds good today. The thoroughbred weed is of no interest to us, since he will lack the stamina for a Three Day Event and the bone that will enable him to stay sound and continue for many seasons. But the Three Day Event horse must be able to gallop sufficiently well to complete the Steeplechase and Cross Country phases without exerting himself unduly, so that he can direct his energy into coping with the demands of the obstacles; if he is struggling to do the required speed as well, he will find things that much more difficult. This implies a thoroughbred or something very near it. On the other hand some thoroughbreds may be too highly strung to be completely reliable in the Dressage test. Some riders feel, therefore, that the 7/8 thoroughbred, by a thoroughbred stallion out of a mare that is not pure thoroughbred but nevertheless has plenty of quality, is better. The ideal, which is not easy to find, is the thoroughbred with good bone, plenty of substance, and an equable temperament.

So now we are ready to telephone perhaps half a dozen likely vendors whose advertisements give us grounds for hope. When telephoning we should have a list of questions to which we would like the answers, which will enable us to decide whether it is worth while going to see the horse. Assuming that the basic points have been covered in the advertisement, we begin by asking the price (if this was not advertised). We then want to know whether the horse moves straight, and whether he has any blemishes, either those which could affect his soundness, such as splints, curbs, thoroughpins, or windgalls, or those which, while they may be a little unsightly, will not affect his performance. We want to know if he has any vices in or out of the stable, whether he is good to shoe, clip, and load into a horsebox or trailer, and whether he is quiet in traffic. We shall seek an elaboration of any claims made in the advertisement regarding his past performance or his future potential, and finally we ask the question – is he likely to make a Three Day Event horse? It is usually worth while to ask this question because, although if the answer is 'Yes' we may be no further forward, if it is 'No' then we can probably save ourselves the trouble and expense of a wasted journey, and be grateful to the vendor for his honesty. We also ask how much bone he has; by this we mean the size of the cannon bone below the knee and above the fetlock joint, and a measurement taken round the leg at this point should read about $8\frac{1}{2}$ inches.

It may be helpful to make a written note of the answers we receive and to take this when we go to see the horse, especially if we are going to see several. We may now find that there are two or three horses that seem worth a visit, and we make appointments to see and try them.

CHAPTER 4

Trying and vetting

Arrival • First impressions • Outside the stable • Conformation
• The head • A good front • The back • Fore limbs • Hind limbs • Blemishes
• Trotting up • Saddling up • Viewing under saddle • Seeing the horse jump
• Evasions • Trying from the saddle • Wind • Jumping the horse
• Concluding the deal • Subject to the vet • Choice of vet • The B.V.A. form
• X-rays • Collecting the horse • Test for soundness • Final questions

Ideally we should visit a horse as early in the day as we can arrange it, partly because it is better to try him before anyone else has done so on that day, and partly because a vendor, though prepared to receive potential purchasers at any time as long as daylight lasts, prefers not to have to clean up his horse late in the evening. If we have several horses to see in the same area, then some will obviously have to be seen late in the day. We should do our best to be punctual, and although it is tempting to arrive early in order to see what is happening to the horse immediately prior to the arranged time of viewing, this is a form of bad manners that few vendors will appreciate. If we are going to be late, then it is sensible to telephone to say so.

On arrival we should find the horse in his stable; if he is not, and is being ridden or led around, then we should ask the reason – many a stiff, even unsound, horse improves if he is kept on the move. First impressions are very important; sometimes it is obvious from the moment that we enter the stable that the horse is not what we are looking for. Assuming that this is not the case, we look him over, then approach him quietly, perhaps feel his legs and run a hand down his back, more with a view to noting his reaction than anything else. At

this stage we may ask to see any documents that relate to him, such as a passport, registration certificate or vaccination certificate.

We shall then ask to see him outside the box. First we should stand back and take in a general view. Does he seem well proportioned? Is the overall picture pleasing? Then we look into the details, remembering that we are looking for a competition horse, not a show horse. The head can tell us much: does he generally have his ears forward and look alert and happy, or are his ears more often laid back, giving him a mean look? Generally speaking, the larger his eyes and ears are, the better. We may not be expert at telling a horse's age but we ought to have a fair idea of what a four- or five-year-old's mouth should look like, and we should note whether his upper and lower jaws meet or whether he is 'parrot-mouthed', which could cause him difficulty when feeding.

He must definitely have a good front, which means that the view from the saddle will give his rider confidence and assurance, and will later mean that in the event of a peck or stumble when landing over a fence, his rider will find it that much easier not to part company. The neck should be reasonably long, in proportion to the rest of his body, and definitely not short. But a good front depends more on the shoulder, which should be long and well sloped. His chest should be deep and wide enough to allow room for heart and lungs.

The back should not be too long, since a horse with a long back may have speed on the flat but will find it difficult to negotiate the sometimes tricky obstacles to be found in Horse Trials. The saddle, when fitted, should appear to lie naturally in the centre of the back. The quarters should appear strong, for this is where the 'horsepower' originates. Now we come to the most important part – his limbs. Starting at the bottom, the feet should be open, and not small and 'boxy'; the wall of the hoof should be sound and not broken, and both the fore and hind feet should be matching pairs – if they are not, then one or the other is unlikely to bear its share of the inevitable strain that falls on this part of the horse's anatomy. The pasterns should neither be too straight, which will give an uncomfortable ride, nor too long, which will place undue strain on the tendons. The fetlock joints should be free from signs of wear, such as swellings or windgalls, and should be angular rather than rounded in appearance.

On the forelegs, the cannon bone should be short rather than long, the tendons should be absolutely 'clean', and the whole leg should feel cool. When the horse is standing square on all four legs, the forelegs should appear to be vertical, so that an imaginary line drawn from the top of his forearm down through the knee to the middle of the fetlock joint should be vertical when viewed from the side. The hind limbs supply the motive power, and in a Three Day Event will be under considerable pressure. They should appear strong, particularly in the second thigh (the part immediately above the hock). When the horse is standing square the cannon bones of the hind legs should be near the vertical. (If they are tucked underneath the body they may in movement give the impression of impulsion to the

uninitiated, but will in fact be liable to strain when under pressure.)

With regard to blemishes, we are not attempting to vet the horse, but we may save ourselves a hefty veterinary bill if we can at least recognise what is definitely not acceptable. Any enlargement, swelling or heat in the tendons, any signs of wear on the fetlock joints, and curbs, thoroughpins or spavins should be cause for concern. All these are signs of strain which should not be present in a young horse – if we were buying a proven older horse with experience and form it might be worth while to have a vet's opinion, but not in this case. A curb appears as a swelling on the back of the hind leg about four inches below the hock and is a strain of the ligament; some horses, however, exhibit a false curb, which is merely an abnormally large bone of the hock joint and may be of no significance. A thoroughpin appears as a soft swelling on either side of the tendon immediately above the hock, and again indicates strain. A spavin is evidenced by a hard swelling on the inside of the hock.

Splints, which appear as bony enlargements on the cannon bone, usually but not exclusively on the inside of the fore legs, are not too important provided that the horse is sound, that they are not so large that they are likely to be struck by the opposite leg, and that they are not placed so as to interfere with tendons or ligaments. Windgalls, too, are unlikely to cause unsoundness, but are signs of wear appearing as soft swellings just above and on either side of the fetlock joint. But in both cases it is safer to obtain a vet's opinion.

This appraisal of the horse will have taken far less time to complete than it has taken to read about here. If satisfied with what we have seen, we now ask for the horse to be walked and trotted up on hard, level ground. At the walk we should note whether he 'covers up' well, which means that he puts his hind feet down well in front of the hoof-prints of his forefeet – a horse that does not do this is unlikely to gallop well. At the trot he must be absolutely sound and must move straight. We must see him trot directly towards us and directly away from us in order to see that he neither 'dishes' (swings either of his forefeet outwards), nor 'brushes' (knocks one joint or leg with the hoof of the other), and watch him trot past us so that we can observe his movement from the side.

If still satisfied, we should now ask that he be saddled up. Any invitation by the vendor for us to ride him straight away should be politely but firmly declined, unless for some genuine reason there is no one available to ride him first. As the horse is mounted we should note whether he reacts in any way, such as by dipping his back, and if he does we should make a mental note to warn our vet – if we reach the stage of having him vetted – to examine his back particularly carefully. Then we should expect to see him walk, trot and canter on both reins on a straight line and on a circle, followed by a gallop. This need not be a flat-out scamper, but should be sufficient to enable us to judge his ability at this pace and to hear any abnormality in his wind.

Next we should ask to see him jump; what and how much will depend on his experience to date, and we shall probably have to be content with seeing him pop over a few low, simple obstacles. All we expect is that he should jump willingly, show a desire to reach the far side, and show some natural ability. This means that he should lower his head and neck, pick up his front, tuck his fore legs in, round his back and lift his quarters, and give an indication that he has some scope. This may sound like asking for perfection, but is really only an indication of what we would hope to see – rather than a young horse that rushes into the fence with his head in the air, dangles all four legs, jumps with a hollow back, and only manages to clear this small obstacle with

difficulty. Height is not important at this stage; a low spread will tell us more.

We must assume that the owner will have schooled him over these obstacles before, so any attempt at evasion, running out or refusing should cause us immediate concern. If he tends to rush at the fences, we must try to assess whether this is due to keenness and is an indication of a healthy desire to reach the far side, or whether it is due to a temperamental defect. If he jumps with his head in the air, not looking at the fence, and hops over it awkwardly with his legs dangling, then we shall probably conclude that he lacks natural ability. If there is a small ditch handy or a small water obstacle, so much the better, and claims that he is not ready for such a test should be food for thought; if the obstacle is there, the chances are that his owner will have tried him over it, provided of course that it is not a mighty chasm!

If all has gone well, we can now climb aboard. Again first impressions are very important; once in the saddle does everything feel right? Is the view between the ears one that gives us confidence? Off we go at the walk; does he walk as if he meant to go somewhere, or does he have to be pushed along? We then work him on the flat at the trot and canter on both reins in straight lines and on circles, and should canter him quite strongly on a large circle on each rein, followed by a gallop. Again this does not have to be flat out, but sufficient to show us whether he likes to go on when asked, whether he can really cover the ground, and whether he gives us a feeling of confidence at speed. At the same time, at both the canter on the circle and at the gallop, we listen to his wind.

Any abnormal noise in the wind should give cause for concern, but we must be able to distinguish between the 'high blower' and the horse with a wind problem. The high blower flaps his nostrils when he exhales, only, and he is usually a sound-winded horse. We must distinguish, also, between the puffing and blowing of an unfit young horse, and any noise due to a constriction in his throat or larynx. It is our vet who will give the final pronouncement on soundness of the wind, but we may save ourselves unnecessary expense if we can recognise the obviously unsound horse. Also, if we think that the horse may have a slight wind problem, it may help our vet if we tell him the circumstances under which we heard it.

Next we should jump him ourselves over a few small obstacles. Whilst we hold him together and give him every chance to jump, we must remember that we are not schooling the horse, but trying to see what he is capable of doing and how he does it. Does he, for example, give us the feeling that with more training he will carry us confidently over any type of obstacle? Is he reasonably keen about jumping? Finally we walk him back to his owner, and this is the moment at which we make up our minds as to whether he is the horse for us or not. If at any earlier moment during our visit we feel sure that he is not, then we should politely say so there and then. There is no point in continuing our examination or trial, when the owner probably has other interested customers. We must bear in mind that no horse is perfect, and there are bound to be pros and cons, but if there appears to be nothing too serious and we feel that it will give us pleasure to own him and that he will in the end make a Three Day Event horse, then we decide to have him. (If there are other promising horses to be visited, we may reserve our decision until we have seen them, though we may risk losing this one if he is sold in the meantime.)

The next step is to conclude the deal, subject to veterinary examination. We must make up our own mind as to whether there is scope for negotiating a lower price than that being asked; some vendors ask one price knowing that they

Once in the saddle, it is important that the view gives one confidence and everything feels right

are going to settle for something less and giving themselves room to manoeuvre, while others initially ask the price that they are determined to achieve. There may be grounds for trying to negotiate a lower price if the horse has some feature not revealed in the advertisement or during our telephone enquiry, or simply if his level of performance is less than we expected. But if the asking price is within our ceiling and the vendor will not take less, then, if the horse seems to be what we are looking for, we should agree to buy him.

If the horse is within reasonable travelling distance of our own vet then we should ask him to carry out the examination, but if the horse is at the other end of the country, we may ask him to recommend a vet in that area instead. We must just make sure that we do not engage the vendor's own vet – to do so is not in the best interests of the vendor, the vet, or ourselves. If possible, whoever vets the horse should have some experience of dealing with competition horses.

The British Veterinary Association has produced a standard form on which the examining vet will record what he finds, and it also lists the five stages of the examination. But perhaps the most significant part of the form is the paragraph headed 'Opinion'. Here the vet is required to state his opinion as to whether the horse is or is not suitable, taking into account all that he has seen, for the purpose for which he is to be bought. It is therefore very important that we tell our vet that we are purchasing a potential Three Day Event horse. If the horse is expensive, and bearing in mind that we are going to put a considerable amount of hard work into him, the question arises as to whether we should have his feet X-rayed. If we were buying an experienced eventer with form this might well be advisable since he will inevitably have been subjected to a certain amount of strain. In the case of a young horse, however, this ought not to be the case, and our best course is probably to say to our vet, 'If you are not 100% sure of his feet and think he ought to be X-rayed, then please go ahead and have it done.' The costs of an X-ray are considerable, and may double the expense of having the horse vetted; the shoes must normally be removed (and replaced), and although portable X-ray equipment can give good results, many vets feel that they can achieve

better pictures if the horse is transported to their surgery. We could say that if a young horse has a question that can only be answered by X-ray examination then we had best leave him alone; but if we are set on having him and our vet recommends X-ray, then it is best to have it done. We shall never find 100% perfection!

Another question may concern his wind. There are horses, other than high blowers, that make a noise of some sort which may not amount to unsoundness. A fat, unfit horse may do so, for example, as may one that is recovering from a cough. If our vet considers that an endoscopic examination, which involves the insertion of a flexible illuminated tube into the larynx, is necessary, then we shall be adding something to the costs of vetting, but it may save us money in the end. If we were buying an older horse with considerable competitive experience, our vet might suggest that a blood test be taken, but in the case of our young horse this should not be necessary.

If all goes well, the horse has no need of any extra examination, and our vet recommends that we buy him. We arrange to collect him and arrive, cheque in hand, and with the gear in which he will travel home. Before loading him into our horsebox or trailer we should ask for his documents: a passport if he is a thoroughbred, and any registration certificates that he may have – B.H.S., B.S.J.A., H.I.S., for example. We should also ask how he has been fed, and whether he has any particular likes and dislikes. We would like to know when he was last wormed, when he last had his teeth rasped, and whether or not he is used to being turned out in a paddock. We should also check whether he has been vaccinated and if so when revaccination is due. Lastly, and this is important, we ask that he be trotted up to make sure that he is sound before we load him. If all is well, the horse is now ours, and our responsibility from this moment on.

CHAPTER 5

Training the horse: preliminaries

Health • Worming • Teeth • Vaccination • Shoeing • Getting to know him
• Training requirements • Paddock or manege • Dressage markers •
Basic saddlery • Saddle • Fitting the saddle • Snaffle • Nosebands
• Martingale • Lungeing kit • Stable kit

Now we have our young horse back at home in our own stable and our first task is to attend to his health and ensure that we have the basic tack that he will need in the stable and when he is ridden. From the questions that we put to his previous owner we shall know whether he is due to be wormed, our vet will have told us whether his teeth need rasping, and from his documents we see whether he is due for vaccination. Modern wormers are easy to administer, either in powder form as an additive to the feed, or as a paste in a syringe which can be inserted into the back of the mouth, and it is wise to administer a dose every 3 months. This should keep the horse free of worms and should not interfere with his training programme.

Teeth generally require rasping every six months, and unless this is done we may have difficulty with his head carriage if he is unhappy in his mouth, and he may go off his feed if it is painful for him to eat. Rasping should either be carried out by a vet or by someone who specialises in this task, and who uses a mouth gag, without which it is almost impossible to do a thorough job.

The rules regarding vaccination against equine influenza are laid down by the Jockey Club for racehorses and have been adopted by the British Horse Society and the Horse Trials Group. The detailed regulations are set out in the 'Rules for Official Horse Trials' and in the Omnibus Schedules for the Spring, Summer and Autumn events. Every horse must have a vaccination certificate, which must accompany him to all Horse Trials, and which in certain cases must be forwarded with his entries, and normally one section at each event is required to produce certificates for inspection before being allowed to start. Since the rules are strict, and since some horses react to an injection, some thought may have to be given to the dates on which injections become due.

If the horse has been previously vaccinated, then all that is required is an annual booster injection not more than a year after his last booster, and this date must not be overlooked. But a horse may not compete within ten days of an injection; this may eventually interfere with our programme, in which case we can consider bringing the date forward. For example, if the due booster date is 1 April, a month into the Spring Horse Trials season, we may decide to give him a booster injection in February, so that in future boosters will always be due in that month. If our horse has not previously been vaccinated, or if his records have not been correctly maintained, then unfortunately we have to start the whole course from the beginning. This consists of two injections given not less than 3 weeks and not more than 13 weeks apart, plus a booster injection between 21 and 30 weeks later. The exact dates are important, as even one day outside the limits is unacceptable, so it is essential to be absolutely clear as to when the injections are due.

If our horse has been regularly shod by a competent farrier, then there should be no immediate problem, but it would be wise to have our own farrier take a look at his feet within a month, if not sooner. Also, we shall want to discuss with him the question of studs. Although horses hunt and race quite happily without them, if a competition horse is to give of his best in all types of going, then he will need studs of varying shapes and sizes. Their object is to prevent the horse from slipping when approaching and taking off at a jump, and to give him a greater sense of security and therefore confidence. They may also be necessary in the Dressage arena if this is slippery, as it may be, for example, when there is early morning dew on short grass on firm going. Studs can be either permanently inserted into the shoe, which gives no flexibility and restricts us to the smallest size, or, as is more usual, can be screwed into holes made in the shoes by the farrier.

When a horse is jumping, his forefeet may slip as he steadies himself for take-off, his hind feet may slip at the moment of take-off, and any of his feet may slip when landing downhill, and when galloping downhill or across a slope. The stud holes should be positioned near the heel of the shoe, and to avoid risk of injury to his own legs should be on the outside only, though some riders like to have them on the inside of the hind shoes as well. The studs should not be sharp, and we should use the

smallest that will give the desired effect; in firm going they will be the smallest available, while larger ones are necessary when it is very wet. Studs normally come in two sizes, 3/8 and 5/16 of an inch, so we must ensure that our studs and the holes made by our farrier match.

The start of our training programme will depend upon the state of the horse when he arrived in our stable, how fit he was, what training he had received, and what experience he had acquired before we bought him. The first week or so will probably best be devoted to getting to know him, and to letting him grow accustomed to his new environment. A new stable and different methods of feeding will require a short period of adjustment, during which it is probably best to hack him gently round the countryside. Then we are ready to start our training, with the aim of preparing him to compete in his first official One Day Horse Trial. Opinions differ as to how soon or late this should be, but unless we want to risk overfacing him by entering him before he is really ready, the autumn of his 5-year-old year is the earliest that we should consider. This will give us time to give him the necessary education and experience in all three tests – Dressage, Show Jumping and Cross Country – so that he produces a reasonable performance on his first appearance.

So, what do we need in order to start our training? The ideal is to have a well drained all-weather manege which is sufficiently large to accommodate both our schooling on the flat and our jumping training. There are several types of surface available, but the essential for them all is good drainage. The only weather that will then prevent us from using it will be snow, but we can usually make use of a field or paddock while snow lies on the ground. An indoor school has obvious advantages when weather is really bad, but it is not essential, and since we are going to be competing out of doors in all weathers, there is much to be said for conducting his schooling in the open air as well. If an all-weather manege is not available, then a well drained paddock with a reasonable covering of grass will suffice, and many a successful Event horse has been produced from such simple facilities.

The minimum useful size for an all-weather manege is 40 × 20 metres, the size of the Novice Dressage arena, but the larger it is the better it will be for jumping training. The actual size will probably be limited by the cost, and although we are aiming ultimately at the Three Day Event, there is not much point in going for a 60 × 20 metre manege, since this is not a very good shape for jumping, where extra width is useful, and we can do all our schooling for the movements of the Three Day Event Dressage test (when we eventually come to it) in a smaller arena, setting out a 60 × 20 arena in the paddock for rehearsing the actual test. 50 × 30 metres is a useful size which will permit us to do all the jumping training that we need to do before either erecting a course in the paddock or taking our horse to jump a small course somewhere else.

It is useful, but not essential, to have a set of the eight basic Dressage markers, together with sufficient white boards to enable us to convert our manege, if it is larger than 40 × 20 metres, into an arena of that size, or to allow us to set up a Dressage arena in the paddock. Nineteen boards, which can either be of wood or white plastic, are ideal, but even eight would allow us to set up the corners. If we have nineteen, then they and the markers, which can either be home-made or of white plastic, should be set up as in Figure 1.

Now for the horse. We need a saddle, a snaffle bridle, a running martingale, a set of lungeing kit, and a set of protective boots for his legs. Although we may later be able to have a Dressage saddle and a Cross Country and Jumping saddle, at this stage what we need is a well made general-purpose or eventing saddle

that fits our horse and is comfortable for his rider. There are several on the market that will accommodate the length of leg necessary for the Dressage, and still enable the rider to pull his leathers up for the Show Jumping and the Cross Country. Even more important is that the saddle should fit the horse. It is difficult these days to find a saddler who will come to the stable and fit the saddle to the horse, but it is as important to have a well-fitting saddle as it is to have a set of well-fitting shoes. At best, a horse will not go freely in a saddle that

Figure 1   Dressage arena, 20 × 40 m.

The position of 8 markers is shown with suggested positions for 19 boards

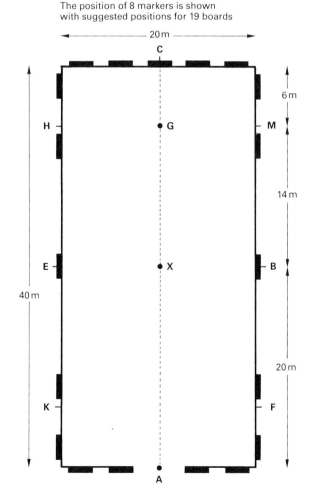

causes him discomfort; at worst, it could cause sores that will make him unrideable. The problem can be alleviated by the use of a good numnah, of which the natural sheepskin variety is the best.

A new saddle will in any case probably need to have the stuffing adjusted after a time, and it is essential to find a saddler who can do this. If the saddler and the horse cannot meet, then a piece of soft lead strip or a flexible strip of rubber used for drawing curves, which can be bought at any large stationer's, should be placed over the horse's withers and moulded into shape. It is then laid flat on a sheet of paper and the outline of the inside of the curve is drawn on the paper. If we repeat the process, placing the strip this time on the horse's back where the centre of the saddle will lie, our saddler will then have two templates from which he can adjust the stuffing of the saddle. Although not as good as a personal visit, it is considerably better than just telling him to 'stuff it up a bit'.

The bridle should be a snaffle, and we have to make decisions regarding two important parts of it, the bit and the noseband, and what is and is not permitted in competition is laid down in the Rule Book. Our initial choice should be a plain snaffle with large free rings and a single joint and the thick hollow type that is the most comfortable for the horse should be tried first. A more severe but useful type is the 'Wels' or 'Fulmer' snaffle, which has small free rings and cheeks, normally used in conjunction with leather keepers that hold the upper part of the cheeks to the cheek-piece of the bridle.

Four types of noseband are permitted, the cavesson, fitted above the snaffle, the dropped noseband fitted below it, and the flash and grackle nosebands which cross over above and below the snaffle and are really combinations of the first two. The dropped noseband is the most commonly used and should be tried first. It must be fitted so that the part which goes over the nose is well clear of the nostril, and should not be too tight. Its object is to encourage the horse to flex his jaw on the correct interaction of the rider's hands and legs, and it should not be a source of discomfort to him. The flash and grackle nosebands are variations which some horses find more comfortable.

A running martingale is required for jumping, as are a pair of tendon boots to protect the forelegs; later a pair may be required for the hind legs too. For lungeing we shall require a lungeing rein approximately twelve metres in length, a pair of side reins, and a lungeing whip. A leather lungeing cavesson is useful but quite expensive, and a horse can be effectively lunged with the lungeing rein correctly attached to the snaffle. However, it is now possible to buy a webbing cavesson with the correct fittings, and we should consider this.

The basic stable kit of a head-collar and rope, night rug, blanket, a set of bandages, and our grooming kit are all that we shall need to start with, and can be added to as we start to travel and to do more serious work. But we shall have to consider the question of clipping for late autumn, winter and early spring work.

We should now be ready to start the serious but enjoyable business of training our horse. Serious and hard work it is, but we should nevertheless try to make it enjoyable both for ourselves and, more especially, for our horse.

CHAPTER 6

Training the horse: Dressage and lungeing

The Dressage test ● Circles ● Corners ● Lengthening the trot
● Hands and legs ● Halts ● The centre line ● Transitions ● The canter
● Help from the ground ● The rider's seat ● Lungeing ● Lungeing kit
● Exercises on the lunge ● Transitions on the lunge ● Maintaining interest

We are now ready to start our horse's basic schooling and to map out a programme that will take him through to his first official B.H.S. Novice Horse Trial. When he does so he will have to perform a simple Dressage test lasting only four minutes, during which he will be required to show the basic paces, walk, trot and canter, on a straight line, through corners, and on a circle. He will have to halt and stand still (twice), and perhaps his most difficult task will be to show a few lengthened strides at the trot. He may also be required to show that he remains balanced when rein contact is relaxed and is not relying on the rider to hold him together.

Assuming that our horse has been correctly broken – and what an unfortunate word has been chosen to describe perhaps the most important part of the horse's early handling – he can presumably execute a normal walk, trot and canter that are perfectly adequate for ordinary hacking. What we now have to do is to develop and refine these paces and condition the horse to performing them in the strange and constricting environment of the 40×20 metre Dressage arena. The first step therefore is to accustom him to this enclosure, so we let him walk round its track on a long rein,

reassuring him should he 'spook' at anything, gradually shortening the reins and driving him gently but firmly forward with our legs until he is walking round the track purposefully and without fuss.

We work him similarly at the trot, concentrating on maintaining an even rhythm and at this stage not asking him to go too deeply into the corners. This preliminary work is best carried out at the rising trot, but we must be careful to change the diagonal on which we rise with each change of rein. Before cantering him in this restricted area we should ensure that we have established an understanding with him on the circle in the larger open spaces of the paddock. We will start with a very large circle which we shall gradually reduce to one of 20 metres. Then, when we canter him for the first time in the manege, we shall not ask him to go deeper into the corners than he does when executing a 20-metre circle. Attempts to force a horse into the corners before he is ready only result in unbalancing him and upsetting his rhythm.

This brings us to the question of circles and

The first and last movements of the test require the horse to halt and stand still. Michaelmas Day, Mark Todd, Badminton

corners. As he passes through each corner of the manege, the horse will have to execute a segment of the smallest circle of which he is capable at the particular pace without loss of balance or rhythm. Since the circle will be smallest at the walk and largest at the canter, it follows that we cannot expect him to go as deeply into the corners at the trot and canter as he does at the walk. The actual size of the smallest circle of which he is capable will depend upon the degree of lateral bend that he can achieve. From an early stage in his life, the young horse can bend his back without too much difficulty in a vertical plane, but finds it very difficult to bend it laterally or sideways. On a circle he should be bent from head to tail so that his fore and hind feet follow the track of the circle, with his head and neck leading him in the required direction. Any attempt to force him into executing circles that are smaller than those of which he is capable will only result in stiffness or evasions which are difficult to correct. Therefore we cannot expect him to go deeply into his corners until he can execute quite a small circle without loss of balance or rhythm.

The trained horse will eventually be able to execute a circle of 6 metres in diameter at the trot, but at his present stage of training we should not expect our horse to be able to do this, and a circle of 10 metres is the smallest that we should ask. So if we draw a 10-metre circle in the corner of our manege we can see on the ground the maximum depth of corner that we can expect him to execute. At the canter all that we can demand initially is a 20-metre circle. Gradually we can reduce this until he can go through the corners correctly at this pace too. Figure 2 shows what 20-, 10- and 6-metre circles look like in the corners of a

On a circle the horse should be bent from head to tail so that his fore and hind feet follow the track of the circle. Accumulator, Richard Walker, Burghley

40 × 20 metre manege. If we have been at pains to emphasise the importance of correct circles and corners, this is because trying to proceed too quickly is a frequent cause of resistance on the part of the horse, and a reason for low marks in Novice Dressage tests.

The next requirement on which we must work is the showing of a few lengthened strides at the trot. This is another movement that is generally poorly performed in Novice tests. What is required is simple – just a few, probably between four and eight, lengthened strides. The same rhythm must be maintained, neither faster nor slower, but each stride covers

Figure 2   Circles of 20, 10 and 6 m diameters in an arena of 40 × 20 m.

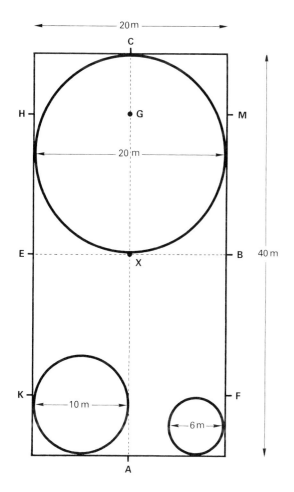

appreciably more ground. The only way that the horse can achieve this is by a greater degree of engagement of his hind legs; in other words he places each hind foot further forward than he normally does at the working trot. His fore-feet will also land that much further forward and in doing so will stretch out slightly more in front of his shoulders. Eventually, a trained horse executing an extended trot will appear to 'float', with his forelegs reaching way out in front of him, but what really matters is the extent to which his hindquarters are actively engaged.

Most horses will produce these lengthened strides of their own accord when following another horse out hacking or in the hunting field. What we have to do is to teach our horse to produce them on demand. It is very difficult to teach this in a small manege, and we should start by asking for it in the wider spaces of the paddock. It is also easy for the horse to become confused as to what we are demanding – more especially if we are not absolutely clear about it ourselves! When we are trotting our horse round the paddock at a normal working trot, if we squeeze him with our legs, we may obtain various reactions according to the actions of our hands. If we take a little, we shorten the trot and increase the collection, or probably, given our horse's state of training, make the trot slower. If we give a little, we allow the horse to lengthen the trot, or probably, at this stage, make the trot faster. What we have to do is to maintain the contact with his mouth whilst allowing him to lengthen his neck slightly so that the increased pressure of our legs encourages him to lengthen his stride.

At first he will try to increase the pace of the trot, and we must then re-establish the working trot. Soon he will realise that an increase in pace is not what is required and will begin to lengthen his stride very slightly. Very slightly is all that we should ask to start with, and after a few strides we should reward him with a pat

The next requirement is the showing of a few lengthened strides at the trot. Flying Rupert, Sarah Wathen

and allow him to relax. Soon we shall be able to trot round the paddock maintaining this slightly lengthened trot and we are then ready to ask for it in the manege. Until this moment arrives it is better to teach the horse to lengthen in the paddock, where frequent corners do not intervene. Throughout this period we must be careful never to ask for too much, otherwise we risk the horse breaking into a canter, which of course makes the whole movement worthless. Unless we ask for too much this should not happen, because the aids for the strike-off into the canter are quite different from those which we use to obtain the lengthening of the stride at the trot.

During the Novice test two halts are required, the first on entering the arena and the second on completion of the test, and each is preceded by a trot up the centre line. Since these two movements constitute the first and final impressions of the judge, they are very important. But too many riders throw away marks in these movements by trying too hard. Let us imagine the movement from the judge's point of view. What he (or she) hopes to see is a horse trotting straight up the centre line, halting square, and remaining still during his rider's salute. What he cannot see is the picture from the side. Too many riders worry as to whether the horse is on the bit, has enough flexion, or is sufficiently collected, when what they should be doing is to push the horse down the centre line towards the judge; the horse is then less likely to deviate from the centre line, or move his head, and will present a better picture as seen from the judge's position. The transition from the trot to the halt must be smooth, with the horse remaining straight and on the centre line, and without throwing up his head as he halts. On no account must we pull the horse back into the halt with our hands; rather we squeeze him up on to our hands with the legs, which will shorten his stride, and our hands then maintain this stronger contact until the movement as it were runs out and the horse comes squarely to a halt. In order to achieve the halt precisely where it is required we must start preparing the horse for it several strides in advance.

This brings us to the question of transitions from one pace to another. Here we should observe three principles. First, we must avoid exciting or confusing the horse; second, we must always prepare our transitions well in advance of the point at which they are required; and third, when schooling we must ensure that our horse makes the transition from one pace to another exactly when we demand it and not when he thinks, by association, that it is due. The horse is very much a creature of habit, and while we shall take full advantage of this during our schooling, if we are not careful it will lead to his anticipating our demands when we in fact have something else in mind.

The transitions likely to prove most confusing to the horse are those from the trot to the canter and from the working trot to the lengthened trot. Fortunately, in the Novice test the transitions from the trot to the canter are always made in a corner, which, as we have seen, is in effect a segment of a circle, and it is much easier to obtain a strike-off into the canter on a circle than on a straight line. But more important is the fact that the aids for these two transitions are very different. With certain exceptions when they apply a degree of persuasion or even compulsion, aids are simply a signal to the horse that we require the execution of something that we have already taught him, and there are several different signals that we could use to obtain a desired effect provided that we have taught the horse to respond to them as required. And if we examined the aids given for the strike-off into the canter by a group of novice riders, we would probably find a greater divergence than with any other aids. However, over the years the experts have generally agreed on those signals which are the easiest for the horse in the early stages of his training, and at the same time can be used with only slight modification right through to the higher levels of schooling.

To obtain the strike-off into the canter from the trot, we first collect the horse a little by squeezing with our legs and holding him with our hands; then we gently take his head to the direction in which we are going, in this case to the right, by a feel on the right rein, and apply our inside leg on or slightly forward of the girth and our outside leg behind it. It will initially help our young horse if we give the rein signal in advance of the leg signal. The timing, too, is important, and we should give the rein signal as the horse's inside foreleg hits the ground, and the leg signals the next time it hits the ground. (When we eventually come on to more advanced work, and require a strike-off on a straight line, we shall gradually reduce the effect of the outside leg, so that there is no tendency for the horse to swing his quarters to the inside when striking off.)

A useful exercise for horse and rider is the clock exercise, in which we imagine a circle to correspond to the face of a clock (see Figure 3). Starting at twelve o'clock, we trot three-quarters of a circle to nine o'clock, where we canter a complete circle. On returning to nine o'clock we trot for three-quarters of a circle to six o'clock, where we again canter a whole circle. We continue trotting three-quarters of a circle and cantering a whole circle until we arrive back at twelve o'clock, when we continue cantering on round the manege. We then repeat the exercise on the other rein. Using this method, the rider will learn to be precise about preparing for the transitions, while the horse will not be able to anticipate them.

In the Novice test, the lengthening of the stride at the trot is always demanded on the diagonal across the arena in a straight line.

Provided therefore that at this stage we only ask for this lengthening on a straight line, and provided that our aids are quite distinct from those for the canter, there is no reason for our horse to become confused. We must, however, ensure that we are established on the diagonal in a straight line before asking for the lengthened strides.

These, then, are the simple requirements of the Novice Dressage test, which demand nothing that we would not ask of our horse in order to make him a pleasurable ride. But it will help us enormously if we can make at least the occasional visit to a knowledgeable instructor, who can correct our faults, help us with any problems that may occur, and prevent us from acquiring any bad habits.

At the very least we ought to engage the services of a friend who rides, preferably in Horse Trials, who can observe our progress and offer useful advice. (This can be anyone other than husband or wife! With very few exceptions, attempts by one spouse to instruct or comment on the performance of the other are more likely to be a recipe for marital strife

Figure 3 The clock exercise: trotting and cantering on the circle.

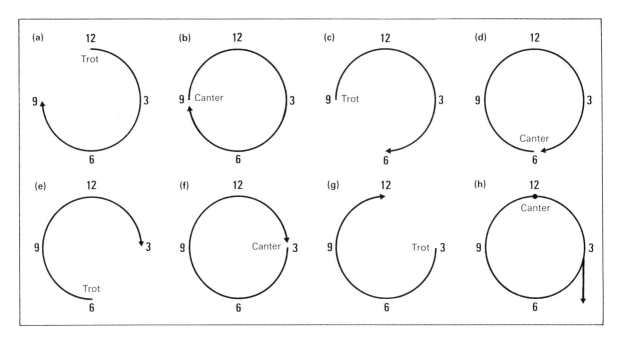

than for progress towards successful competition in Horse Trials!)

One particular area in which the help of an instructor in the early stages is invaluable concerns the rider's seat and the length of stirrups. For Dressage the seat should be as 'deep' as possible, and the function of the stirrups is to provide a 'foot-rest' for the feet. (Our feet hate hanging in space; if we try sitting on a bar stool from which we cannot reach the ground, our feet will search for a foot-rest either on the stool or in front of the bar.) The best way to achieve the correct length of stirrup on our own is to walk round for a few minutes without stirrups, pushing the knees as far down the saddle as they will go, letting the ankles hang loose with the toes pointing downwards, and with the stirrups hanging so that the stirrup bar is level with the ankle bone. Then, without raising the knees, we place the toe on the stirrup bar. If we have to raise the knee to do this, then the stirrups are too short and should be let down a hole. However, we must at this stage be comfortable, and it may be necessary to start with the stirrups a hole shorter; later, when we come on to schooling the horse without stirrups, we shall be able to ride 'deeper' and with a longer stirrup.

Opinions differ as to the value of lungeing and the part that it ought to play in the training of the young horse, and some riders prefer to do as much as possible from the saddle. Carried out correctly, lungeing accustoms the horse to obeying the rider's voice, it teaches him to balance himself, and it helps the development of his muscles. There may also be occasions when it is necessary to lunge the horse rather than to ride him, and at a Horse Trial some young horses settle more quickly on the lunge than under saddle, and it may therefore be helpful to lunge them for a period before mounting.

For lungeing we need a lungeing rein, some 12 metres long, and a lungeing whip. The rein should have a swivel clip on one end and a small hand loop at the other, and the whip should be sufficiently long from the bottom of the handle to the far end of the lash to enable us to reach the horse's quarters if necessary. It is possible to make use of a hunting whip or even to dispense with a whip altogether with a trained horse, but a proper lungeing whip is essential for a young horse. A lungeing cavesson, though not absolutely essential, is very useful, and it is now possible to buy one in a webbing material with all the correct fittings. We shall certainly need a pair of side reins, with a swivel clip at one end for attaching to the rings of the snaffle, or to the cavesson, and an adjustable loop at the other for attachment to the girth, to the rings of a lungeing roller if we have one, or to the rings of a stable roller if we have not.

Lungeing should have featured in the process of breaking in our young horse, so we should have no difficulty in resuming this exercise. If we are using the snaffle, and are going to start on the left rein, then the clip of the lungeing rein should be passed through the snaffle ring on the left or near side, passing from outside to inside, then over the top of the horse's head and down onto the outside (right) snaffle ring. In this way any direct sideways pull on the horse's mouth is avoided, and the sensation for the horse is the nearest that we can achieve to the feel of the normal reins on the bit. If we are using a lungeing cavesson, then we attach the lungeing rein to the inside ring.

Useful work can be done without side reins, but the horse is then free to put his head where he pleases, which, if we are lungeing on grass, may well be as near as he can get to his favourite snack. With correctly fitted side reins, the head will remain in approximately the same position as it holds when the horse is ridden; they must not be used to try to force the head into any other position, and they are better fitted too long than too short. When the horse is ridden on a circle, his whole body should be bent in a gentle curve from muzzle to croup or tail, and the degree of bend should be such that we can just see the horse's inside eyelashes when viewed from the saddle. We should therefore fit the side reins so that this slight degree of bend is allowed, with the outside rein a few holes longer than the inside one, and both of them long enough to permit the horse to carry his head in a natural position with his nose in advance of the vertical. Any attempt to force the horse to bend on the circle by shortening the inside rein will merely force his quarters outwards, cause resistance, and defeat the object of lungeing. Shortening both reins in an attempt to 'collect' the horse will cause him to be overbent and to leave his hindquarters behind instead of engaging them.

Standing to the left of the horse and level with his withers, we take the loop of the rein in the right hand, together with the slack of the rein and the whip, holding the rein in contact with the snaffle in the left hand. We encourage him to walk forward with the voice aided by the whip, paying out the rein as he responds. We push him out on to the circle by pointing

the whip at his quarters and if necessary by 'rippling' the rein as well. (In order to 'ripple' the rein, we move the left hand up and down smartly several times, which will produce a ripple travelling along the rein towards the horse's head.) We must keep ourselves in a position that enables us to continue driving the horse forward, for only then can we control him and prevent any attempt at evasion. This means that we must be, not opposite his head, but opposite his quarters, as shown in Figure 4. If we position ourselves too far forward, then we cannot control him if he swings his quarters outwards and turns to face us, whereas if we are in the correct position opposite the quarters we can continue to drive him forward. To maintain the correct position, we cannot stand still but must walk round in a small circle, and this too helps to keep the horse moving forward. The tension on the rein should be such that there is a gentle loop from the hand to the snaffle.

With the horse walking round on the circle we give the command 'trot', supported by a flick of the whip towards his hocks. Our tone should be such as to galvanise him into action, and is best given in two syllables with a sharp

Figure 4   Figure lungeing.

Wrong
The trainer is standing in one place

Wrong
The trainer is moving round with the horse but is opposite the head

Correct
The trainer is moving round with the horse and is opposite the quarters

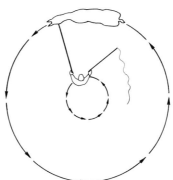

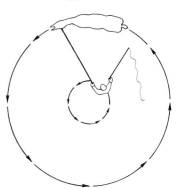

accent on the second – 'Terrrottt!'. Eventually only the voice will be required to produce the desired reaction. To return him from the trot to the walk, the voice clearly has a calming, slowing-down sort of tone – 'Waaaaalk', accompanied by a slightly increased feel on the rein. As soon as he comes back to the walk, we must ensure that he continues to walk forward and does not stop or turn towards us. We say 'Walk on!', pointing the whip at his quarters, and take a step to the right to ensure that we are in a position to drive him forward at the first sign of hesitation on his part.

Most of our work on the lunge will be done at the trot, and the canter should not be attempted until the horse is proficient at the trot on the lunge, and at the canter under saddle. When we do ask for the canter on the lunge, we want him to strike off into it as a result of the correct application of aids, or signals, that he recognises, and not by increasing the speed of the trot to such an extent that he runs into a canter. When we are ready to canter him on the lunge, we first establish a working trot and then ask for one or two transitions from trot to walk in order to prepare him. Then we increase the activity of the trot by use of the voice supported by the whip. Remembering that our preparatory signal for the canter under saddle was a feel on the inside rein, we feel the lungeing rein, give the command 'Canter', and flick the whip towards his quarters. On this first occasion he may well have to be 'driven' into the canter, but he will soon understand what is required. To return to the trot, our command will this time be a slowing-down, long-drawn-out 'Tro–o–o–o–t', and again we must be ready to drive him forward in the new pace until we are ready for another canter or a walk.

To achieve a halt, our command 'Ha–a–alt' is accompanied by a raising of the left hand, much as a traffic policeman might halt the traffic, having transferred the rein into the right hand, and we must be ready to use the whip to prevent him from coming in to us until we call him. A lungeing session ought to last for between twenty and forty minutes, with periods of ten minutes between changes of rein. Two points should be borne in mind: on the lunge he must be made to work and not be allowed just to amble round in a sort of idle jog-trot; and we must retain his interest by rewarding him when he works well. Good work on the lunge can be pleasurable for both horse and rider, and can do much to facilitate communication between them.

CHAPTER 7

Training the horse: jumping

At our first Novice One Day Horse Trial, the second test will be the Show Jumping, which will involve a course of between eight and ten obstacles up to 1.10 m, including a combination. This is a simple test, but too many riders at all levels reduce their chances in the overall competition by not paying sufficient attention to the preparation and schooling for it. The Cross Country test which follows is set at approximately the same height, though here the outline and type of obstacle and the approach to it may be more influential than the height. (We may note at this stage that the heights shown in the Official Rule Book are metric; a conversion table for feet and inches is provided in Appendix B.)

While it may be possible to undertake these tests on a horse with natural jumping ability, a degree of courage, and not much experience, the process of registering both horse and rider and of entering for Horse Trials is quite expensive, and we should therefore aim to give the horse the best possible preparation before we launch him into his first competition. He should certainly be capable of jumping clear in a Newcomers competition under B.S.J.A. rules, and ideally he should have learned to cope with a Foxhunter course. If he can do

that, then he will have the jumping ability to cope with both the Jumping and Cross Country tests at a Novice Horse Trial, and the only additional schooling needed will be to accustom him to water obstacles, bounces, banks and ditches.

Our first step will be the basic schooling over simple jumps at home, and this is possibly the most important part of our horse's training. For at this stage we shall have two objectives: first, to teach him to jump in good style, which simply means that he will make the most economical use of his energy in negotiating a fence; and second, to develop his confidence, both in his own ability and in his rider. When we eventually reach Advanced level or start to compete in Three Day Events, we shall find that a number of obstacles can only be jumped by the horse if he has complete confidence in his rider, since the horse himself will not know, and will not be able to see during the approach or at the moment of take-off, exactly where or on what he is about to land.

The equipment that we shall need for this basic schooling can be kept quite simple to begin with, and can be added to later. Our minimum requirement to start with consists of the material to build one upright and one

First it is important to teach the horse to jump in good style, which means that he will make the most economical use of his energy in negotiating a fence. Shannagh, Lucinda Green

spread fence, some cavaletti and some trotting poles. This amounts to six stands, six 3.65 m poles, four 2.75 m trotting poles, and four cavaletti. Later we can add the components of different obstacles such as a wall, a gate, and a brush fence together with extra stands and poles, so that we can build in the paddock a small course of between six and eight obstacles. Alternatively, we may be lucky enough to live near a riding establishment whose facilities we can hire occasionally when we need them. For our manege, the standard B.S.J.A. wing stands, though durable, are not really necessary, and there is an advantage in having something lighter that can more easily be moved, bearing in mind that we are probably going to have to

The first exercise involves the use of trotting poles

Figure 5 Trotting poles: each pole is 2.75 m × 10 cm in diameter, and 1.25 m apart.

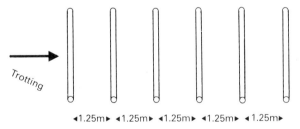

Trotting

◄1.25m► ◄1.25m► ◄1.25m► ◄1.25m► ◄1.25m►

enlist the help of a friend during our jumping sessions, and the friendship may be strained or the help may diminish if the equipment is too heavy!

Although our new horse may already have reached the stage of jumping over small obstacles with his previous owner, as part of the process of gaining his confidence we shall start at the beginning with the basic schooling exercises, which are in any case beneficial to him throughout the early stages of his training. For all jumping work we should have the services of a helper. He (or she) can range from someone who is an instructor to just a willing pair of hands, but it is only sensible to have someone present in case of accidents, and it is extremely difficult to make progress unless someone is available to raise or lower fences, retrieve poles that are knocked down, and adjust distances.

Our first exercise involves the use of trotting poles (see Figure 5). These should be round poles 2.75 m long and at least 10 cm in diameter. We begin by trotting over a single pole placed across the track of the manege. If our horse jumps or hops over it, we come back to the walk, and only when he trots quietly over it do we add a second pole about 1.25 m from the first. The horse should now lower his

head and lengthen his neck as he trots over the two poles, and should also pick up his feet sufficiently to clear them. Then we add the third and fourth poles; we can add a couple more if we have them, but with four we can achieve our object, which is to calm him, make him lower his head and lengthen his neck so that he looks at the poles, and encourage him to be careful – it will be quite uncomfortable for him if he treads on them. The exercise will also, incidentally, produce a beautifully cadenced trot, especially if we space the poles a few inches wider than his normal stride at the trot requires. If our horse starts rushing, or tries to jump over the poles, we go back to the walk, and when retaking the trot we give the reins as we approach the first pole; if we try to restrain him with a firmer contact this will merely encourage him to take off; if we yield the reins he has nothing against which to

lean, and he will drop his head and pay attention to what is required.

It is very important that we make it clear to the horse when we are pleased with his performance – we are usually quick enough to display our dissatisfaction – and when he does what we ask of him we should reward him with a pat, a few kind words, and perhaps some small titbit that he particularly appreciates. The use of the voice is especially important. Throughout our horse's training we should use it to reinforce other aids, to express displeasure, and to show him that we are pleased with his efforts.

We are now ready to pass on to the next stage, but before doing so we should remember never to ask our horse to do too much at one session. Where jumping training is concerned, 'little and often' should be our guiding principle, and our horse will enjoy both his flat

The next stage is to place a small jump about 2.5 to 2.6 m beyond
the trotting poles

A second cavaletto is added some 60 cm beyond the first

work and his jumping training more if we end each period of flat work with a few jumping exercises. In this way he will enjoy both aspects of his schooling and never become bored with either.

The next stage is to place a small jump about 2.50 to 2.60 m beyond our trotting poles (Figure 6). (The distances that we give for these training exercises are approximate, and should be varied to suit the size and stride of the horse; they will not be the same for the 17-hand thoroughbred and for his 15-hand cousin!) This can be either a cavaletto (an Italian word used to describe a 'knife rest' with the pole approximately 60 cm high), or a pole of the same height on a pair of stands. When our horse trots calmly over the trotting poles and this small obstacle, we add a second cavaletto or pole some 60 cm beyond the first, thus making a small spread. It is very important now to give the horse almost total freedom of his head and neck over this small jump. We

say 'almost', because we should remain in control and should therefore retain a light contact. But the horse must nevertheless be allowed to lower his head and stretch his neck as much as he wishes at this stage. We shall thus ensure from the very start that our horse jumps with a rounded, not hollow, back, which will be important when we come to jump larger fences and when, much later, the horse has to extricate himself from difficult situations that may arise on the Cross Country.

Before asking our horse to jump larger obstacles we shall further develop his muscles and increase his agility by using variations on this theme of trotting poles, cavaletti and small spreads. We can place a single pole on the ground 2.50 to 2.60 m in front of the fence, and another the same distance beyond it (see Figure 7); this is particularly useful for a horse that tends to throw up his head on landing, often merely a sign of exuberance or *joie de vivre*.

Figure 7   A pole is placed 2.5 m in front of a small fence and another the same distance beyond.

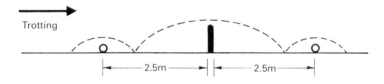

Figure 6   A small fence is placed 2.5 m beyond the trotting poles.

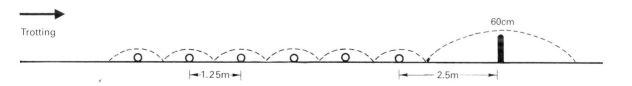

Next we introduce him to what is in effect his first small bounce. We lay out the trotting poles as before, with a cavaletto 2.50 m beyond. As soon as he has trotted quietly over these, we place a second cavaletto about 3.20 m beyond the first. Then, as we are about to take off over the first, we squeeze slightly harder with our legs so that he bounces straight out over the second.

We are now ready to introduce our horse to the grid. This is simply a line of six cavaletti or poles at the same height, with a distance of

A single pole can be placed on the ground 2.5 to 2.6 m in front of the fence, and another the same distance beyond it

approximately 3.20 m between each (see Figure 8). We start by trotting over one, then add another and so on until we have a line of six. We must again give the horse almost total freedom of his head and neck, whilst retaining sufficient contact to keep him straight and using our legs to keep him going forward. This is a most beneficial exercise for the development of the horse's muscles, and for the rider's balance.

Figure 8   A grid. Six cavaletti are placed 3.2 m apart.

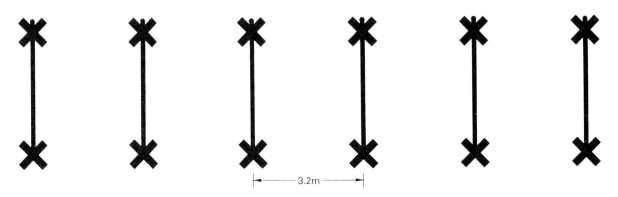

A second cavaletto is placed 3.2 m beyond the first

The grid is a most beneficial exercise for the development of the horse's muscles and for the rider's balance

A cavaletto is used in front of the fence so that the horse takes off from the correct position without intervention

Now is the moment to start asking our horse for a bigger effort. But we do not simply build a bigger fence and ride him at it. In all our previous agility work, and right through to schooling him over much larger fences, we want him to approach the obstacle correctly and take off at the precise spot that will enable him to negotiate it with the minimum of effort. What we do not want to do at this stage is to have to adjust his stride in the approach either by urging him on with our legs in order to lengthen it, or worse, by using the bit to shorten it. We therefore use a pole or a cavaletto in front of the fence so that this causes him to take off from the correct position without our intervention. (We can later use the same device to produce a take-off nearer to the fence or to make him stand off further away from it.) When using a cavaletto in this way to regulate the take-off, we always approach at the trot, and on landing over it the horse then takes one canter stride before taking off.

So we place a cavaletto about 6 metres from a low spread of two poles about 75 cm apart and 60 cm high. Then we gradually increase the spread, eventually adding a third pole, so that we are asking our horse to jump, from a trot, a spread of nearly two metres (see Figure 9). Now if we were to stand at the side and watch him jump, we would see that in order to clear this low spread, he is in fact raising himself to a height of perhaps 1.10 m, or even 1.20 m, which is the maximum height of a Three Day Event Show Jumping or Cross Country fence! Yet if we were to put a 1.20 m upright obstacle in front of him he would probably knock it down, or at the best produce an awkward and ungainly jump. But by jumping these low spreads, he is in fact teaching himself to clear height without realising it, and this is something of which we can take advantage during his training.

In order to clear this low spread, the horse is in fact raising himself to a height of 1.1 or even 1.2 m (the stands are 1.6 m high)

Figure 9   Increasing the effort over low spreads. By jumping low spreads, the horse is in fact teaching himself to clear height without realising it.

We shall continue this training using a cava-letto or take-off pole in front of a small parallel spread and then, when he has developed the ability to clear a certain amount of height, place one in front of an upright of two poles. Because there is no pole at the back to lift him over the obstacle, he may start by knocking this upright down, so we will make it easier for him by placing the cavaletto a little bit further away from the fence in order to make him take off earlier – another illustration of the way in which we use this device to achieve a precise point of take-off without having to intervene from the saddle. We can now start to ask our

horse to jump higher obstacles, so we replace the low parallel spread by an ascending spread, in which the front pole is lower than the back one. Using this method, in which he will always arrive at the correct point for take-off, we shall be developing both his jumping ability and his confidence, and we should now find progress relatively easy.

But alas, in competitions, both in the Show Jumping arena and across country, and indeed in the hunting field or out on a ride, any fences that we jump will not have the benefit of an aid that ensures a correct take-off. So now we have to train him, and maybe ourselves too, to

Figure 10   Teaching the 'bascule'.

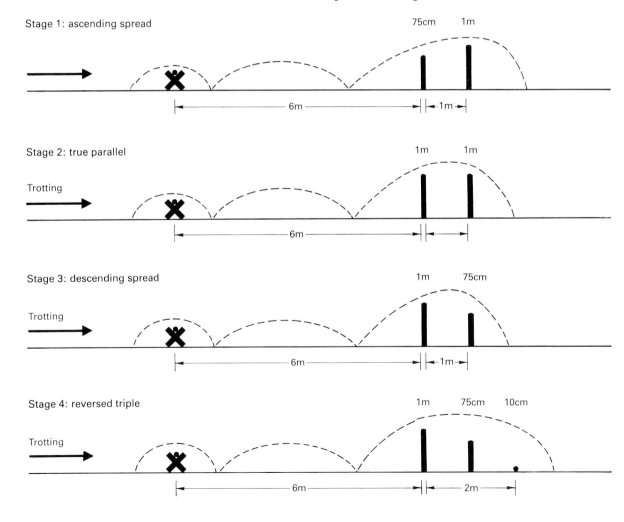

negotiate obstacles without this aid, and also teach him that however he may arrive at a fence, he is still expected to take off and clear it, whether it be upright or spread. To enable him to do this he needs two things – confidence in himself and his rider, and increased mobility and agility of his shoulders. If he arrives at a take-off point that is too close to a fence, he must still clear it with a rounded back and the minimum of effort; an awkward jump will take more out of a tired horse on the Cross Country than a stylish effort.

What we now aim to achieve is for the horse to take off close to an obstacle, lifting his body no higher than is necessary, which implies jumping with a rounded back, folding his forelegs, and then lifting his hindquarters as his forelegs come down. As is so often the case, we have no word in the English language that adequately describes the movement, and we have borrowed the French word 'bascule', though as its literal translation is 'see-saw' even this is not an entirely satisfactory term. In order to achieve a bascule, we set up our cavaletto in front of a low spread but about 50 cm closer than usual (see Figure 10, stage 1). In order not to hit the front pole, the horse must

When the horse has developed the ability to clear a certain amount of height, a cavaletto is placed in front of an upright

The horse is being assisted by the back pole of the spread

It can be made more difficult by raising the front pole and lowering the back one, thus making a descending spread

lift his shoulders more than usual, and we will have achieved the first step. But he is being assisted by the back pole of the spread, so we will make it slightly more difficult for him by raising the front pole slightly and lowering the back one, thus making a descending spread (stage 3).

Next we increase the differential between the front and back poles and place a third pole on the ground, so that the obstacle is now what amounts to a triple bar in reverse (stage 4). Having arrived at the take-off point that our cavaletto prescribes, our horse must lift his shoulders and retract his forelegs in order to clear the front pole, and then stretch his neck forwards and downwards in order to clear the second and third poles, which will enable him

Next the differential between the front and back poles is increased, and a third pole is placed on the ground, making a triple bar in reverse

to lift his hindquarters. He will lift his body no higher than is necessary and his back will be rounded – in other words, we have achieved a bascule. In order to let him do this, our hands must follow the movement of his head and neck, otherwise we shall restrict his freedom and his back will be hollow instead of rounded. It is important that we carry out this exercise over a descending spread or reversed triple bar only in the presence of an assistant and over a lower obstacle than the horse is accustomed to jumping. We shall, however, have laid the basis of a good style of jumping which our horse should retain for the rest of his career.

Our horse is now ready to tackle fences at the canter without any assistance in deciding the point of take-off. We start with the easiest form of obstacle, the ascending spread. During his previous schooling, he has been trotting over a cavaletto or take-off bar, which will have allowed him one canter stride before the take-off. We allow him to do this again, and then remove the cavaletto and approach the fence at a controlled canter. Much that happens from now on will depend upon our ability to 'see a stride'. Some riders seem to be born with this ability; with others it develops with experience; some, alas, never achieve it. Probably the greatest difference between the very top riders and the 'also rans' is this ability to see a stride. The real expert sees it so far in front of the obstacle that he appears never to have to make any adjustment to his horse's stride during the approach; in fact he may be doing so unobtrusively during the last five or six strides. His less talented colleague may be seen either to check his horse or to push him on during the last one or two.

In Show Jumping, the d'Inzeo brothers, Piero and Raimondo, from Italy, Bill Steinkraus from the U.S.A., and Peter Robeson from Great Britain are among those great riders who in their heydays were brilliant judges of a stride. In steeplechasing, Fred Winter, in his riding days, Bryan Marshall, winner of three Grand Nationals and probably one of the best natural horsemen to come out of Ireland, and John Francome, a member of the British Junior European Show Jumping Championship Gold Medal Team before he took to racing, are among those for whom horses seldom seemed to arrive wrong at a fence. In eventing, Bruce Davidson, America's former World Champion, Mark Todd, New Zealand's Olympic Gold Medallist, and our own World Champions Lucinda Green and Virginia Leng are among those for whom fences consistently seem to come right.

Most of us do not come into this class, and so for us it is important to train our horses to

Figure 11 Straight approach and take-off (side view).

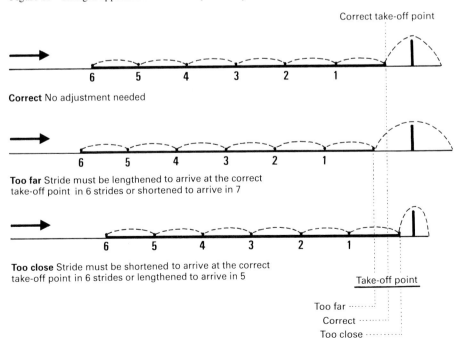

think for themselves. We have already used a cavaletto to teach our horse the correct take-off point, and we can also use one to teach him to take off close to a fence, or to stand back from a distance, by placing it closer to or further away from the obstacle. Now he has to learn to take off on his own, however we may bring him into it. So we approach the fence at a steady canter, and ideally our horse will arrive at the correct take-off point without our intervention. But if at some point we recognise

that he will not, then we have three options: we can do nothing and let him do the best he can, we can check him and shorten his stride so that he arrives at the correct take-off point by putting in an extra stride, or we can squeeze him forward with our legs so that he arrives at the take-off point with one stride less (see Figure 11). Since our priority at this stage is to keep the horse going forward, if in doubt we should adopt the last course. If we really cannot see a stride at all, then it is better to do

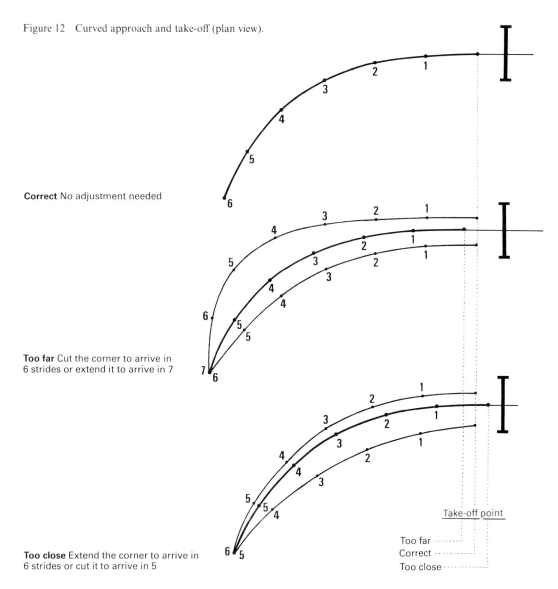

Figure 12   Curved approach and take-off (plan view).

Correct No adjustment needed

Too far Cut the corner to arrive in 6 strides or extend it to arrive in 7

Too close Extend the corner to arrive in 6 strides or cut it to arrive in 5

Take-off point

Too far

Correct

Too close

nothing and let the horse sort out the situation for himself, for in that case there is a 50% chance that the stride is not wrong anyway, and if it is wrong there is a 50% chance that we shall make the wrong correction!

There is, however, another way of ensuring that we arrive at the right point for take-off, and which is easier to put into effect than lengthening or shortening our horse's stride. If we are jumping two fences in a straight line, then we have no option other than to shorten or lengthen the stride between the first and second, but when we are approaching a fence on the turn, we can adjust our approach very easily either by cutting the corner, which will bring us to the take-off point sooner, or by turning later, which will have the opposite effect (see Figure 12). It is also much easier to judge the approach when coming in on an angle than when on a straight line.

We should now be ready to teach our horse to jump combinations of either two or three fences with one or two strides between them.

Since we have already introduced him to small bounces and grids, this should not be too difficult. All we need to do is to place a cavaletto in front of our low spread and place the second ascending spread one stride away from the first. Now the question of distances in combinations could easily fill a whole chapter on its own; but useful working distances are 7.50 m for a one-stride combination and 10.50 m for two strides, measured in each case from inside to inside, or from the last element of the first obstacle to the first element of the second (see Figure 13). (The cavaletto we place only about 6 metres in front of the first fence because we shall only be trotting over it.) We then vary the obstacles in our combinations, and eventually remove the cavaletto.

Ideally we should have at home a variety of small obstacles and fillers – small walls or more simple wooden boards painted in bright colours – plus a brush fence and a gate, so that we can gradually introduce strange shapes and colours into our schooling fences. We are then

Figure 13   Training distances for combinations. The distances will be varied according to the height and type of obstacle and the stride and experience of the horse.

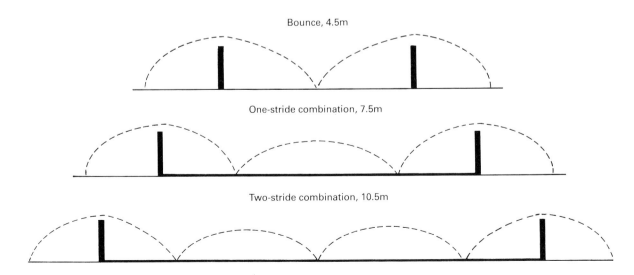

Bounce, 4.5m

One-stride combination, 7.5m

Two-stride combination, 10.5m

ready to tackle a small course which we can erect in the manege if it is big enough, or otherwise in the paddock. If our preparation has been correct, this will not prove difficult for him, though the first time we ask him to jump a course in the open we must be on our guard against any attempt to evade an obstacle by running round it. Once our horse can jump a small course at home cleanly and without fuss, we should take him to a local riding establishment or to friends who have some show jumps, so that he can be introduced to a course of strange fences. Once he has negotiated these confidently, we are ready to take him to his first small show.

We now need to consider the rider's seat and length of stirrups for jumping. The same basic considerations apply to the Show Jumping and the Cross Country, though we shall have to modify our seat for the latter in order to give extra emphasis to the need for security. An examination of the top riders in action will show that over the jump the rider's position is such that a line drawn from the shoulder to the knee will continue down through the ankle, and that over normal fences this position is maintained throughout the jump. The weight is taken on the ball of the foot, or sometimes the toe, which rests on the stirrup; the ankles and knees, together with the hip joint, allow the body to follow the movement of the horse. A second line drawn from the shoulder to the hands will continue through to the horse's mouth. The upper body position allows the arms and hands to follow the horse's mouth as he stretches his neck and lowers his head over the fence, and the rider's weight is at this moment off the saddle.

Such perfection, however, is not always achieved; if the rider is too far forward, with his legs too far back, his weight will probably have been thrown onto the horse's shoulder just as he was about to lift his forehand over the fence, and in the case of a peck on landing the rider may well be thrown 'out of the front door'. If he is too far back, then his weight will be down on the saddle, and it will be difficult for the horse to lift his quarters over the fence. In either case it will be less easy for the horse to clear the fence, and in the case of a combination obstacle the rider will not be in the best position in which to regulate his horse for the second element.

The length of stirrup, which will vary from rider to rider and from horse to horse, needs to be short enough to enable the rider to maintain the correct position over the fence, and yet not so short that he cannot comfortably sit down in the saddle when he requires to drive his horse forward during the approach. During our schooling of the young horse at home, it may be wise to have the stirrups a hole longer than we shall have them when riding in a competition, and when schooling the young horse we should be ready to make use of the neck strap of the running martingale in case an unexpected take-off upsets our balance – better to catch the neck strap than our horse's mouth!

CHAPTER 8

Training the horse:
Cross Country and general

Introduction to Cross Country • *New types of obstacle*
• *Banks, ditches, water, drops* • *Bounces* • *Corners* • *Hunting* • *Hunter Trials*
• *Riding Club events* • *Problems* • *Psychology* • *Reward, correction and punishment*
• *Bit, spur, whip and voice* • *Jumping problems* • *Rushing and head-throwing*
• *Jumping to one side* • *Carelessness* • *Maintaining enthusiasm*
• *The Cross Country seat* • *Ready for action*

If our basic jumping training has progressed according to plan, we should not experience too much difficulty in introducing our horse to the Cross Country, since he will have both the technical ability and the confidence necessary to face this new challenge. The maximum height of fences on the Novice Cross Country course is only 1.05 m, but the siting of them, and the approaches to them, which may be uphill or downhill or across a slope, may present extra difficulties for a young horse. For this reason his jumping should be firmly established before he tackles an official Horse Trial, which means that he should be capable of jumping a B.S.J.A. Foxhunter course, or at the very least a Newcomers. But his introduction to Cross Country obstacles can begin long before he reaches this stage.

If we are lucky enough to live near a riding establishment that has a small Cross Country schooling course, or even just a few obstacles, then our task will be relatively easy. It is not the size of the obstacles that will bother him, nor – since they will be rustic or natural – their colour, but their shape and siting. Used to coloured poles, walls, planks and gates, he must now accustom himself to banks, ditches, water and drops, all of which require rather different techniques. In addition to combinations of fences set at one or two strides apart, he must now learn to cope with bounces, where the landing-point of one fence is also the take-off point for the next. Accustomed to jumping fences straight, he must learn to jump them at an angle when required.

Fortunately, the basic jumping schooling that we have already carried out will also serve us well when it comes to introducing our horse to the Cross Country. Bounces, for example, formed part of our agility training, and when it comes to negotiating rather higher ones on the Cross Country, it is usually the rider who is more apprehensive than the horse. In fact many of the problems that arise on a Novice course are due more to apprehension on the part of the rider, which quickly communicates itself to the horse, than to doubts on the horse's

Jumping into water: French Blue, Richard Meade, Bramham

72

part. The rider's approach should therefore be one of confident forward movement; given this encouragement, a young horse that has received the correct basic training will overcome these new challenges without too much difficulty.

The obstacles used for Cross Country schooling should not be too large. We are only trying to accustom the horse to a different set of problems, and there is not the motivation, for either horse or rider, to attack large fences. In competition, horse and rider are wound up to do as well as possible, but schooling over large Cross Country obstacles in cold blood has probably been responsible for as many falls as competitions. Another reason for keeping schooling fences fairly small is that above all we must ensure that the horse retains the desire to be onward bound, so that if he does not meet an obstacle right, he can still negotiate it provided that he has the necessary forward movement. With larger obstacles, the rider may feel that it is necessary to check his horse, who may then suspect that undue caution is required. Throughout this stage of schooling, the obstacles, though strange, should always be within the horse's capability.

One type of obstacle that we must introduce

A bounce fence can be gradually increased in height to 1.05 m and the distance to 4.5 m

(a) Start with poles 90cm high and 3.5m apart

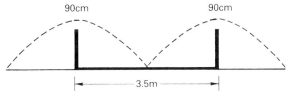

(b) Gradually increase the poles to 1.05m high and 4.5m apart

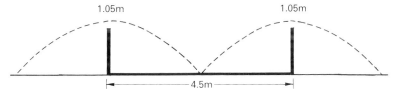

Figure 14   Setting up a bounce at home.

to our horse at an early stage is water, since he will eventually meet it in various forms, and to cope with the problems that it will present he must first lose any fear of water, then learn to trust his rider, and finally develop the strength and agility necessary to negotiate obstacles into, in and out of water. If we are lucky enough to have near us a wide but shallow ford with a firm bottom that we can ride through on hacks, this will quickly accustom him to water, as will a sandy beach by the sea. (Few ponds have a firm enough bottom, and nothing will put a horse off water more surely than an uncertain footing.)

We may be able to erect a small jump – two stands and a pole will suffice – on the lip of the water so that we can pop in and out of it, and we may even be able to fix up a small jump in the middle of the water by resting a pole on an oil drum or any makeshift stand other than one that will float. The important thing at this stage is to give our horse confidence, and also to let him overcome the effects of splashing water which may unsight him just as he is about to take off.

Two obstacles that we can prepare our horse for at home are bounces and corners. The normal distance in a bounce fence on a Novice Cross Country course will be between 4 and $4\frac{1}{2}$ metres. We start by exercising over the grid, and then set up a bounce fence with poles about 90 cm high and 3.50 m apart, gradually increasing the height to 1.05 m and the distance to 4.50 m (see Figure 14). We can set up a corner by placing two poles on three stands as shown in Figure 15, with the back pole slightly higher than the front, and a fairly acute angle in the corner. Gradually we widen the angle and raise the poles.

Most errors at corners on Cross Country courses are caused by riders taking the wrong approach and so confusing the horse. Unfortunately, course builders have a habit of constructing corners as 'island' fences in the

middle of a field, usually because they cannot often be sited conveniently as part of a natural hedgeline. If there happens to be a tree on the corner itself the obstacle is easier, since there is less likelihood of the horse trying to run out

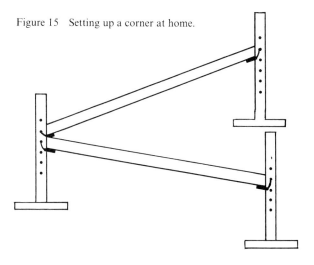

Figure 15   Setting up a corner at home.

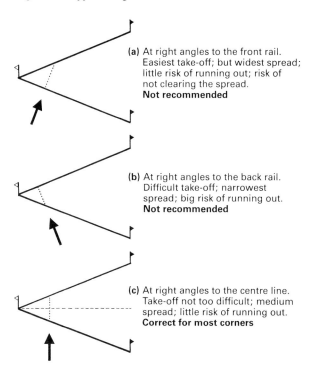

Figure 16   Approaching a corner.

(a) At right angles to the front rail. Easiest take-off; but widest spread; little risk of running out; risk of not clearing the spread. **Not recommended**

(b) At right angles to the back rail. Difficult take-off; narrowest spread; big risk of running out. **Not recommended**

(c) At right angles to the centre line. Take-off not too difficult; medium spread; little risk of running out. **Correct for most corners**

A corner can be set up by placing two poles on three stands with
the back pole slightly higher than the front

Gradually the angle can be widened and poles raised on the corner

at the open end; if there is no tree, then the course builder ought in fairness to plant a shrub or Christmas tree on the corner, since without one he is almost asking an unfair question of the Cross Country horse. However, we are often going to be faced with this problem, with only a flag on the corner, so we had best prepare to deal with it.

It is possible to approach a corner fence in three ways: first, we can approach at right angles to the first pole (see Figure 16a). This produces the easiest take-off but, for any given take-off position, the widest spread. We can alternatively narrow the spread by approaching at right angles to the back pole (see Figure 16b), but this increases the danger of running out. The best course is to approach at right angles to an imaginary line bisecting the angle of the corner (see Figure 16c). The distance of our point of take-off from the corner will depend upon the configuration of the fence and the angle of the corner. Ideally it should be, in the case of an 'open' corner without a tree, as far from the corner as possible without increasing the spread too much. In practice we should aim at a point that gives us a spread of about 1.10 to 1.25 m.

Our next step will be to enter a Hunter Trial or similar Cross Country competition. But first it is worth while to consider the merit or otherwise of educating our horse in the hunting field. Much, of course, will depend on where we live. We may not live in hunting country at all, and our horse's Cross Country education will gain little from trotting round the roads or following the horse in front round endless hock-deep ploughed fields. If, however, we are fortunate to have access to country with a fair percentage of grass there is much to be gained, since grass implies fences. Few of them, admittedly, will be similar to the majority of obstacles met on Cross Country courses, but, especially if there are ditches, his boldness and his scope will be developed. With our young horse, we shall be careful to follow those who know the country and whose horses are more experienced, so that we are given a lead, and so that we do not inadvertently put our horse at unjumpable places. In this way, he will gain confidence and learn to look after himself – and his rider! And although many successful Three Day Event horses have never set foot in the hunting field, it is to the hunting field that we in this country owe our predominance in the production of Cross Country horses, and it is the reason why British horses are eagerly sought after by riders of other nations (Lucinda Green makes a habit of sending her horses to be hunted in Leicestershire by 'Joss' Hanbury, Master of the Quorn and Cottesmore Hunts).

Our first Cross Country competition will probably be a Hunter Trial. In the past, Hunter Trial courses mainly consisted of natural fences, with a proportion of posts and rails that could be knocked down; not particularly suitable for the embryo eventer, since at Horse Trials it is (usually) the horse that falls rather than the fence should there be confrontation between the two! But today Hunter Trial courses tend to resemble Horse Trial courses, for three main reasons. First, Hunter Trials are very popular, and to withstand the onslaught of perhaps two or three hundred horses in a day, the fences must be strengthened so that they are no longer natural; second, many Hunter Trials are now sponsored and are qualifying events in a national series culminating in a championship, and there is therefore the money available with which to build a solid, imposing and interesting course; and third, most Hunter Trials are conducted in order to make money for the hunt or other organisation that runs them, and courses are often designed with a view to attracting entries from the eventing fraternity, who regard them as useful pre-season pipe-openers.

We should now be ready to put all three

aspects of our training together – schooling on the flat, over jumps, and across country. Before we take the serious (and expensive) step of entering for an official Horse Trial, however, we may be able to find a local Riding Club that runs its own Horse Trial, and we may be able to enter for one of these. If it is run by a Riding Club that is affiliated to the British Horse Society, the Official Rules permit this, and if not, then the only stipulation is that the prize money may not exceed a certain limit.

Although we are now ready to enter our first official Horse Trial, let us suppose that during our training all has not gone according to plan, and that we have experienced difficulties en route. We must continually bear in mind that there are two elements in the training of the young horse – the physical, by which we mean the development of his muscles and his athletic ability, and the psychological. The psychological aspect is very important and has many facets. It entails the building of the horse's confidence, both in his own ability and in his rider. He must trust his rider so that when he is presented with an unforeseen challenge he trusts his rider's judgement in presenting it, and his own ability to overcome it. We must remember that the horse has a very good memory but very limited power of reasoning, and every step that we take in his training must reflect this. Each step forward must be built upon the last, and we must regulate the speed of our progress according to our horse's ability to understand what we are asking and to remember what we teach him.

We must be as generous in rewarding him when he responds to what we are asking him to do as we are in rebuking him when he does not. The pat on the neck, the vocal expression of pleasure, and a handful of grass or a mint or other titbit will all reap dividends. When he fails to do what he is asked, we have to decide whether it is because he is naughty – and what young child, human or equine, is not naughty

at some time or other? – whether it is due to discomfort or pain, caused either by ill-fitting tack or by some ailment, or whether it is simply because we have tried to move forward too quickly and he has either not understood what we are asking him, or is physically incapable of responding.

We then have to decide whether correction or punishment is required, or whether, in the case of pain or discomfort, we can eliminate the cause. If the horse has misunderstood our demand, then we must correct him by retracing our steps to the last point at which the correct response had been firmly established. If punishment is required it must be immediate, definite and very short: immediate, because the horse's brain can only associate punishment with something that has occurred seconds, not minutes, before; definite, because he must be in no doubt that it is punishment that we are inflicting; and short, because prolonged punishment will cause him to forget the original cause and will merely make him seek ways to escape from or overcome this unpleasant experience, and we may lose his co-operation. There are four readily available methods of punishment which the rider can use; one of them should never be used, one seldom, if ever, and the remaining two should be used when necessary.

The one that should never be used is the bit. We spend much of our time trying to lighten the horse's mouth, steady his head carriage, and get him to accept signals from a piece of ironmongery which is placed on one of the most delicate portions of his anatomy, the bars of his mouth. To use the bit as a means of punishment will undo much of this training and make him frightened of what we are trying so hard to get him to accept. The one that should seldom be used is the spur. The spur is an aid, and is again something to which we are training the horse to respond; to use it as a means of punishment therefore is something that should seldom, if ever, be done. The whip is first and foremost an aid, used primarily to reinforce the signals given by the legs and the spur. For example, when teaching our horse to turn on the forehand, one of the essential steps in teaching him to open a gate, we apply our leg in order to move his quarters, and if he does not respond, probably because he does not understand, a sharp tap with the whip will make our purpose clear. We may also use it as a reinforcement to the leg to achieve increased impulsion. It is also a legitimate means of punishment, which, provided that it is used correctly, will not do the horse any harm.

For example, during our jumping training, our horse should never refuse, provided that we match each step forward to his ability and experience to date and never ask him for too much. But a young horse, fit, well and full of *joie de vivre*, may suddenly try to evade the obstacle and run out. Perhaps this morning it occurs to him that it might be easier, or more fun, to go round the obstacle rather than over it. If we have not been sufficiently alert to prevent this, then a couple of sharp strokes from the whip applied to his quarters is a necessary and salutary punishment. The strokes must be immediate, strong enough to hurt, and few in number. The whip should never be used as a means of punishment anywhere except on the quarters, and its use should never be prolonged.

The fourth and often the most effective means of punishment for the young horse is the voice. Horses, like dogs, do not easily understand words, though they can be taught to respond to them through repetition, but they do react to tone, and the short, sharp, verbal expression of displeasure, in contrast to the tone that we use when we are pleased, will often be sufficient punishment. We have already taught our horse to obey our voice when on the lunge, so he will be used to interpreting the shades of tone that we can display.

If our jumping training progresses step by step, and we do not try to hurry the pace of learning too much, then ideally few problems should arise. But life seldom conforms to the ideal, so we must try to understand the cause of any problems that do confront us and do our best to remedy them. A refusal or a run-out should always be punished, but at the same time we must ask ourselves whether it was our fault for asking our horse to do something for which he was not ready, in which case we must retrace our steps and progress more slowly, or whether it was due to naughtiness, in which case after correct and salutary punishment we can proceed again. There are, however, several problems which may arise, and which must be corrected before they become established habits.

Rushing at a fence is at least a sign that our horse is keen to jump it, but it can land us in trouble and it certainly makes the task of ensuring a correct take-off more difficult. In some situations it can be extremely dangerous. Sometimes this habit is combined with that of throwing up the head, either in the approach, during the final strides before take-off, or on landing. This means that the horse is not really looking at the obstacle, his rider's vision may also be obscured, and there is a fair chance of the rider receiving a nasty blow in the face on landing. The remedy is to revert to the use of trotting poles or a grid, and to place one or other in front of a fence, the poles about $2\frac{1}{2}$ to 3 metres in front, or the last element of the grid about 6 metres in front. The horse cannot then continue to rush, and must also lower his head to see what he is doing. For the horse that throws up his head on landing, a single pole placed on the ground $2\frac{1}{2}$ to 3 metres in front of the fence, and another on the ground about the same distance beyond it on the landing side will again cause him to lower his head. We may find that we have to resort to these reminders occasionally during our training.

Jumping to left or right over a fence can lead to all sorts of problems if not corrected. In the Show Jumping arena it may cause a fence to be knocked down by the rider's leg hitting the wing stand; across country it may produce a more serious problem, especially in combinations, where the line through them may be very important; and in both tests the horse may be considerably increasing the spread which he has to negotiate. The habit is sometimes caused initially by the horse coming too close to an obstacle and then trying to make room for himself, but it can also be caused by the rider being stronger on one side than on the other, or by some soreness or pain in one side of the horse's mouth. Having eliminated the possibility of the last by having his mouth and teeth examined, it is then not too difficult a fault to correct.

Figure 17   Straightening the crooked jumper.

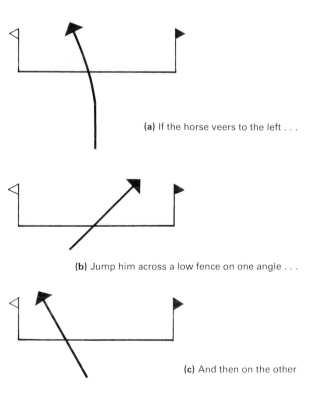

(a) If the horse veers to the left . . .

(b) Jump him across a low fence on one angle . . .

(c) And then on the other

Let us suppose that our horse has started jumping to the left (see Figure 17a). Starting with a pole at about 75 cm, we trot him across it several times at an angle (Figures 17b and c). We must be strong with our outside or open-side hand and leg to prevent him from running out. We gradually increase the height to about 1.05 m, and then vary the exercise with approaches in a straight line. Our horse will soon understand that he must jump the fence at the point and in the direction of our choosing.

Finally there is the problem of carelessness. If our horse has natural jumping ability, and if our basic jumping training has been on the correct lines, then we are more likely to find that over-exuberance or extravagance in jumping provide early problems rather than carelessness, which may however develop as he becomes more familiar with jumping and as his style becomes more economical. Fortunately, we have on our side the fact that a horse does not really like hitting an obstacle, because the average Show Jumping pole is fairly heavy, and to hit it with any part of his leg above the hoof causes a degree of pain – and all the more so if it is a fixed Cross Country obstacle. Nevertheless, some horses do become careless, and this is unacceptable.

The best way to overcome this is to make the horse associate the hitting of a pole with a startling noise and rather more resistance than is offered by the ordinary pole. To this end we replace the top pole of our schooling fence with an ordinary scaffold pole or metal drain pipe of the same length, and painted in the same way as our normal poles. If our horse hits this with his toe, the noise will startle him, and if he hits it with any part of the leg above the hoof, then he will recognise that he has been in contact with something considerably less yielding than the customary wooden pole. (It will still fall down if he hits it really hard, and the lesson will be that much better learned!)

An occasional reminder of this sort, coupled with continued agility schooling, will cure most horses of a tendency to be careless.

We have touched upon various technical aspects of training, dealt with some of the problems that may arise, and emphasised the importance of the psychological aspect. It is now extremely important that we keep our horse interested and keen about his work. To this end we must never bore him, must vary his work, reward him when he responds to our demands, and let our watchword be 'little and often'. If we work him for six days of the week, letting him rest on the seventh, then only three, or at the very most four, should be spent in the manege; on the others he should enjoy a hack round the countryside, which can be just as important as his work at home. Work in the manege should only last for thirty to forty minutes, with the last ten minutes or so devoted to jumping work, so that he does not become bored by work on the flat and will also enjoy his jumping exercises at the end of the session. Each session of flat work or jumping should be planned to achieve a specific and limited objective. When we have achieved it we should reward our horse, leave the manege, and take him out for a hack.

Although our hacks will be in the nature of a relaxation for our horse, there are several aspects of his training which we can practise whilst out in the country: lengthening of the stride, halting, reining back, opening gates, and later even lateral movements – a half-pass executed from one side of the road to the other, for example, may seem to have more point than the same exercise performed in the manege. But most important is to work on his walk, pushing him along and making him extend himself instead of just ambling along at his own pace.

To lengthen his stride at the walk, we use our legs alternately in order to make him place his hind legs further forward than he would otherwise do. We can influence his hind legs only when they are on the ground; once they are in the air it is too late. But fortunately when the hind leg is on the ground, the foreleg on the same side is moving forward, so if we apply our left leg as the horse's left (near) foreleg is moving forward, and our right leg as his right (off) foreleg is moving forward we should achieve a lengthening of his stride. This may sound complicated, but in practice it is not, and since a horse that walks out well will usually gallop well, this is a most important area of our training.

Having considered the rider's seat and length of stirrups for Jumping, we should now see whether we need to modify these for the Cross Country. Basically the principles of a correct seat remain the same for both tests, but when we come to the Cross Country there are two factors that outweigh all others in our considerations. The first of these is security. 'Handsome is as handsome does' was never more true than when applied to a rider's Cross Country seat. This does not mean that we can toss our principles to the wind, for an elegant style implies that a rider is both giving his horse every chance of clearing the obstacle and is himself secure in the saddle. What it does mean is that security on landing must be a prime consideration. Very few show jumpers fall on landing after they have cleared a fence; and while, if a horse falls on the Cross Country either through hitting a fence or through losing his feet on landing, there is little that his rider can do to avoid a separation, in the case of a peck, or stumble on landing, a secure seat can make all the difference between 'getting away with it' and the impossible handicap of 60 penalties. And in extreme cases at a Three Day Event a secure seat may just enable a rider to hang on long enough for his horse to clear

Over Cross Country obstacles and especially those with a drop, the rider's centre of gravity must be further back, and the reins appreciably longer. Sir Wattie, Ian Stark, Badminton

the penalty zone before he parts company, so avoiding any penalties at all!

This implies that over Cross Country obstacles, and especially those with a drop, the rider's centre of gravity must be further back, and his feet further forward, than over a Show Jump, and that the reins must be appreciably longer if he is not to interfere with his horse's mouth. When jumping into water these considerations apply even more strongly, for the sudden deceleration experienced when a horse lands in 50 cm of water, as anyone who has stood at the Lake at Badminton will know, can decant the rider who is not prepared for it, and at the same time the length of rein required to give the horse freedom of his head means that the reins must be virtually out to the buckle – and yet the rider must quickly collect his horse to jump out of the water, or another obstacle in it. It is hardly surprising, therefore, that riders landing over Beecher's Brook in the Grand National and those jumping into the water at, for example, the Trout Hatchery at Burghley adopt much the same seat!

The second factor is 'drive'. On the Cross Country course there is a much greater need to be able to sit down and drive the horse forward into an uninviting obstacle than is normally the case in the Show Jumping arena, certainly with the simple type of course usually facing the Horse Trials competitor. At the same time, for most of the Cross Country course we shall want to take the weight off the saddle, and this applies especially to a Three Day Event, where the course may be several miles in length. This implies a shorter length of stirrup than for Show Jumping, but not so short that we cannot sit down and drive our horse forward when required. Because Horse Trials riders spend most of their time in the saddle with their stirrups at Dressage length, the tendency is to ride too long across country, which makes it difficult to take the weight off the horse's back, and is consequently more tiring for him.

It is interesting to note that, if we observe the top riders in action across country, the principle of shoulder, knee and ankle being in line still seems to apply, even when the centre of gravity is shifted back in order to cope with a big drop. Style can therefore be practical as well as elegant!

We have now trained our horse up to Novice standard; we have taken part in Riding Club or unaffiliated Dressage competitions, completed some Hunter Trials, and he is confidently jumping clear rounds in jumping competitions at small shows, hopefully up to Foxhunter level or somewhere near it. We are now ready to enter him for his first official Horse Trial.

Part 3

COMPETING

CHAPTER 9

Our first official Horse Trial: preparations

Registration • *The Rule Book* • *The Bulletin* • *The Omnibus Schedule*
• *Entering* • *The ballot system* • *Entry forms* • *Acknowledgement* • *Withdrawals*
• *Start times* • *Assistance* • *Timetable* • *Saddlery* • *In the stable*
• *Rugs* • *Bandages* • *Grooming kit* • *First aid kit* • *Dressage*
• *Show Jumping* • *Cross Country* • *Dress*

Competing in an official Horse Trial involves a certain amount of long-term planning. First, the rider must be a member of the British Horse Society (B.H.S.). This is an organisation to which every rider should belong, for it is the one body that represents the interests of all riders and the welfare of all horses; sadly, many do not, though they are happy to enjoy the benefits that the work of the Society gains for them. But membership is a prerequisite for competing in Horse Trials. So too is membership of the Horse Trials Group, the body that controls the sport of eventing and regulates some 160 official Horse Trials in the annual calendar. Finally, the horse must be registered, which requires the completion of a vaccination certificate or passport.

In order to complete these formalities, we apply to the Horse Trials Office at the British Equestrian Centre at Stoneleigh, Warwickshire, and we shall then receive the Rules for Official Horse Trials, the Omnibus Schedule for the Spring, Summer or Autumn events, the Horse Trials Group Bulletin, and a supply of entry forms, together with our membership card and a registration card for the horse. Our first task should be to read the rules – ignorance

may, in other circles, be bliss, but in the world of Horse Trials it may not get us very far! Apart from that, we are going to considerable trouble and expense in order to compete, so we may as well ensure that we do not have our entries rejected, get ourselves eliminated in competition, or worse, incur suspension, through ignorance of the Rules.

Next we should study the Omnibus Schedule and plan our campaign. The rules relating to entries are contained in the Rule Book and repeated in the Schedule, and we must familiarise ourselves with the detailed procedure for making entries and with the ballot system. Although there are over 130 Novice One Day Horse Trials in the annual calendar, many of these are vastly oversubscribed and are therefore subject to a ballot system in order to reduce their entries to manageable proportions. Several systems have been tried over the years, and a new one was introduced in 1988. The rules must be studied in detail, and since they are liable to amendment each year, not too much reliance should be placed on those in force in 1988, which involve two types of entry form and three categories of entry. The system may seem complicated, but the aim is to try to ensure that every competitor will be assured of a competition in each two-week Ballot Period during the season.

In brief, there are Normal entry forms, with no priority, Special entry forms (of a different colour), which give priority, and Super Special entries, using both forms, which confer the highest priority of all. If we now look at the fixture list, we shall see that the whole year is divided into Ballot Periods, most of which cover a half-month. Against each fixture is shown a Ballot Date, which replaces the old Closing Date and which is about three weeks before the event. We need, however, to make a note of yet another date, fourteen days before the Ballot Date, because entries must not be posted before that date, otherwise they may be rejected.

Having selected the Horse Trials at which we would like to compete, and noted the various dates which we must observe in making our entries, we then have to decide for which of our chosen events in each Ballot Period we will use our Special entry form, which should normally give us a high probability of acceptance, and for which ones we will take our chances with the Normal forms. We can discover which events are normally oversubscribed and liable to ballot either from the Bulletin or from the organisers shown in the Schedule. Some, especially in the Spring, are so heavily oversubscribed that a Special entry may still be balloted out, but in that case we become eligible for a Super Special entry.

When making our entries, it is important to read the detailed schedule for a chosen event carefully, and in particular to note the paragraph headed 'Special Notices'. It is also wise to look for a note below the paragraph headed 'Approximate Times' in case it indicates that some competitors will be required to do their Dressage on the afternoon of the previous day, and requesting those who are unable to do so to say so on their entry forms; it can be very

annoying, having planned to travel to an event on a Saturday, to discover that in fact your Dressage test takes place on Friday afternoon, because you failed to notice this request! The entry form itself should be read carefully and completed correctly – at an oversubscribed event, an incorrectly or illegibly filled-in entry form arriving on the desk of a harassed secretary is likely to find its way quickly into the 'balloted out' tray! For the same reason, it is important to note whether or not the entry fees, which are higher for events which take place before Badminton than for later ones, are subject to V.A.T. Finally, if we have any special requests, the time to make them is now, on the entry form, and not at the last moment when all the arrangements have already been made.

If our entry is accepted, we will receive an acknowledgement which will include our approximate timings. The next point to note is the deadline for and the method of withdrawing, in case circumstances make this necessary. If we do not withdraw it is assumed that we shall compete, but forgetting to withdraw and then failing to start is likely to be penalised by the Disciplinary Committee of the B.H.S. Our next step will depend upon the distance that we have to travel to the event. If it is local, and we have the time, we may go and walk the Cross Country course when it is officially open for inspection on the previous afternoon, and we may be able to collect our starting times then. If it is far afield, then we telephone for our starting times according to the instructions laid down in the schedule, and we must fit in our course inspection on the day of the competition itself. Telephoning for starting times can be frustrating and time-consuming, for there may be up to 300 horses running on the particular day in question, which means that the telephone lines may be jammed with calls – when a telephone with a repeat dialling facility becomes a distinct advantage. Having eventually established contact, it is as well not to begin by exchanging pleasantries, but to come straight to the point and ask for the starting times for 'Section 3, Number 123, Hopeful Optimist' – the numbers will have been sent to us on the form of acknowledgement.

Having received our timings, we then know whether there will be time to walk the Cross Country course after the Dressage, or even after the Show Jumping, or whether we must arrive in sufficient time to walk it before the Dressage. A Novice course can normally be walked comfortably in an hour, sometimes less. The distance may vary by up to 1,200 metres, but the maximum number of obstacles is twenty, many of which will be simple at this level. On arrival we have to park our vehicle, which may take a little time if we arrive during the 'rush hour', collect our numbers, which sometimes involves a lengthy walk to the secretary, and tack up our horse. The time taken for all this will depend on whether or not we have an assistant, and although it is possible to compete in a one-day Horse Trial without help, a Novice rider should always try to enlist the services of someone who can help throughout the day and – and this is not pessimism but common sense – who can drive the whole party home should we be unlucky enough to have a fall.

The Rules stipulate a minimum of 30 minutes between the three tests, and though in practice this would entail an unholy rush, between 45 minutes and an hour is ideal, and this is what most organisers try to achieve. But when riders with two horses, perhaps in different classes, have to be slotted in, the intervals for a particular rider may be longer. But unless there is a gap of at least an hour and a quarter between tests, the Cross Country course will have to be walked before the Dressage. Assuming that we want to be on our horse for between 45 minutes and an hour

before the Dressage, then our timetable will look something like this:

1000	Arrive and park.
1015	Walk the course.
1115	Tack up.
1130	Mount.
1230	Enter the Dressage arena.

We now have to be certain that we have all the necessary tack for horse and rider. Questions regarding what is necessary and permitted are governed partly by experience, partly by custom or tradition, and mainly by the Rules. These lay down the permitted and required dress for the rider and tack for the horse for each of the three tests – Dressage, Show Jumping and Cross Country. The Rules are further elaborated by guidelines published from time to time in the Horse Trials Group Bulletin, which explains what attire for the rider is correct and what is incorrect. We have already briefly considered what tack we need in order to start training the horse, and we now need to take note of what we actually require in order to compete at an event.

First of all, in his stable our horse requires a top rug, which can vary from a plain jute rug to a coloured thermal rug, of which there are several types on the market. When he is clipped out in winter, he will need one, sometimes two, blankets, of which the warmest are probably the yellow ones with a red and black stripe at each end, and for the summer he will need a washable summer sheet. A sweat rug, for use after hard work and after he has been washed down, can be either like a string vest or one of the newer thermal rugs made for this purpose. A coloured woollen day rug, bound in a contrasting colour, is nice to have, but we could well add this after our horse has won a point or two! A leather head-collar with brass fittings is a sound investment, but again is expensive, and we can start with a smart webbing one, and a rope with a swivel clip at one end.

Bandages have four functions: to give the legs support and protection when galloping and jumping, to protect them when travelling, to keep them warm in the stable after hard work, and to hold dressings in place in case of injury. The first two functions have now largely been taken over by tendon boots for competitions, and by leg guards for travelling, and certainly for Novice One Day Events a good pair of tendon boots made from material that does not hold water, thick enough to give protection from a blow from another hoof, and fastened with velcro straps, saves considerable time over bandages. In the stable we need a set of four stable bandages made of flannel or wool, which are applied over a length of gamgee tissue or a more modern washable bandage pad, for use after hard work, while for poulticing or for use with dressings we require a couple of elastic crepe bandages. To complete the kit we need an elastic tail bandage.

To our basic grooming kit of body brush, curry comb, dandy brush, hoof pick and hoof oil, we must add plaiting kit, stud kit, and a sponge and scraper for washing down. For plaiting we need strong thread of the same colour as our horse's mane, scissors, and a supply of small rubber plaiting bands of the same colour for emergencies or quick plaiting. The question of studs we shall have arranged with our farrier, and if we have screw holes, then we need a selection of large, medium and small studs of the same measurement, a tap for cleaning out the holes, a spanner for inserting and removing the studs, cotton wool for plugging the empty holes, and a nail or something similar for packing and removing the cotton wool. (It is also wise always to have a cloth on which we can lay the kit whilst we are using it in the stable, in the horsebox or trailer, or in the open, since it can be frustrating to have to grovel about in the straw for a vital stud – the

proverbial needle and haystack come to mind, but are not much consolation when we are in a hurry!)

No horse should travel anywhere without a basic first aid kit that will enable us to do just what its name implies – give immediate first aid that will suffice until we can obtain the services of a vet, should that seem necessary, or until we can get our horse back to his stable. It will also enable us to treat minor injuries, which if left untreated may assume more serious proportions. At an official Horse Trial a vet is always in attendance during the Cross Country and Jumping tests, so it is mainly to deal with minor injuries and those that occur at other times that we need our first aid kit. Its basic contents should include disinfectant, wound powder, aerosol antiseptic spray, a healing ointment, vaseline, cotton wool, lint, crepe bandages and bandage pads (already part of our stable equipment), scissors, and an animalintex or similar poultice dressing. We should also include an effective fly-repellant.

For winter work, and certainly if we are going to hunt our horse, we shall need to have him clipped, so unless we can arrange for someone to clip him for us, we shall need an electric clipping machine.

What we are and are not allowed to use on the horse during competitions is laid down in the Rule Book, though we do have to refer to the Official Dressage Rules or to the F.E.I. Three Day Event Rules in order to discover exactly what bits are allowed for the Dressage test. For the Novice test, we are limited to a plain snaffle, and we shall already have chosen this, together with one of the four permitted nosebands, when we started schooling our horse. For the Show Jumping test, we may add a running martingale and tendon boots, and for the Cross Country a breast plate or breast girth if the course is hilly or the shape and conformation of our horse make this necessary. Also optional is a surcingle, its object being to give added security beyond that afforded by the girth. For a rider who must later on carry lead in order to make the required weight, this may be necessary, but, by holding the saddle firmly down on the horse's back, it counters the effect of a spring tree, which allows the saddle to have the minimum weight on the horse's back during a jump, and we would be better to ensure that the girth and girth straps are sound.

At a Novice Horse Trial the rider should wear for the Dressage test a black or dark blue hunting cap, a tweed coat with a coloured hunting tie (stock) or with collar and tie, buff or fawn breeches and plain black boots; brown boots are also permissible with a tweed coat. Gloves (which must be of a light colour) and spurs are optional, as is a bowler hat, but a whip is not allowed. A lady rider may wear a black or dark blue coat, but in that case with a white stock – never a white tie! Strictly speaking, a man should wear a black coat only in Intermediate or Advanced classes.

For the Show Jumping we wear the same dress, but we must now replace the hunting cap with a hard hat (jockey skull or riding hat) with a navy blue or black cover and a correctly fitted harness, and it is as well to check the Rule Book to ensure that we have a hat that conforms to the current B.S.I. standard. We may now carry a whip, but its length must not exceed 75 cm. For the Cross Country, the jockey skull is mandatory, and we either remove our coat or replace it with a sweater. A back protector is now compulsory; there are several types on the market, and in the event of a fall they give protection from the horse's hooves and in those cases where the rider is thrown against part of the obstacle. In all three tests we wear our allotted number on a bib which we have to buy in advance from the Horse Trials Office at Stoneleigh – an item of equipment which we must not forget.

CHAPTER 10

At the Event

Before walking the course we should collect our number and obtain a programme, which normally contains a map and a description of the obstacles, together with the distance and the Optimum Time. We should also check the official course plan at the Secretary's office in case there have been any changes since the programme was printed, since sometimes these are forced upon the event by the weather.

On walking the Cross Country course, whether we do it on the previous day or on the day itself, we have five points to bear in mind. First, the route; we must not have to think about this on the way round once we have started. Second, the places where we can gallop and make up time. Third, the places where we have to reduce speed because of the going or any natural hazards, which may be defined as anything other than a numbered obstacle that may affect horse or rider on the way round. Fourth, those obstacles that are straightforward. And fifth, those that require a special approach or a particular route through them. Into the last category come obstacles with water or dry ditches, which may cause our horse to 'spook' or to decelerate sharply, corners, and all types of combination obstacle including bounces, some of which may have alternative routes through them. And in the case of these last, we must not only plan our chosen route, but must also have a plan to put into operation should we have a refusal or run-out at any part of the combination. At the end of our inspection, we should have a clear picture of the course and the obstacles in our mind, including the line from one fence to the next.

The amount of time that we spend on our horse before the Dressage will vary according to his experience and temperament, as will the type of work that we do during that period. In general, the young horse will need more time spent in getting used to the atmosphere and the scenery, and only a short time in preparing for the test itself; often too much actual Dressage work will cause him to go over the top and 'die' on us in the arena. We should give him plenty of work on the previous day, so that he is not over-fresh on the day itself. We may start by letting him wander round for a few minutes getting used to the tentage and other distractions. Next we should work him at the trot and canter on a long rein for perhaps ten minutes. Gradually, as we get his attention, we ask him for a little more collection, both on a circle and on a straight line, until he is working to our satisfaction up to the standard that he has achieved at home, and until his transitions from one pace to another are reasonably smooth. We should not, however, be looking for perfection!

There are four Novice tests, and while we should not rehearse the whole test, we should go through some of the individual movements. If we are preparing for Test 'A', for example, we should rehearse the halt from the trot, the move-off at the trot, the lengthening of stride at the trot, some medium walk, and a few transitions from trot to canter. For Test 'D', we would add some shallow loops at the trot, and the giving and retaking of the reins. There is now rather less than half an hour left before we are due to enter the arena, and we may now return to our box for a final spruce-up before going up to the collecting ring for the Dressage arenas. Whilst we are doing this preliminary work we must ensure that we abide by the rule that limits what tack we may use on the horse during this period.

On arriving at the Dressage collecting area, we should find the Steward for our section, who should be wearing a tabard or number bib with our section number or letter on it, give him our number, and ask whether our section is on time, ahead of time or behind time. If it is ahead of time, we can still start at our appointed time, though the judges would probably appreciate it if we went as soon as they were ready. We should now let our horse wander round on a long rein for a few minutes, then, as the horse in front of us is doing his test, start to collect him. As the previous horse completes his test, we should trot forward and make maximum use of the couple of minutes or so that will elapse before we hear our signal to start, trotting and cantering round the outside of the arena, close to the markers, and letting our horse get used to the judge's car. As the signal goes, normally a toot on the car's horn, we should establish a working trot and when ready turn towards the entrance giving ourselves plenty of room to get straight and

to settle our horse on a straight line before entering.

Now is the moment when our basic schooling on the flat is put to the test. But more Novice tests are spoiled as a result of over-tenseness on the part of the rider who is trying too hard than by mistakes on the part of the horse. So on entering the arena, we should make a conscious effort to relax. As we move up the centre line we must try to keep our horse straight, and this can more easily be done if we drive him forward rather than try to collect him too much – after all, the judge in his car is not in an ideal position from which to assess the degree of collection of the horse, but he will immediately see any deviation from the centre line. We must prepare our horse for the halt, easing him into it so that he halts square, does not throw up his head as he does so, and stands still while we salute. When we retake the reins he must not move off until we give the signal, and must go straight into the trot.

Now for any given standard of performance by the horse, we can gain or lose marks by executing the movements accurately or otherwise. In riding Test 'A', for example, our corners should be smooth rather than too deep, and our circles should be true circles and not 'lozenges', and should go out on to the outside track of the arena when required to do so. When turning across the arena for the lengthened trot, the turn should be made precisely at the quarter marker, and the horse straightened before the lengthening is demanded, and the return to the working trot made before reaching the far side, where the track should be met slightly before the quarter marker, so that the horse is straight as his shoulder passes the marker. Our transitions must be made precisely where they are due, which means preparing our horse a few strides in advance and giving the aids before we reach the appointed marker. The two half-circles at the medium walk must be true half-circles and not flattened

The horse must be prepared for the halt, so that he halts square. Murphy Himself, Virginia Leng, Burghley

out, and there should be one stride on the centre line when our horse is absolutely straight and facing the judge. When we turn on to the centre line for our final movement we must be careful not to overshoot it and have to turn back to it.

If our horse misbehaves or makes a mistake we must correct him calmly and quickly and carry on with the rest of the test. Throughout this, his first test, we should err on the side of pushing him forward rather than looking for too much collection. Finally, we must remember that the test is not over until he has left the arena, and that, should he have performed well, lavish displays of pleasure are not in order until then!

The Show Jumping test should present no special problems if we have followed a sensible course of preparation, since our horse will be well able to deal with jumping courses at this level. Yet it is surprising how many riders incur unnecessary penalties in this test, a fact of which we should be able to take advantage. Before going to the jumping ring, we return to our box, put tendon boots and a running martingale on our horse, ensure that we are wearing the correct hat, collect our whip and shorten our stirrups. We may sometimes have to jump without having walked the course, because, unless we have walked it after our inspection of the Cross Country course on the previous day, there may be no opportunity for us to do so on the day itself, since breaks between sections for this purpose may not fit in with our allotted times for the three tests. In this case we should first study the official course plan, and then walk or ride round outside the ring, observing the turns and the approaches to the fences and watching other competitors jump. The course will be simple and the distances in combinations standard, so this should not present too much of a problem. If we do get the chance to walk the course in the arena we should certainly do so.

In the warming-up area, we prepare our horse by first trotting over a low pole, then by jumping the upright practice fence a few times followed by the spread, noting that these fences are flagged and can only be jumped from one direction. We should not make the mistake of overjumping our horse in the practice area, and should be satisfied when he has jumped both fences well at roughly the same height as

those in the ring. If he knocks one down we should of course remonstrate with him, but this is not the time nor the place in which to start schooling. When our turn comes to enter the ring, we should go in as soon as possible and make use of the time before the bell goes to let our horse get used to the ring, trotting him smartly round, but without, however, showing him the obstacles, for which we could be eliminated. Finally, we must not make the mistake of starting before the bell! If our preparation has been sound, hopefully we shall complete this test without adding to our Dressage score.

Before the Cross Country, we have to replace our coat with a sweater or whatever it is that we intend to wear under our number bib, put on our back protector, again check that we have the correct hat for this test, check our horse's tack, and perhaps shorten our stirrups another hole or two. (The length of stirrup that we adopt for each test we have considered in Chapters 6, 7 and 8.)

We should report to the Cross Country start about 10 minutes before our allotted time, though it is again wise to discover in advance whether they are running ahead of time, behind time or on time. We are going to ask our horse to set off on his own at a strong canter or gallop and to start jumping fences almost immediately. Although he has already done a fair amount of work, he must be thoroughly warmed up, and should be jumped a few times over the practice fence. In Novice events horses are normally despatched on the Cross Country at $1\frac{1}{2}$-minute or 2-minute intervals, sometimes even at intervals of 1 minute. The start is from a 'box' about 5 metres square, with the start line across the open side. The starter will call us into it about 30 seconds before our start time and will count down from 5 seconds. In the box we may walk round or stand still, with the help of an assistant if necessary, who must leave the horse alone as soon as the starter says 'Go'. Should we inadvertently cross the start line before this, the starter will recall us and we must re-enter the box and start again, though the clock will not be stopped. With a horse that is excitable at the start, it may be best to enter the box after the starter has called '10 seconds'.

One of the secrets of success, especially with a novice horse, is to concentrate on every single fence; our concentration and determination, or lack of them, will communicate themselves to our horse, who will respond accordingly. Although we are unlikely to win our first official Horse Trial, we shall be out to do our very best, and if we have acquired the right type of horse and have prepared him properly by giving him experience in lesser events, then he should be able to negotiate a Novice Cross Country course at the required speed of 520 metres per minute, which will put him inside the Optimum Time, which will be between 3 and 5 minutes depending on the length of the course. There is no point whatsoever in going faster than this, but we shall add to our score one penalty point for every 3 seconds by which we exceed the Optimum Time.

With luck, the first few fences will be fairly straightforward, and so on crossing the start line we must quickly establish a pace which will put that Optimum Time within our reach. Bearing in mind that there will probably be some places on the course where we must go more slowly, we must cover the open and easier stretches at rather more than 520 metres per minute. If all goes according to plan, if we have walked the course properly, if our preparation and training have been on the right lines, then, if luck is on our side, we shall complete the Cross Country test without adding to our penalty score.

Although we should never leave anything to chance, luck, or the lack of it, may spoil the best laid plans. Moreover, we are riding a horse, not a machine, and a young horse at that, and we cannot guarantee that he will not make a mistake. It is important that he should enjoy his first event; at the same time he must learn the lessons of any mistakes that he may make. If we ride him with determination and give him time to jump the more tricky fences all should go well. If he does run out or refuse, then the reason is likely to be either that our approach to that particular obstacle has been at fault, or that we have lost control in the middle of a combination. Whatever the reason, we must make it absolutely clear that such disobedience is totally unacceptable; this demands a couple of strong blows with the whip behind the saddle – no more – after which we retake the obstacle.

If our horse makes a serious mistake at a fence while negotiating it, hitting it hard or pecking badly on landing, we should not punish him, but make it perfectly clear to him by use of the voice that his performance has fallen short of what we require! This is also one of the rare occasions on which it is sensible to use the whip other than behind the saddle; a couple of sharp taps on the shoulder without taking our hands off the reins will reinforce our use of the voice and should make our dissatisfaction apparent. (It is perhaps at this juncture as well to remember that other ears than those of our horse may be the recipients of our verbal castigation, and that our language should be moderately controlled!) Pecking on landing over a fence may be due to the going and not to any mistake on the horse's part, in which case it may be wise to ease the pace for a few hundred metres while he recovers. Equally important, our horse deserves praise and encouragement when he has jumped well, and a pat on the neck after a particularly good jump will convey the message.

Having finished the course, our horse's task may be over, but ours is not. After crossing the finishing line we should let him gradually come back to the walk, then dismount, loosen his girths and noseband, and look him over to see if he has acquired any obvious injury. Then we should lead him round, or back to his box, until he has stopped blowing. What we do next will depend upon the weather, how much he has sweated, and what help we have. Ideally, as soon as he has stopped blowing, and not before, we should wash him down completely using a sponge and plenty of water, remove the water with a scraper, cover him with a sweat sheet with a light sheet or rug over the top, and walk him round until he is dry. He may then be allowed to graze, which will help him to unwind, before being put back into the box. If there is a very cold wind, then it is best not to wash him down except for the legs if they are muddy, but simply to walk him round with a sweat sheet under a light rug. (Although horses do not object to cold water in the same way as humans do, if we fill a water container with hot water before leaving the stable in the early morning, and wrap it well in sacking, or place it with some straw inside one of the paper sacks

in which most forage is now delivered, it will remain warm enough for most of the day, and our horse may appreciate it when he is washed down.)

Now is the moment to go to the scoreboard to see how we have fared. Hopefully we shall not have added to our Dressage penalties, but there will be others in our section with the same hope. If we find that we have, in spite of a clear round, incurred time penalties on the Cross Country, it may be that others have done so too, and that this is a course that has been tightly measured, or is one on which the Optimum Time is difficult to achieve because of gradients, twists and turns, deep going or other factors.

If we find that we have in fact finished among the prizewinners, then we must find out when the prizegiving is due to be held, and return then, properly dressed as for the Dressage test, to receive our prize. We have started on the long road to success.

It is important to work the horse at the trot, concentrating on maintaining an even rhythm. Shannagh, Lucinda Green, Badminton

The horse must pass through each corner of the manege without losing balance or rhythm. Fair Enough, Sally Carson, Boekel

Over the jump the rider's position is such that a line drawn through the shoulder and knee will continue down through the ankle. Glentrool, Lorna Clarke, Burghley

Over the highest part of the jump: Robert The Devil, Liz Purbrick, Burghley

Landing: Any Chance, Mark Todd, Badminton

In ... Bolebec Miler, Anne-Marie Taylor, Chatsworth

And out ... Tivoli Gardens, Diana Cabbell Manners, Chatsworth

The horse must stand still while the rider salutes. General Bugle, Michael Tucker, Burghley

Corners. If there happens to be a tree or bush on the corner it is easier. Hector James, Vanessa Ashbourne, Gatcombe

The horse deserves praise and encouragement when he has jumped well. Lutin V (U.S.A.), Karen Lende, Burghley

The medium trot is a development of the lengthened strides demanded in the novice test. Newfield, Karen Straker, Burghley

The Dressage Test: entry, halt and salute. Friday Fox, Rachel Hunt, Badminton

Medium Trot: Oxford Blue, Ian Stark, Gawlor

Extended Trot: Artful Dodger, Claire Mason, Chatsworth

Half Pass: Aloaf, Rachel Hunt, Luhmuhlen

Extended Canter: Glenburnie, Ian Stark, Burghley

Some riders like to smother their horse's legs in grease. J.J. Babu, Bruce Davidson (U.S.A.), Burghley

The Start – Phase A. 5, 4, 3, 2, 1, Go – and off they go at the trot. Night Cap, Ginny Leng, Badminton

Phase B – The Steeplechase. 5, 4, 3, 2, 1, Go – and this time they set off at the gallop. Tivoli Gardens, Diana Cabbell Manners, Chatsworth

Hopefully they will meet the fences right. Clarence II, Melanie O'Brien (Ire), Chatsworth

There may be a few straightforward fences on the course which require no great effort on the part of the horse. Woden, Mandy Jenkins, Burghley

There will be some big spreads that require boldness, speed and accuracy. J.J. Babu, Bruce Davidson (USA), Stockholm

There will be drop fences, and one must allow sufficient length
of rein and adopt a seat that offers security. Badminton

CHAPTER 11

Progressing to the Three Day Event

So far so good • *Novice experience* • *Upgrading* • *Intermediate requirements*
• *Cross Country speed* • *The need for 'blood'* • *The Intermediate Dressage test*
• *Medium trot* • *Smaller circles* • *Loops at the canter* • *Simple change of leg*
• *Rein-back* • *Shoulder-in* • *Collective marks* • *Show Jumping and Cross Country*
• *Fitness* • *Open Intermediate* • *Open Novice* • *Two Day Events* • *Planning*
• *Speed and pace* • *Weight* • *Novice, Intermediate and Open Championships*

So far so good! We seem to have chosen a promising horse, our basic schooling appears to have been on the right lines, and our first competitive effort has been rewarded with enough success to give us hope for the future. We are still, however, a long way from our ultimate goal, the Three Day Event.

Our next step is to give our horse further experience as a Grade III horse in Novice classes, then to upgrade him to Intermediate. This involves earning 21 points, and points from 6 down to 1 are awarded to the first six horses in a Novice section. Thus we could in theory win our first four Novice events and then find ourselves, with 24 points, with a Grade II horse competing in Intermediate classes. But competition is hot, and it is more likely that we shall pick up points here and there, and thus give our horse sufficient experience in Novice classes to enable him to make the step up into Intermediate when the time comes without too much difficulty. But even if we were to upgrade quickly, the Rules provide that a Novice horse can compete in a Novice class for which he has been entered when he

has been upgraded after the close of entries, except in the unlikely event that he has actually won four Novice classes.

The step up from Novice to Intermediate does not on the surface seem a very big one. For the Dressage test, the additional requirements are the medium trot, for which the lengthened strides of the Novice test have been a preparation; a reduction in the size of circles; a 5 metre loop at the canter without change of leg; a medium canter; a simple change of leg at the canter; a rein-back – something we will in any case have had to teach our horse for normal riding and hacking; and the introduction of lateral work in the form of the shoulder-in – not really as difficult as it sounds.

The maximum height of the Show Jumping and Cross Country goes up 5 cm to 1.15 m, and on the Cross Country slightly bigger spreads and drops are permitted, while the maximum length of the course is increased from 2,800 m to 3,620 m with the possibility of four more obstacles. The next significant difference lies in the speed necessary to achieve the Optimum Time on the Cross Country, which goes up from 520 to 570 metres per minute, which is the same speed as is required for a Three Day Event at Intermediate, Advanced or Championship level. Thus, whereas in a Novice class it should not normally be too difficult for a well bred fit horse to achieve the Optimum Time, in the Intermediate class it is a different story.

It is for this reason, if we are serious about eventing, and if we have aspirations beyond having fun in Novice classes, that we have strongly advocated the thoroughbred or something very near it. Novice classes are won by all shapes and sizes, and a look at the scoreboard at a Novice event will usually show that the leading prizewinners have finished on their Dressage scores. In other words, while there are plenty of competitors who pick up penalties in the Show Jumping and on the Cross Country, it is the Dressage score that sorts out the leaders. (It also emphasises, incidentally, how important it can be to pick up those few extra marks by riding the test accurately and for presentation.)

The step up into Intermediate is in practice quite a steep one, but not too steep for the right type of horse. There are many horses that win Novice classes, but which, when upgraded, find that they have already reached their limit. Although the Dressage still plays a most important part, in Intermediate and Advanced classes Cross Country ability, and especially speed in this test, really begin to determine the result. And this remains true right through to Three Day Eventing at Championship level, where the standards of the leading competitors are so high that, except where weather conditions accentuate the difficulties of the Cross Country course, they tend to finish on their Dressage scores. But that need not concern us at this stage!

Before taking part, then, in our first Intermediate Horse Trial, there are certain aspects of our training to which we shall have to give special emphasis. Although there are five Dressage tests at Novice level (four for One Day trials and one for the Novice Three Day event), at Intermediate level there are only two, and although both of them have more movements the approximate time taken to do the test is the same – four minutes. Of the new movements, the medium trot is a development of the lengthened strides demanded in the Novice test, and the fact that these were always demanded on the diagonal through the centre of the arena is a help, for that is where the medium trot is required in the new tests. Although in principle we must of course school our horse to respond to our aids when we give them and must not allow him to anticipate our demands, nevertheless his memory will be helpful to us here. In every Horse Trials Dressage test, from Novice up to Intermediate Three Day Event level, whenever we traverse the arena from one side to the other on a diagonal at the trot, we do so with a degree of extension – at Novice level, a few lengthened strides, at Intermediate and Advanced, the medium trot, in the Intermediate Three Day Event, the extended trot.

It should not be too difficult to increase the lengthened strides into a medium trot, provided that we check any tendency to increase the tempo, in other words to run. We must always prepare for the transition, ask for it gradually, and never ask for too much – better to receive 6 marks out of 10 (satisfactory) for showing less extension than our horse is capable of performing when he is at his best, than the 3 (fairly bad) that we shall receive if he runs, or the zero or 1 that will be awarded if he breaks into a canter.

The smaller circles should not present much difficulty at this stage, nor the 5-metre loop at the canter, our introduction to the serpentine and the counter-canter (the canter with the outside foreleg leading). Provided that we introduce it gradually, starting with a 2-metre loop, maintaining quite strongly the leg position that we use when giving the aids for the strike-off at the canter, our horse should not change legs. The medium canter is something that will come easily to the horse, since he will frequently perform it when out hacking. Again we have to teach him to lengthen his stride on command, whilst not increasing the tempo. What may be difficult initially will be the maintenance of balance and rhythm at the medium canter through a corner, and the immediately following transition back to the working canter.

The simple change of leg at the canter between two half-circles we must introduce gradually; to try to execute it without adequate preparation will at best produce an untidy performance, and may upset our horse. From the canter, the horse has to be brought back to the walk, and after two or three steps must strike off into the canter directly from the walk with the other leg leading. Between the two circles, there will be a moment at 'X' when, at the walk, our horse is absolutely straight. We should start by progressing from the canter to the walk via the trot, which means that if we are to be walking at 'X' (see Figure 18), we must trot at the imaginary point 'T' and walk at 'W'. As soon as our horse is straight at 'X', we give the aids for the canter to the right (Stage 1). Gradually we move points 'T' and 'W' closer together and further towards 'X', reducing the number of trotting strides until we can dispense with them altogether, bringing the horse smoothly back from the canter directly into the walk (Stage 2). At this stage it is in fact permitted to pass through a trotting stride or two during the downward transition, but the strike-off into the canter must be straight from the walk.

The rein-back is something our horse needs to be able to execute merely in order to be a pleasant ride, and so we shall certainly have taught him to do this earlier during his basic schooling. However, what the Dressage judge expects to see may differ from what has been necessary to enable us to open a gate! The horse must first halt and stand still momentarily from the working trot, then rein back four steps, and without a pause go forward into the medium walk. In moving backwards the horse must remain straight, must not deviate from the track, and the steps, which are virtually in two-time as in the trot, but without elevation and at the speed of a walk, must be distinct and unhurried. Throughout the movement his head carriage must remain steady. (We say that the movement is 'virtually' in two-time, because if we rein back on a hard surface such as concrete we shall hear the hoof beats not as 'one ... two ... one ... two', but rather as 'one/one ... two/two ... one/one ... two/two', as the forefoot of each diagonal touches the ground very slightly before its opposite hind hoof. But for all intents and purposes we can consider the rein-back as a movement in two-time.)

Figure 18   Teaching the simple change of leg at the canter.

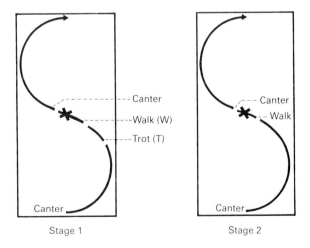

Stage 1   Stage 2

Gradually move points (T) and (W) closer together and nearer towards X, reducing the number of trotting strides, until they can be dispensed with altogether

When teaching the rein-back, we start by bringing our horse to a halt facing a barrier such as a wall, hedge, or gate. With the halt established, we squeeze with our legs. The horse cannot go forward, and we increase the feel of our hands through the reins to the bit, at the same time using the voice – if the horse was correctly driven in long reins when he was broken in he will have learned the meaning of the command 'Back', and we should obtain a backward step or two, and we shall reward him for this. It is important that we initiate the movement with our legs and not with the hands, whose function is to translate the impulsion being generated by our legs into a backward movement, not to pull our horse backwards. If he resists initially, we must resist the temptation to pull on the reins, but should execute a few 'give and take' movements, gently 'rippling' the fingers, and the horse will usually then respond. When executing this movement during a test, a slightly stronger feel on the inside rein and a firmer pressure of the inside leg will help to keep the horse straight on the track. On completion of four strides we must drive our horse immediately forward into the medium walk – a fifth stride is not only not required, it will result in marks being deducted.

The shoulder-in is the first lateral movement that we encounter in the Dressage test, and is a step towards the half-pass that will later be required in Advanced and Three Day Event tests. It is reached via the exercise of leg-yielding, in which the horse moves away from the rider's inside leg, with his head very slightly bent away from the direction in which he is moving, and with his body straight (see Figure 19). It can either be performed on the diagonal, in which case the horse's body remains parallel to the long side of the arena as he moves on a diagonal across it, or along the side of the arena, when the horse moves along the outside track with his body turned inwards at an angle of about 30°. The shoulder-in is

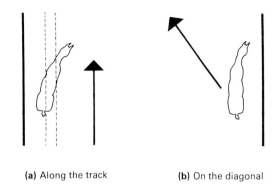

Figure 19 Leg-yielding.

(a) Along the track   **(b)** On the diagonal

The horse's body is straight, with his head very slightly bent away from the direction in which he is moving

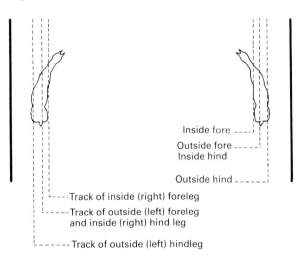

Figure 20 Shoulder-in.

Inside fore
Outside fore
Inside hind
Outside hind

Track of inside (right) foreleg
Track of outside (left) foreleg and inside (right) hind leg
Track of outside (left) hindleg

The whole body of the horse is bent round the rider's inside leg. The degree of bend is only sufficient to allow the outside foreleg to move on the same track as the inside hind leg

performed along the outside track, with the whole body of the horse slightly bent round the rider's inside leg, as it would be on a large circle, and again the bend is slightly away from the direction of movement (see Figure 20). The degree of bend is only sufficient to allow the outside foreleg to move on the same track as the inside hind leg. If the word 'slightly' appears rather frequently here, it is because too often this movement is spoiled by an attempt to produce too much bend, resulting in resistance and stiffness, whereas the object of this exercise is to increase collection and suppleness.

In the Intermediate test, the shoulder-in is demanded after a 10-metre circle, and it is on completion of a circle that it is easiest to obtain this movement. On the 10-metre circle, the horse is bent round the rider's inside leg, with the outside leg maintaining the correct bend. A helpful preparatory exercise is to ride several circles, alternating between 10 and 15 metres, and using the inside leg assisted by an outward feel on the outside rein to increase the size of the circle. Then from the 10-metre circle, at the moment when we retake the track, instead of straightening our horse we maintain the bend by allowing his forehand to move off the track just enough to allow the outside foreleg and the inside hind leg to follow the same track, at which moment we increase the pressure of our inside leg so as to move him down the outside track of the manege or arena, assisted by an outward feel on the outside rein (see Figure 21). This outward feel on the outside rein is very slight, and must not interfere with the correct bend of the head and neck.

Another aspect of the Intermediate Dressage test is worthy of note. At the end of the Novice test, 30 collective marks are awarded by the judge for (a) general impression, obedience and calmness, (b) paces (freedom and regularity) and impulsion, and (c) position and seat of the rider and correct use of the aids. At the end of the Intermediate test 40 marks are allocated to four opinions expressed in greater detail. And although as a percentage of the total marks for the test, these collective marks are in fact slightly lower in the Intermediate than in the Novice, judges are relatively more severe and

more critical of faults in the Intermediate.

An extra 5 centimetres in the height of the Show Jumping should not worry us, but the spreads may be considerably increased, and we may find additional combinations, all of which will require a little more accuracy on the part of horse and rider. Similarly, the Cross Country obstacles are only 10 centimetres higher, but the spreads can be much wider and the drops can be higher. But it is not the dimensions of the obstacles so much as their siting and presentation that are likely to be a cause for concern. Consider the difference between a tiger trap, for example, of ascending poles at a height of 1.05 with a spread at the base of 2.15 – quite an easy Novice obstacle – and a single telegraph pole at the same height over a dry ditch 1 m deep and 2.15 m wide. Even a

Figure 21   Shoulder-in from a 10 m circle.

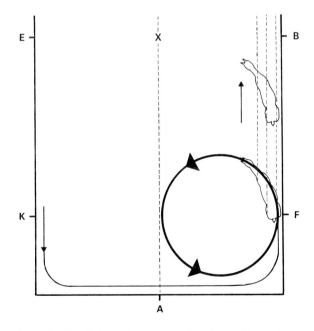

From the 10m circle, at the moment when the track is retaken, the bend is maintained by allowing the forehand to move off the track just enough to allow the outside foreleg and the inside hind leg to follow the same track

water-filled ditch would be easier, and this illustrates that the difference between a typical Novice obstacle and an Intermediate one is often a matter of presentation rather than size.

But not only are the Intermediate obstacles more difficult; the course is longer and the required speed considerably faster. It is therefore now necessary to ensure the fitness and stamina of our horse to an extent not required in a Novice class. To achieve the Optimum Time, or even to come somewhere near it, at the increased speed of 570 metres per minute over a distance of up to 3,620 m, we now have to give serious consideration to fitness training. This does not, however, mean that we have to start galloping our horse all round the country. The basis of fitness is long, slow work, on top of which it is only necessary to give our horse a few short, sharp bursts to clear his wind and exercise his lungs.

Better still, if there is a fairly long and steep hill within reach of our stable, a trot up this will do wonders for our horse's fitness. It will exercise all his muscles, especially those in the 'power pack', the hindquarters, and will at the same time give his lungs a good blow – and all this without the possibility of placing any strain on his forelegs.

Intermediate classes are divided into Intermediate and Open Intermediate in order to provide competitions for Grade I horses beyond the fairly limited number of Advanced classes, and to enable events which do not have the facilities to construct an Advanced course to attract a higher standard of entry. Open Intermediate classes also allow the riders of Grade I horses to give them a fairly easy run on occasions, especially at the start of the season or after a rest. Both classes perform the same three tests, though it is often the case that an event with an Open class will have a more difficult Intermediate Cross Country course than one which caters only for Grade II horses, even though the fences will be no higher, a

point that should be borne in mind when entering our first Intermediate events after upgrading. However, a few Horse Trials now have what are called Open Novice classes, which are confined to Intermediate horses that have won between 21 and 35 points, and have therefore been recently upgraded. Here the Dressage and Show Jumping tests are of Intermediate standard, but the Cross Country course is that for the Novice class, and we should perhaps enter for some of these before tackling the full Intermediate event.

It is at this stage that we should consider entering a Two Day Event or even a Novice Three Day Event. In the (1988) calendar there were half a dozen Novice Two Day Events and two Novice Three Day Events. The only qualification for a Two Day Event, whether at Novice or Intermediate level, is that both horse and rider should have completed four official Horse Trials. The Dressage and Show Jumping tests are both held on the first day, and the Speed, Endurance and Cross Country test on the second, and it provides a most useful stepping-stone for both horse and rider towards the Three Day Event. The second day's test includes the same four phases, but all are considerably shorter. Nevertheless, our horse will have to be fitter than for an Intermediate One Day Event.

The Two Day Event Speed, Endurance and Cross Country test starts with a Phase 'A' of between 2,200 and 4,400 metres, to be carried out at a speed of 220 metres per minute, which involves both trotting and slow cantering. Phase 'B', the Steeplechase, is up to 1,675 metres in length, or just over a mile, with five or six fences and a required speed of 650 metres per minute. Phase 'C' is another stretch of roads and tracks about twice as long as Phase 'A', and after a 10-minute halt and a brief veterinary inspection, the competition finishes with Phase 'D' over a Cross Country course of up to 3,200 metres at a speed of 540 metres per minute. Thus we have a total distance of just over 18,000 metres, nearly $11\frac{1}{4}$ miles. On the Steeplechase, a decent gallop is required, for the speed of 650 metres per minute is significantly faster than the 520 metres per minute required for the Novice One Day Cross Country test and the 570 metres per minute of the Intermediate, while on the Cross Country the speed of 540 metres per minute comes somewhere between the two.

Perhaps the most significant aspect of the Two Day Event, however, is not the increased requirement for speed and stamina, but the necessity for the rider to undertake the planning and preparation that will eventually be required in the Three Day Event. At a One Day Event, at whatever level, there is relatively little planning to be done, whereas at a Two Day Event the rider must work out his timings for the four phases and commit them to a form in which he can conveniently refer to them whilst on the course. For the first time he must learn to judge his horse's pace with some degree of accuracy, so that he neither collects penalties for exceeding the Optimum Time for the phase concerned, nor asks his horse for unnecessary effort by completing a phase too early, which does his score no good whatsoever.

A further complication at a Two Day Event is the necessity to carry a set minimum weight on the second day's Speed, Endurance and Cross Country test. At One Day Events it is not until a horse reaches Advanced level that this is required. The minimum weight to be carried is 75 kg (11 st. 11 lb), and if the rider cannot make this weight, dressed as for the Cross Country, plus all his saddlery except the bridle, then he must acquire a weight cloth and lead. In the case of someone who has just to carry a few kilograms of lead, the normal racing weight-cloth with two or three pockets on each side into which are placed flat slabs of lead will suffice. In the case of an ultra-lightweight rider and some ladies find them

selves carrying well over 10 kg of lead – carrying a large amount of lead in this way can prove uncomfortable for both horse and rider over the extended distance of a Three Day Event. The solution then lies in a specially shaped weight-cloth into which is put a quantity of lead shot in pockets that are moulded to the saddleflaps. The extra weight then lies in a position in which it neither interferes with the rider nor causes discomfort to the horse.

Before the competition, and before leaving home if it is the first competition of the season or the first in which it has been necessary to carry weight, the rider should carry out a trial weighing, dressed and equipped as for the Cross Country. At the event there should be a set of scales for trial weighing somewhere near the start of Phase 'A', and then each rider must weigh out on the official scales in the presence of a steward and sign the official sheet confirming that they have been weighed. Care must be taken to ensure that every item of equipment needed for horse and rider is taken to the weighing area if it is not actually taken on the horse; it has been known for a rider to go separately to the scales, and then to find when it comes to saddling the horse that a vital item of equipment is missing, but failure to cross the start line of Phase 'A' at the appointed time is likely to lead, at the best, to an accumulation of penalties on this phase, and at the worst, to elimination. At the end of Phase 'D', the rider must not dismount until told to do so by the steward in charge of weighing in, and must then weigh in and sign the sheet. Usually, if it is very wet and muddy, the rider will have added to his weight rather than lost weight, but if he is under weight he may add the bridle in order to make it up. If the weather is very hot, and he thinks that he may lose weight on the way round the course, then it may be wise to start a pound or two overweight at the start.

Before turning to the Three Day Event in detail, mention must be made of the various

One Day Event championships. Apart from Scotland and Wales, who have their own National Championships, there are in England Novice Regional Finals, open to the winners of Novice sections at One and Two Day Events, and the British Novice Championship. At Intermediate level, there are Northern and Southern Finals and the British Intermediate Championship. The Novice and Intermediate Championships are held at Locko Park, and finally for Advanced competitors there is the British Open Championship currently held at Gatcombe Park.

So now to our ultimate goal – the Three Day Event.

Part 4

THE
ULTIMATE GOAL :
THE THREE DAY
EVENT

CHAPTER 12

Preparations

Entering • Qualifying • F.E.I. Rules • Planning ahead
• The Novice Three Day Event • Intermediate Dressage • Extended walk
• Serpentine at the canter • Strike-off on a straight line • Fitness
• Slow and fast work • Increasing the effort • Interval training
• Planning our competitions • Training programme • Equipment

In the Horse Trials calendar there were (in 1988) eight Three Day Events; two Novice (Holker Hall and Tweseldown), two Intermediate (Windsor and Osberton), two Advanced (Bramham and Chatsworth), and two Championship (Badminton and Burghley). Entering and starting in a One Day Horse Trial is a relatively simple process, but in the case of Three Day Events not only do the terms 'Novice', 'Intermediate' and 'Advanced' have a different significance, but there are also additional qualifications, both to enter and to start, which have to be taken into account, and so participation in Three Day Events needs rather more planning.

The Novice Three Day Event is open to Grade II and Grade III horses of at least 6 years of age, but to enter and to start both horse and rider (not necessarily together) must have completed an Intermediate One Day or a Novice Two Day Event without jumping penalties on the Cross Country. An Intermediate Three Day Event is open to Grade I and Grade II horses, with stiffer qualifications to enter and start, and for an Advanced event the qualifications, again for horses in Grades I and II, are stiffer still. The two Championship events are confined to Grade I horses, and the qualifications for horse and rider are such as to ensure that only those who have thoroughly

proved themselves at Advanced level are entitled to take part. All these qualifications are laid down in the Rule Book, and should be carefully studied, as they do change from time to time. It is now, however, advisable to acquire an additional set of rules, for Three Day Events in the United Kingdom are conducted in accordance with the General Rules for Official Horse Trials, and F.E.I. Rules for Three Day Events, and anyone who is serious about taking part in Three Day Events should have a copy of the F.E.I. Rules, which can be obtained from the Horse Trials Office at Stoneleigh or from an equestrian bookseller.

Owing to the qualification system, it is necessary to plan ahead when considering which Three Day Event to enter, and especially those at the higher levels, where the qualifications have to be current, in other words obtained within a specified period of time before the event. There are also qualifications to start, their object being to ensure that both horse and rider have some recent form to back up their entry qualifications. It is worth noting that both Intermediate and Advanced Three Day Events are open to the same grades of horses (I and II), but the qualifications to enter and to start differ. The speeds required are also the same for both classes, as are the Steeplechase obstacles. But in the Advanced event the dimensions of the Cross Country obstacles will be higher, as in One Day Horse Trials.

We should if possible start with a Novice Three Day Event, but circumstances may force us to start at Intermediate level. Provided that our horse has had adequate experience at this level in One Day Events, and has preferably completed a Two Day Event, and provided that we take steps to ensure that he is really fit, then this should not present too much of a problem.

The first additional requirement for the Intermediate Three Day Event concerns the Dressage, for of the two Intermediate events, Windsor requires the F.E.I. Young Rider test for its senior section and the F.E.I. Junior Three Day Event test for all others, while in the case of Osberton the tests are the Advanced and the Intermediate. However, in our first Three Day Event we will not be among the entrants with the highest number of points, who normally comprise the senior section, so entry for Osberton would not require any Dressage movements that we had not already performed elsewhere. But if we entered for Windsor, we would encounter a new test, and, for the first time, the larger 20 m × 60 m arena. Although this larger arena gives us more room, it does mean that we cannot rely on corners to help us as much as they do in the smaller arena, and we shall have to be more accurate in timing our transitions.

There are three new movements, and the first is the change of rein at the extended walk. Previously we have used the free walk on a long rein, in which our horse has been allowed to relax and to lower and stretch his head and neck. In the extended walk his stride must be lengthened, with the hind feet striking the ground well in front of the hoof-prints of the forefeet. In order to do this the horse must be allowed to lengthen his neck, but the rein contact must be maintained, and the rhythm of the walk must continue. This is something

that our horse will do naturally when, for example, he catches sight of another horse when out hacking, but which, like the medium and extended trot, will require practice at home in order to produce it on demand in the Dressage arena.

Also required for the first time are two serpentines at the canter, one on each rein (see Figure 22). Starting at 'A', the entrance, the serpentine consists of three half-circles, each going right to the outside track and ending at 'C' opposite the judge. Since the length of the arena is 60 m, each half-circle will be 20 m in diameter. Previously we have encountered the 5-m loop down the long side of the short (40 m) arena, which would be the equivalent of part of a very large serpentine indeed. If we have been able to take part in a Novice Three Day Event, we shall have met in Test 12 the serpentine at the trot, and also a half-circle at the canter followed by a return to the track in counter-canter. In this full serpentine we have to guard against the horse changing legs as the counter-canter loop meets the outside track. It is also important to ride the serpentine accurately, taking each loop right to the outside track, and ensuring that when the horse crosses the centre line he is for a brief moment straight and facing directly across the arena. If our horse does break the canter or change legs on the counter-canter loop when we are teaching him this movement, then we should reduce the depth of the loop, and perhaps go back to one of 5 m, gradually increasing its depth until we are back to the full serpentine.

The final new movement comes towards the end of the test. The second serpentine at the canter, which starts and finishes on the left rein, is followed by a change of rein across the diagonal at medium canter. On reaching the far side of the arena, we change to the working trot, and, now on the right rein, turn up the centre line. At 'L', which is sufficiently far up the centre line for the horse to be properly established in a straight working trot, we have to strike off into the canter, with the off foreleg leading. This is the first time that we have to do this in a test without the benefit of a corner or even the outside of the arena to help us. Our horse must therefore be established in his response to the aids for the canter in a straight line.

More serious are the steps that we need to take to ensure that our horse is absolutely ready for the second day's Speed, Endurance and Cross Country test. We have already done a certain amount towards this during our preparations for the Two Day Event, but it is only

Two serpentines are required at the canter, one on each reign. Master Chester, Katie Parker, Bramham

when we come to our first Three Day Event that we must take into account, not just the extended distances, but also the need to conserve our horse's energy for the third day's Jumping test. No longer can we ride the Cross Country as if there were no tomorrow, and at the end of it relax, seeing only to our horse's comfort and the treatment of any injury that he might have incurred. In the Three Day Event, not only do we have to ensure that our

Figure 22   Serpentines at the canter in the 20 × 60 m arena.

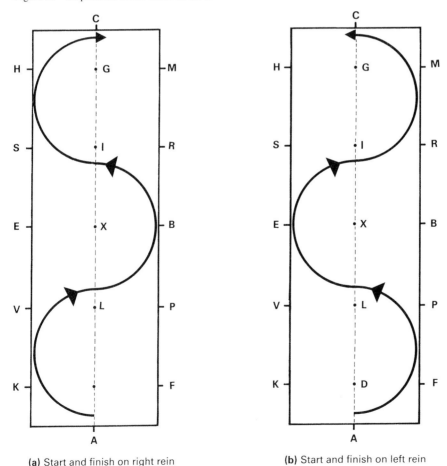

(a) Start and finish on right rein

(b) Start and finish on left rein

When the horse crosses the centre line he is for a brief moment straight and facing directly across the arena

horse is considerably fitter, but we have to plan and ride the second day in the light of the weather and ground conditions, with the final horse inspection and the Show Jumping test very much in mind.

The subject of fitness training, together with the associated subject of feeding, could easily fill a whole book on its own – and indeed it has done so, and there are whole libraries of books on the subject. Not all, however, are written with the particular requirements and problems of the Three Day Event in mind, and in any case both fitness and feeding have become such specialised and personal matters that there are as many theories as there are authors, and the conclusion that the uninitiated can draw is that no hard and fast rules can be laid down! Perhaps this is just as well, for each horse must be treated as an individual and his personal tastes and requirements studied. But by the time that we come to enter our first Three Day Event, we should know enough about our horse to have developed a programme that suits his personal idiosyncrasies.

Much will depend upon the type of horse that we are training – how well bred he is, what sort of conformation he has and what his temperament is like. We have already expressed our preference for the thoroughbred or something very near it, since the required speed will come naturally to him and he can then devote his efforts to negotiating the obstacles. But the Three Day Event is also about endurance, and the thoroughbred weed is unlikely to have sufficient room for heart and lungs, which means he may find it difficult to stay the course. Temperament will have its effect too: the lazy horse will require more work, the over-zealous rather less. The less well bred he is, the more work he is likely to need. For the Three Day Event, especially with a thoroughbred horse, the accent will be more on long, slow work and less on fast gallops, and if our slow

work can include hills, which exercise the lungs and muscles without straining the legs, then relatively little fast work will be required. The Three Day Event will in any case come at the end of a programme of events that will in themselves have developed our horse's fitness and stamina.

So if, for example, we are aiming at a Three Day Event at the end of May, and assuming that our horse has been let down and rested for some period during the winter months, we select the events that we want to enter, and plan our fitness training around them, bearing in mind also that we have to complete the necessary qualifications to enter and to start. A plan is important, for if fitness training is to be fully effective it must be organised so that each piece of work that we do carries our horse's development forward by a small amount. Haphazard work may produce a peak of fitness before it is required, after which, since he cannot become fitter, he will deteriorate – he will have gone 'over the top'. (It is very difficult to maintain peak fitness, and it can really only be done by competing, and then only for a limited period of time.) An admirable comment on the subject of fitness training was made recently by an expert on the subject in a different field, though his remarks are equally applicable to the training of horses. Talking about fitness training during a television programme concerning sport in schools, a Royal Navy Petty Officer said, 'What we have to do is to ask the body to do a little more than it is capable of doing, then let it rest a while, and then ask it for a little more again.' If this applies to humans, whose training can be discussed with them and who know what they are aiming at, how much more it must apply to horses, who can have little idea of what they are being aimed at, and who must sometimes wonder what on earth we are trying to achieve.

There are basically two ways of approaching

this development of basic fitness. One is formal and works to a strict timetable, and is called interval training; the other is less formal and more variable and has no special name. Interval training originated in athletics, and has been successfully adapted to the training of the Three Day Event horse. It formalises the system of asking for a little more effort each time we work the horse, and of granting him precise and gradually diminishing periods of rest or recovery, normally at the walk, in between the periods of effort. It requires the use of a stopwatch to time the periods of effort and rest – the intervals – and it is easier to conduct over set distances on the ground which have been marked out, so that we can more easily check our horse's speed in metres per minute. A further sophistication is to monitor the horse's heart during the recovery periods in order to measure the speed of recuperation, and it is even possible to have equipment that enables the rider to do this from the saddle during periods of work.

It is perfectly possible, however, to achieve the level of fitness necessary for a Three Day Event without recourse to this formal system, though we shall still be basing our training on the principle of gradually asking for increased effort, coupled with gradual reductions in the periods of rest. In order to develop our programme, we shall work backwards from our planned Three Day Event, which is an Intermediate event in the last week of May. Our last competition should be about two weeks before this, and should be one that builds our horse's confidence, and that he enjoys, rather than a particularly gruelling one, either as regards hills, the going, or the obstacles. This takes us back to mid-May. We then come to the question of how often an event horse can, or should, compete. The tendency today, when there are so many events, is to do too much, since it is possible to compete almost every week. But added to the strain of competing, there is also

the stress of travel to be considered. Two hours, for example, is not an unreasonable amount of time to spend on the road travelling to an event, but a total of four hours spent on the road in addition to the time spent on the ground is something that should also be taken into consideration. If we are alone with our horse, we are likely to spend a minimum of four hours on the ground; if we share transport with another horse in a different class, then up to eight hours may have to be spent there, and this adds up to a very long time out of the stable.

When we eventually reach Championship class, and can enter for Badminton in mid-April or early May, then we may have to enter for every possible event in the calendar prior to that date, because there are only about 6, or at the most 8, weeks available, and some events may be cancelled owing to the weather; in 1987 this applied not only to several of the early events but also to Badminton itself. But with our aim of a Three Day Event at the end of May, we have about $2\frac{1}{2}$ months in which to work up to our goal, and we shall have a fresher and keener horse if we aim to compete about once a fortnight. With the season opening around 7 March, our programme will look something like this:

6 March	Intermediate Horse Trial
20 March	Intermediate Horse Trial
3 April	Intermediate Horse Trial
17 April	Intermediate Horse Trial
1 May	Intermediate Horse Trial
15 May	Intermediate Horse Trial
27–29 May	Three Day Event

This programme gives us $2\frac{1}{2}$ months between our first One Day Event and the Three Day Event, and it will normally require about 3 months to produce a horse at his peak fitness if we are starting from scratch. But if we are in fact planning to run him on 6 March we shall have to start work more than three months before the Three Day Event, so time will not be a problem. If we have let our horse down during the winter, then we shall start walking exercise soon after the New Year, trotting and Dressage 'refreshment' towards the end of January, and cantering work a month before the first Horse Trial, about 7 February. We are not aiming for peak fitness at our first event, and we shall not necessarily go very fast across country at it, since everything that we do this spring is going to be geared to producing our horse at his peak for the Three Day Event at the end of May. Our two March events we shall therefore regard as part of our planned build-up in which we shall not be demanding 100% performance, but our gradually improving level of fitness should allow us to win a One Day Event in April should that appear within our grasp after the Dressage and Show Jumping tests.

Our cantering work begins, then, about 7 February, and we fit this in with Dressage schooling, Jumping exercises, and possible visits to an indoor Jumping competition and a Hunter Trial if one with a suitable course can be found locally, and if the ground conditions are good. During this time our normal weekly work programme will look something like this:

Monday	Dressage, ending with Jumping exercises
Tuesday	1½-hour hack including some canter work
Wednesday	Dressage and Jumping exercises
Thursday	1½-hour hack with cantering
Friday	Riding a Dressage test and jumping a short course
Saturday	2-hour hack including cantering
Sunday	Rest

In a week in which we have had some sort of small competition to enter on the Saturday or Sunday, we will have varied our programme accordingly. On the days devoted to Dressage and Jumping, we should start by letting our horse canter for a few minutes on a loose rein, on each rein. This not only helps to relax and settle him before we start serious work, but also gradually helps in the building up of his fitness. The Jumping exercises should be restricted to achieving one particular aim in each session, such as the jumping of upright fences, or spreads, combinations, bounces or work on the grid. If he works well our horse may only jump three or four times, and he should always be allowed to end the session with an enjoyable jump over an inviting spread. In this way he will become neither bored nor careless and will enjoy these exercises.

On our hacks we should demand more as the week progresses, with our strongest cantering work on the Saturday. By 'strongest' we mean 'longest', for it is quite unnecessary and may be positively detrimental to do any fast work at this stage. But our Saturday work will include longer stretches at the canter, with shorter rest periods in between. This work should be done with our stirrups at the Cross Country length, so that our weight is off our horse's back, and the cantering should be done on a long rein, for our horse must learn to canter slowly with a very light rein contact on the roads and tracks section of the Three Day Event. He must also learn to do this even when another horse is in sight in front of him, for sometimes on Phase 'A' or 'C' the horse in front, only 4 or 5 minutes ahead of us – perhaps even less if he has been slow over the Steeplechase – will be visible, and nothing is more annoying on these phases than a horse that exhausts himself and his rider by trying to catch up with the horse in front. Once we have started competing in events, then the intervening weekends can be devoted to working up to the level of fitness required for our Three Day Event. Our programme has been based on preparation for an Intermediate event; for a Novice event the same basic considerations apply.

The equipment that we need for our first Three Day Event will not differ much from what we have been using already, especially if we have taken part in a Two Day Event. A stopwatch is now an essential part of our equipment, and we must remember that spurs must be worn for the Three Day Event Dressage test. We must also include a spare set of shoes with stud holes. If our programme of training and competing has gone according to plan, we are now ready for this ultimate test.

CHAPTER 13

The Three Day Event: briefing and Dressage days

Arrival • Horse examination • Official briefing • Course inspection
• Phase 'A' roads and tracks • Phase 'B' Steeplechase • Phase 'C' • The Box
• Phase 'D' Cross Country • 1st course walk • Penalty zones • Alternative routes
• Method of scoring • Coefficients and multiplying factors •
Cross Country penalties • 1st Horse Inspection • Order of starting
• Preparation for the Dressage test • Riding the test • 2nd and 3rd course walks
• Timings • Timetable • Stopwatches • Final checks

The modern Three Day Event in fact usually involves the attendance of horses and riders for five days, since the number of starters may necessitate two days of Dressage. The test itself takes about 8 minutes to perform, so not more than six horses can be scheduled to the hour, and there is a limit to the number of horses that the Dressage judges can be expected to judge in a day without losing their concentration or their objective capacity. If a Three Day Event is scheduled to end on a Sunday, therefore, the Cross Country will take place on the Saturday, with Dressage on the Thursday and Friday.

On arrival at the stables there is a brief horse examination to establish identity and check the horse's health, and the first official engagement for competitors is the official briefing on the Wednesday morning. Most will therefore have arrived on the Tuesday evening. At the briefing the Director will run through the programme, give details of any administrative arrangements affecting competitors, brief them on the arrangements for inspecting the course, issue maps, remind competitors of any social engagements and invitations, especially those involving the event sponsors, and generally issue any dos and don'ts necessary to ensure the smooth running of the competition. The British Horse Society Steward, in the case of a national event, or the F.E.I. Technical Delegate if it is international, will probably also have something to say.

There follows the official competitors' inspection of the course for the Speed, Endurance and Cross Country test, for which riders, often accompanied by their owners and trainers, will assemble at the start of Phase 'A'. This may either be in the 'Box' , where Phase 'C' ends and Phase 'D' starts and finishes, or it may be set up on its own. Here competitors will climb into four-wheel-drive vehicles to drive round Phase 'A'. This consists of a stretch of roads and tracks usually varying in length from 3,300 to 4,500 metres to be covered at a speed of 220 metres per minute, which involves travelling at a trot or slow canter and completion within an Optimum Time of between 15 and 20 minutes. There is no advantage in going faster than the speed laid down, but penalty points start to be incurred for exceeding the Optimum Time. However, the next phase, the Steeplechase, follows immediately after the end of Phase 'A' without any pause, so it is necessary to time our arrival so as to have between $1\frac{1}{2}$ and 2 minutes in which to check our girth, shorten our stirrups, and prepare to set out on the Steeplechase. Since the kilometres are marked on the ground, there should be no question of incurring time penalties on Phase 'A'.

On arrival at the start of the Steeplechase, competitors will leave their vehicles and walk round the course. The distance will be between 2,070 and 2,415 metres, these apparently odd distances being laid down in order to produce Optimum Times in whole or half minutes at the required speed of 690 metres per minute. There will be about a dozen fences similar to those at a race meeting or Point-to-Point, and the course may consist of two circuits over the same six fences, or it may be laid out in a figure of eight. Again there is no advantage to be gained by completing the course in less than the Optimum Time, but penalties are incurred for exceeding it. This is one of the two crucial phases of the second day, and when walking it riders will take note of any gradients, the position of the fences in relation to the bends on the course, and any particular features such as sharp bends or slight curves which might cause a galloping horse to change legs, and the half-way point.

Then back into the vehicles for Phase 'C', another stretch of roads and tracks similar to Phase 'A' but about twice as long, between $6\frac{1}{2}$ and 9 kilometres. It starts from the moment that the horse passes through the finish of the Steeplechase, so that completing Phase 'B' in more or less than the Optimum Time will not affect the time available in which to complete Phase 'C'. If the Steeplechase is completed in, say, 15 seconds under the Optimum Time, then Phase 'C' must end 15 seconds before the time shown on the timetable; if half a minute over the Optimum Time, then Phase 'C' ends half a minute after the published time. He will therefore enter Phase 'C' at the gallop and will gradually slow down through a canter and trot to a walk, probably taking half a kilometre to do so. (Some riders like to dismount and walk beside their horses for a while at this point, but most prefer not to risk any difficulty in remounting.) For the clock ticks on inexorably, and the required speed, alternating between trot and canter, must be regained before long. Whilst driving round this phase, which is again marked off in kilometres, riders will note differences in the going and any significant gradients.

On Phase 'C', there is no need to save precious minutes, because at the end of it comes a horse inspection to determine that the horse is sound and fit to continue, followed by a 10-minute halt in the Box. We should therefore aim to arrive at the end of Phase 'C' not more than half a minute before the due time. (If we were to arrive three minutes early, we would then have to wait for thirteen minutes in the Box in order to start Phase 'D' at the correct time; if we arrived three minutes late, we would incur time penalties for Phase 'C', but would still have ten minutes in the Box, starting Phase 'D' three minutes late.) In the Box, the organisers will have provided water for washing horses down, and a vet, a doctor and a farrier will be in attendance. Riders will be met here by their grooms or helpers, will prepare for the final crucial Cross Country phase, and receive information on what has been happening out on the course, which fences have been causing trouble, and what is proving to be the best line to take at problem fences.

Competitors now leave their transport and set out to walk Phase 'D', the Cross Country, which will consist of up to thirty obstacles over a distance of between $4\frac{1}{2}$ and just over $5\frac{1}{2}$ kilometres, to be completed in an Optimum Time of between just under 8 and 10 minutes.

There will be a wide variety of obstacles, which will test the horse's jumping ability, agility, fitness and courage. The courage of his rider will also be tested, together with his judgement of pace and his ability to present his horse to each obstacle so that he can negotiate it with the minimum of effort. Many obstacles will have alternative ways in which they can be jumped and will require considerable thought as to how they should be approached.

Most riders will probably walk the course three times, and on this first visit they will be concentrating on the course as a whole, noting the most difficult fences and those that have alternatives that must be considered in more detail later. At the same time they will take note of the going and the gradients, and those parts of the course where they can go fast and make up time, and those parts where they must conserve the horse's energy. At some time during the Dressage days they will return for a second inspection to consider the obstacles and the lines of approach in more detail, and

then a third visit will be made to particularly difficult fences. On this occasion they will want to make sure that they are absolutely clear in their minds about two important points, penalty zones and alternative routes.

Up to now, faults at Cross Country obstacles have been penalised only if in the opinion of the fence judge they have been connected with the negotiation of the obstacle: if, for example, a horse has jumped a fence, and his rider has parted company with him some distance beyond it, it has been up to the fence judge to decide whether the fall is penalised or not. At Three Day Events, each obstacle has a penalty zone, which extends for 10 metres in front of it and to each side, and for 20 metres beyond it, and which is marked on the ground by sawdust or something similar (see Figure 23). Faults are then only penalised when they occur inside a penalty zone, and if, for example, a horse pecks on landing over a fence, and his rider can hang on and not touch the ground – or anything else – until he is clear of the penalty

Figure 23   Penalty zones.

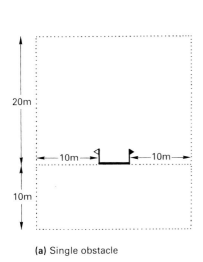

(a) Single obstacle

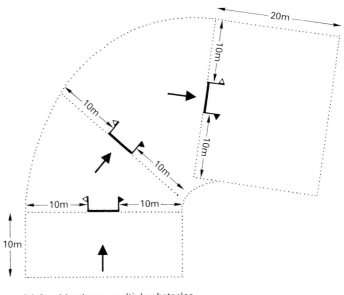

(b) Combination or multiple obstacles

zone, then he will incur no faults. A complication arises, however, in the case of combinations and other single obstacles which are sited so close together that their penalty zones overlap. For here the competitor must remain within the penalty zone from the moment that he has entered it in front of the first fence until he leaves it having jumped the last, except that after a run-out or refusal he may leave the zone in order to retake the obstacle without penalty. Thus a rider must be absolutely clear as to exactly where the limits of the penalty zone are, especially if his intended line of approach or his route through the obstacles is likely to take him near the boundary.

The second important consideration concerns alternative routes, both at difficult single obstacles and at combinations. First of all he will plan his first choice of approach and route through an obstacle, but in case this does not work out as planned, either because of a refusal or because the horse does not follow the intended line, he must be clear as to what alternatives are available, so that he can switch to one of them without delay (see Figures 24, 25 and 26). After his final inspection, the rider should have a very clear picture in his mind of the whole course; if he does not, then a further visit should be made to clear up points of doubt.

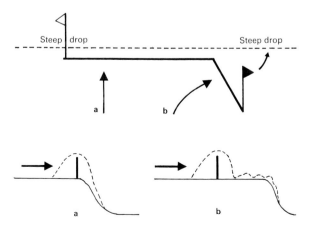

Figure 24   Planning alternative routes at single obstacles.

At this stage it may be helpful to clear our minds as to the exact method of scoring. In the early days of the sport, until 1971, marks gained in the Dressage were converted into penalties as at present. To these could be added penalties for late arrival on Phases 'A' and 'C' of the second day. But on both the Steeplechase and the Cross Country, competitors could also earn bonus marks for going fast, which were then deducted from their penalty scores, so that it was possible for the leading competitors to finish with bonus scores. The system was difficult for most spectators and some riders to understand, and in 1971 the change was made to the present system of penalties only.

The Dressage judges, of whom there are normally three, mark each movement of the test out of ten. Their scores are added together and then divided by three and subtracted from the total possible score for the test, to give the competitor's score in penalties. However, this is not the figure that appears on the scoreboard, because it is now multiplied by a coefficient of 0.6, thus effectively reducing the spread of the top and bottom scores and hence the relative influence of the Dressage on the whole competition, which should be in the ratio of Dressage 3; Endurance 12; Jumping 1. But we are not home yet! Now the severity or otherwise of the Cross Country course is assessed, and a further multiplying factor is applied to the Dressage scores with the object of maintaining these ratios in the light of the expected influence that the Cross Country will have on the whole competition. Thus, if the course is thought to be especially difficult, a multiplying factor of 1.5 will be used; if it is considered relatively easy, then the factor will be 0.5. This enables due account to be taken of adverse weather conditions, for example.

Each competitor therefore starts the second day with a penalty score, which can be increased by the addition of time penalties for going too slow on any of the four phases of

Figure 25 Planning alternative routes at a combination obstacle.

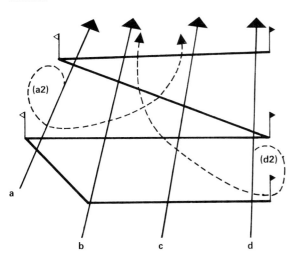

a 2 corners as a 2-stride double
b 2 one-stride combinations and a bounce
c One-stride combination – bounce – 1-stride combination
d One-stride combination to a corner – 2 strides out

Plans must be made for refusals or run-outs at any element,

e.g. **a2** Refusal at second corner
d2 Refusal at centre corner

Figure 26 Alternatives at a corner.

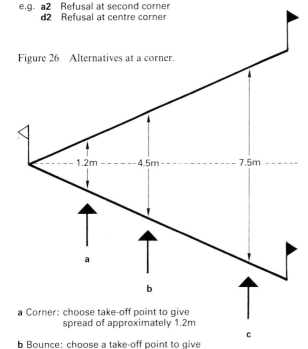

a Corner: choose take-off point to give spread of approximately 1.2m

b Bounce: choose a take-off point to give a distance of approximately 4.5m

c One-stride combination: choose take-off point to give a distance of approximately 7.5m

the Endurance test, and of any penalties incurred at the Steeplechase obstacles or the Cross Country fences. Finally, any jumping penalties picked up on the third day are added to the total. A competitor's score might therefore build up as follows over the three days:

1st Day: Dressage —Maximum marks 240

Judge A	138 marks
Judge B	150 marks
Judge C	144 marks
Total	432 marks
÷ 3	= 144 marks
Subtract from 240	= 96 penalties
× coefficient 0.6	= 57.6
× multiplying factor 0.75	= 43.2 penalties

DRESSAGE SCORE = 43.2

2nd Day:
Speed, Endurance and Cross Country

Phase	Time	Jumps	Total
A	-	-	-
B	4.8	-	4.8
C	-	-	-
D	16	20	36

CROSS COUNTRY SCORE 40.8

SCORE AFTER TWO DAYS
Dressage	43.2
Cross Country	40.8
TOTAL	84

3rd Day: Jumping
Jumps 5, Time 0 = 5
FINAL SCORE = 89

Hopefully we are not going to incur those 20 penalties for jumping on the Cross Country, so our time penalties will be reduced as well, and we hope not to have a fence down in the final Jumping test. If we can finish our first Three Day Event by adding less than ten time penalties to our Dressage score, we shall be very happy.

The time has now come to prepare for the First Horse Inspection. The object of this is to ensure that all the horses entered are sound and, as far as can be told from a visual inspection, fit to take part in a Three Day Event. Each competitor in turn produces his horse in front of an inspection panel which consists of two experienced and knowledgeable officials, often former competitors themselves, and a veterinary surgeon, all appointed by the Organising Committee. First the horse is inspected standing still, then it is walked away from the panel and trotted back past them. Now no competitor is likely to produce a horse at a Three Day Event that is actually lame or in some other way unfit to compete. But sometimes a horse may have sustained a minor injury while travelling to the event, and the rider may have worked hard to get him sound, knowing that he has a clear day before the Dressage and two days before the Cross Country; perhaps the panel may detect that he is not 100% sound and turn him down. In doubtful cases they may put the horse to one side to await a more detailed examination at the end of the inspection.

The order of starting, which is maintained for the Dressage and Endurance tests, is drawn, with those riders who have two horses seeded so as to allow time between them. (Sometimes in the past, riders have entered two horses, deciding in which order they wished to run them, so that when riding their second, and probably better, horse, they had the advantage of a late draw and of having had a trial run round the course. Now a new F.E.I. rule requires that the order in which the two horses run must be drawn, which may reduce the advantage slightly.) Unless conditions are very bad on the second day, it is usually an advan-

tage to be drawn late; on the other hand, if we are drawn early enough to do our Dressage on the Thursday, where there are two days of Dressage, it does mean that we can work our horse that much harder before the Dressage in the knowledge that we have a spare day before the Cross Country. Although we have by now done plenty of Dressage tests, never before have we done one with our horse at the peak of fitness, nor have our previous outings taken place in quite the same atmosphere; there will be more tents, more flags, and definitely more people, all adding up to more distraction. The rider, too, is likely to be more keyed up, and this will communicate itself to the horse. We shall probably therefore have to give our horse considerably more work before the Dressage than we have done in the past, and, just as we did at our first One Day Horse Trial, make a conscious effort to relax ourselves and our horse as we enter the arena.

Our Dressage behind us, and at a Three Day Event the Dressage scores are usually available much more quickly than at a One Day Event, we now turn our minds to the Cross Country, fitting in our second and third course inspections. Our next task is to work out our timings, and commit them to paper in a manner in which we can refer to them while riding round the course, a task which has been simplified by the marking of Phases 'A' and 'C' with kilometre markers on the ground. All riders will have been issued with a large-scale map of the entire course with these kilometre markers on it, which will help to refresh our memory of the route. We must now prepare a piece of card, which we shall tape to our wrist before we set off on Phase 'A', showing our starting and finishing times for each phase, together with the times at which we are due to pass the kilometre markers on the roads and tracks.

Now our timings will be issued as real times, but various things may cause these to be upset, and so we must also have these transposed into

elapsed times starting from zero, with both sets of times clearly written on our card, in figures large enough to be read whilst cantering. Let us suppose that our issued timings are as follows:

	Phase 'A'	Phase 'B'	Phase 'C'	Phase 'D'
Distance	4,950 m	2,070 m	8,140 m	4,895 m
Optimum Time	22'30"	3'	37'	8'35"
Start	1212	1234.30	1237.30	1325
Finish	1234.30	1237.30	1314.30	1333.35

The required speed of 220 metres per minute on the roads and tracks allows just over $4\frac{1}{2}$ minutes per kilometre. But we want to arrive at the start of the Steeplechase with about $1\frac{1}{2}$ minutes in hand, so we shall adjust our timings accordingly. Similarly we shall adjust the timings of Phase 'C' to take into account the running-down period after the Steeplechase, and since this phase starts as we go through the finish of the Steeplechase, we shall start our elapsed times for it again from zero, and remember to reset our stopwatch as we go through the Steeplechase finish. On the Steeplechase itself we want to know the time at which we should be at the half-way point, which we have already noted on the ground.

For the Cross Country, we may wish to know approximately how we are doing relative to the Optimum Time, so we divide the course into sections – two, three, or four according to its length – and make a note of the time at which we should complete each, taking into account the gradients, the going, and the obstacles. So our card, with the figures bold enough to be read as we ride, and with the clock times in, say, black and the elapsed times in red, will look something like this (since we shall have plenty of time in the Box in which to reorganise, we may put the times for Phase 'D' on a separate card, which we carry initially in our pocket or fix to the other wrist):

The last movement – Halt and Salute: The Moroccan, Julian Wathen, Burghley

The exact form of the card will depend on personal preference, and is not important so long as it is clear. The card will then be covered with clear plastic tape so that rain or sweat cannot cause the figures to run, and taped to the wrist.

Watches are also a matter of personal choice, some riders preferring digital models and others the type with a conventional face and

A	4,950 m	$22\frac{1}{2}$'	C	8,140 m	37'
S	1212	0	S	$1237\frac{1}{2}$	0
1	1216	4	1	$1243\frac{1}{2}$	6
2	1220	8	2	$1248\frac{1}{2}$	11
3	1224	12	3	$1253\frac{1}{2}$	16
4	1228	16	4	$1257\frac{1}{2}$	20
F	1233	21	5	$1301\frac{1}{2}$	24
			6	$1305\frac{1}{2}$	28
			7	$1309\frac{1}{2}$	32
B	2,070 m	3'	8	$1313\frac{1}{2}$	36
S	$1234\frac{1}{2}$	0	F	1314	$36\frac{1}{2}$
$\frac{1}{2}$	1236	$1\frac{1}{2}$			
F	$1237\frac{1}{2}$	3			

D	4,895 m	8'35"
S	1325	0
X	1328	3
Y	1331	6
F	1333'35	8'35"

hands; either must be large and clear enough to be read while galloping. Some may dispense with a normal watch and the clock times and work entirely from a stopwatch, but it is safer to have both. The normal watch must then be synchronised with the official clock at the start of Phase 'A', and we must remember to reset our stopwatch to zero at the end of Phase 'A', to restart it as we cross the start line for the Steeplechase, and again as we finish.

All that now remains is to carry out a final check of all our saddlery and equipment for the next day. Lucky is the rider who, having done all that he can for his horse, can then switch off and sleep soundly for the night before the Cross Country. As a newcomer, we may find ourselves riding the course in our minds until sleep finally overtakes us!

CHAPTER 14

The Three Day Event: Cross Country and Jumping days

Assistance • Preparing the horse • Dress • Equipment for the Box
• Weighing out • Phase 'A' • The Steeplechase • Phase 'C' • 2nd Horse Inspection
• In the Box • Briefing • The Cross Country • On the course • Weighing in
• 2nd horse examination • Debriefing • Care of the horse • Veterinary assistance
• Forbidden substances • 3rd Horse Inspection • The Jumping test
• Preparation • Jumping • The prizegiving • The future

Before going to the start of Phase 'A' there is much to be done. Hopefully for this event we shall have the services of a groom, or at least a willing and reasonably knowledgeable helper, and if we have another friend who can also be at the start of Phase 'A' and in the Box, so much the better. In the morning our horse will have had a light feed – its size depending on our start time – his water will have been removed as soon as he has had a chance to drink after his feed, and he will not have had any hay. He must be groomed, his mane plaited, his shoes studded, his legs bandaged or booted, and finally he must be tacked up. If bandages are used they must be sewn in position, and the headpiece of the bridle should be attached to the top plait with plaiting thread so that in the event of a fall the bridle cannot come off – this can happen on its own, or the rider can sometimes push it off in trying to avert a separation!

Some riders like to smother their horse's legs in grease, so that if the horse hits a fence and drags his legs over it there is less chance of injury, and the horse may be able to pull his legs free a fraction of a second earlier, which could just make the difference between a peck and a fall on landing over a fence. Others feel that the grease adds to the weight that a horse must carry on his legs and prefer to do without it.

We must now dress ourselves for the fray! We need a regulation helmet and cover, back-protector, jersey, number bib, breeches, boots and spurs, gloves if it is wet, whip, watch and stopwatch, timing card, and finally a spare piece of lead or two in case we need it in order to weigh out, though we shall already have done a trial weighing. We must also assemble everything that will be needed in the Box and arrange for it to be transported there. Then, off to the start, where we will be officially weighed out and will sign the weighing sheet. We will be weighed dressed for the start but without our whip, and with all our horse's saddlery except for the bridle, which we shall be able to use at the weigh-in if necessary to make up weight that we have lost on the way round the course. On a wet day, we shall probably gain weight as our clothes become soaked, but if it is very hot we may lose a pound or two, and it may be wise to allow for this by starting very slightly overweight. Failure to weigh in at the required weight, using the bridle if necessary, entails elimination.

Having resaddled our horse and mounted, we wait to be called to the start by the starter. The final count-down begins, '5 seconds, 4, 3, 2, 1, Go', and off we set at the trot – an anti-climax if ever there was one! As we cross the start line we set our stopwatch going, and on Phase 'A' we alternate between trotting and cantering, and aim to arrive at the Steeplechase with $1\frac{1}{2}$ minutes to spare. Here we may or may not meet our helper, but we shall check our girth, saddle and weight-cloth, shorten our stirrups, and set our stopwatch to zero. The starter will give us a minute and a half-minute warning, and at about 15 seconds we should enter the starting box, and either stand still or walk quietly round it, being careful not to cross the line early, which would entail re-entering the box and starting again while the clock continued to run. Although our horse may normally be quiet, he may be excited by the horse in front of us passing the finish just as we are about to start, and we must be ready to guard against starting too early.

'5, 4, 3, 2, 1, Go', and at least this time we set off at a gallop! To complete the course within the Optimum Time we must average something approaching 25 miles per hour, and we must therefore get into top gear straight away, and as we cross the line we must set our stopwatch going. We should by now have a fair idea of how fast we need to go to do the time, and hopefully we shall meet the fences right, so that our horse neither uses too much energy in jumping them nor risks falling through standing off too far or taking off too

close. If we should see that a lengthening of our horse's stride is going to allow him to stand back safely we should ask for this; if he is approaching 'dead wrong', we must on no account try to shorten him, but should sit still, hold him together, and remember to put our legs further forward than usual in case he hits the top of the fence or pecks on landing.

At the half-way mark, which will not be marked but which we will have noted during our course inspection, we glance at our stopwatch to see how we are doing, and will take another look as we are approaching the end of the course, but in neither case as we are approaching a fence. Our aim will be to cross the finishing line a few seconds, not more than 10, before we are due. If we go too fast we shall take more out of our horse than is necessary, a fact that is likely then to become apparent half-way round Phase 'D', and if we go too slowly we shall incur time penalties at the rate of 0.8 for every second over the Optimum Time. As we pass through the finish we must stop and restart our stopwatch in order to start our timekeeping for Phase 'C'.

We now have just over 8 kilometres of roads and tracks ahead of us, and we gradually let our horse slow down through a canter and a trot to the walk, at which pace we continue until he has stopped blowing. We have allowed on our time card 6 minutes for the first kilometre, and 5 for the second, before resuming our normal speed of 4 minutes to the kilometre – and resume it we must, for the clock ticks on! We may slacken our girths a hole, though this may be difficult if we are using a surcingle. The trot-and-canter ritual must now be resumed. If there is a steep incline on this phase, we should let our horse get to the top at the pace that suits him best, which is probably a sharp canter; it is a mistake to force him to walk up it, but we may let him walk for a short while on reaching the top.

We hope to arrive at the end of this phase

Phase C – they now have just over 8 km of roads and tracks ahead of them. Gorky Park, Katie Meacham, Chatsworth

with half a minute in hand; there is absolutely no point in being early, unless for some particular reason we require more than the stipulated 10 minutes in the Box. As we approach we will be met by the 2nd Horse Inspection Panel, who will probably signal us to trot the last 20 yards or so, and who will then briefly examine our horse to make sure that he is fit to continue. We now have 10 minutes in which to prepare for the crucial part of the whole competition, and exactly what we do will depend upon the temperament of our horse, on the weather, and on how much help we have. As a minimum we should loosen the girths, check the saddle and weight-cloth, pick out his feet and check his shoes and studs, sponge his nostrils and mouth, and check his boots or bandages. If it is hot, we may remove all his tack except for the bridle, wash him down completely, dry him with a scraper, and resaddle him; if there is a cold wind we may just sponge his head and neck; if it is pouring with rain, we may just remove what mud we can. We then put a light sheet on him and have him walked round the Box.

Ideally our helpers should do most of this for us, leaving us free to find out all we can about what has been happening out on the course, what fences have been causing trouble and what routes at the combination fences have ridden best – in the light of which we may decide to modify our original plans and put our second options into operation. We may have asked someone to take note of what has happened at certain fences, and at major events there may well be a closed-circuit television monitor in a tent in the Box which will provide a fair amount of useful information. But in the absence of positive information which leads us to believe that our plans should be modified, we should stick to the plans that we made on our course inspections. Not less than 2 minutes before we are due to start, we should remount, tighten our girths, ensure that our stopwatch is reset, ask our helper to clean the mud off the soles of our boots, and compose ourselves for this crucial test. Again the count-down, and away we go, not forgetting to trip the stopwatch as we cross the line, quickly setting up the speed and rhythm that will put us within reach of the Optimum Time.

There may be a few straightforward fences on the course which will require no special approach and no great effort on the part of the horse. There will be some big spreads which demand boldness, speed and accuracy, and there will be drop fences which require control,

whilst at the same time we must allow our horse sufficient length of rein to balance himself and recover from any mistake, and must adopt a seat that offers security in the event of a peck on landing. There will almost certainly be water, perhaps requiring a jump into it, in the middle of it, and out of it to dry land on the far side. Again, if we watch the experts we note that, as over drops, they are concerned with a secure seat, adequate length of rein, and the maintenance of control and impulsion – all this when flying spray can distract or blind both horse and rider. Some obstacles will slow us down considerably, and we must aim to make up time elsewhere on the course, glancing at our watch at the pre-arranged points to monitor our progress. But as important as speed on the flat between fences is speed in getting away from them on landing.

In an ideal world, we will negotiate the course according to plan, and will approach the last fence with some 20 seconds in hand. The last fence seldom constitutes a serious problem, but many a good round has been ruined by too casual an approach to it! Hopefully our and our horse's concentration will be maintained, and we shall gallop through the finish with a few seconds to spare. Before we do anything else – and in the euphoria of the moment it is all too easy to forget this – we must weigh in. We must not dismount until told to do so by the steward, and should have no contact with anyone else until we have been on the scales and have signed the sheet. Although most stewards might take a sympathetic view of a young girl receiving help as she staggers exhausted from her horse under the weight of her saddle and 10 kg of lead, according to the rules this could lead to elimination.

We are now likely to be approached by the

As important as speed on the flat between fences, is speed getting away from them on landing. Friday Fox, Rachel Hunt, Gatcombe

official responsible for debriefing riders at the end of the course. He will ask whether we incurred any faults on the way round, so that a provisional score can be passed to the commentary box, together with our time over the course – all subject to confirmation when the official score sheets are collected. Meanwhile our horse will have been briefly examined by a vet appointed by the organisers in order to see whether he needs immediate attention or is fit to return to his stable. He should now have a sweat-sheet on him, and should be walking quietly round the Box. This he should continue to do until he has stopped blowing, when he should be completely washed down, dried off with a scraper, covered with a sweat-sheet and a light rug, and led round until he is completely dry, when he will be only too pleased to be allowed to get his head down and graze. If it is very cold, or if there is a chilling wind, he should not be washed down in the open but should be led back to his stable where this can be done in a wash-box or in a sheltered place. If we do this there should be little chance of him breaking out in a sweat later in the evening.

From now on our prime consideration must be our horse's welfare, and producing him sound and fit to jump at the 3rd Horse Inspection tomorrow morning. First we should trot him up to see that he is still sound, then we must give him a detailed inspection to ensure that we have not overlooked any minor injury such as an overreach which if not treated could blow up overnight. Any cuts or grazes should be cleaned with warm water and mild disinfectant and then sprayed with wound powder or a purple spray, or if necessary bandaged. Our main worry will be whether there has been any strain to the legs or any bruising to the joints. In both cases heat and swelling will tell us that something is wrong, but unless the injury is very serious it will take an hour or so before the signs become apparent. If all seems well we should then bandage his legs, give him

a drink and a feed, and leave him quietly in his box.

If there are signs of injury other than small cuts or grazes, then we should call a vet. At a Three Day Event there are normally two teams of vets: the official vets acting on behalf of the Organising Committee and including members of the examination and inspection panels who carry out their duties according to the F.E.I. rules, and another team who are present to help competitors throughout the competition, and who will be in the stable area after the Cross Country. They will do all they can to ensure that a horse is fit to pass the next day's inspection, and will advise a competitor if the horse should be withdrawn. In a case of obviously serious injury, such as a damaged tendon, there is no question of the horse continuing to compete, and it would be impossible, and quite wrong, to try to patch it up to enable it to pass inspection. But between this and complete soundness there are degrees of minor injury which can be successfully treated and which will not be aggravated if the horse competes in the Jumping test. But there are very strict rules regarding the use of medications and drugs – for both horse and rider, incidentally – and this is one reason why treatment should only be carried out by or under the supervision of a vet, who will know exactly what is permitted and what is on the list of forbidden substances, which is in fact published in both the B.H.S. and F.E.I. Rules, which also provide for the testing of horses and riders at events.

Hopefully these problems will not arise, and early next morning our horse will trot up sound, and will be groomed and prepared for the 3rd Horse Inspection. This is a part of the event that is interesting to spectators, and a large crowd usually assembles to watch. We must present our horse looking his best in order to show the panel that he is fit to continue the competition, and he should therefore be as alert as possible. The majority of horses will

There will almost certainly be water requiring a jump into it. Dylan II, Polly Schwerdt, Badminton

In the middle of it: Gelert of Wales, Jane Holderness-Roddam, Burghley

Jumping into water requires a secure seat and adequate length of rein

Control and impulsion

Flying spray can distract or blind both horse and rider

with unfortunate results

Show Jumping: Accumulator, Richard Walker, Burghley

Show Jumping: Alibi, Richard Burns, Bramham

Show Jumping: Autumn Venture (Hol), Eddy Stibbe, Burghley

The helpers too, without whom so much could not be achieved, will also be happy. Sir Wattie, Badminton 1986

Watching the winner receive his trophy. Sir Wattie, Ian Stark, and Badminton's Whitbread Trophy

Croft & Co Ltd sponsored the British Open Championships at Gatcombe Park. J.J. Babu, Bruce Davidson

Windsor Three Day Event had as its Sponsor Beefeater Steak Houses – now replaced by Polly Peck

So is it worthwhile? The answer is a resounding 'yes'

MacConnal-Mason sponsored a series of horse trials. Stowell Park

Carphone Group sponsored two Three-Day Events, two One Day Horse Trials and a team of four riders and twenty horses

Olympic Games, Seoul, 1988

The Dressage Arena

Karen Lende, The Optimist (USA)

Mark Todd, Charisma (NZ)

Olympic Games, Seoul, 1988

Ginny Leng, Master Craftsman (GB)

Mark Todd, Charisma (NZ)

Claus Erhorn, Justyn Thyme (FRG)

Olympic Games, Seoul, 1988. Team Gold medal: West Germany
Matthias Baumann, Shamrock II
Thies Kaspareit, Sherry 42
Ralf Ehrenbrink, Uncle Todd
Claus Erhorn, Justyn Thyme

Olympic Games, Seoul, 1988
Gold Medal: Mark Todd, Charisma (NZ)
Silver Medal: Ian Stark, Sir Wattie (GB)
Bronze Medal: Ginny Leng, Master Craftsman (GB)

pass without any difficulty, and no rider will present a horse that is clearly lame. But often there are a few borderline cases, and there will be much heart-searching on the part of the members of the Panel, who are as keen as anyone not to exclude a horse from the final test unless he is clearly unfit to continue. In cases of doubt, they will put a horse to one side in a box reserved for this purpose, and will reconsider him at the end of the inspection.

Having passed this inspection we return our horse to his stable until the time comes to prepare him for the Jumping test. This is run in reverse order of merit according to the placing of competitors after the Cross Country, and if there is still a sufficient number of horses left in the competition some will jump in the morning, leaving the last 25 or 30 to jump in the afternoon. Our preparation for this final test is most important, for on the previous day our horse has been galloping and jumping solid obstacles, and apart from the fact that he may be less exuberant even if not actually tired, he may tend to stand too far off

the fences and risk lowering them with his hind legs. Conversely, if he does arrive too close to an obstacle he may lack that 'snap' that normally enables him to clear it. We must therefore prepare him particularly carefully outside the arena, and ride him more definitely than usual when we take him inside. Exactly how we prepare him will depend on what practice obstacles are available; ideally we would use a cavaletto or take-off pole in front of a fence in order to encourage him to look at the obstacle, and also to place him for take-off rather closer than he may have in mind after yesterday's gallop. If this is not possible, then we may use a pole on the ground, but sometimes even this is difficult without interfering with the preparations of other competitors.

The Jumping test is usually preceded by a parade of those competitors remaining in the competition, which can prove a problem to some highly strung horses, and we must do our best to keep our horse calm and relaxed. After

The Final Horse Inspection: Priceless, Ginny Leng, Gawlor

a satisfactory round yesterday, we have added just a few time penalties to our Dressage score, and, whilst unlikely to be among the prizes, we should finish well in the top half of the competition, and will have gained useful experience and qualification for future Three Day Events. The scores above and below us are close, however, and we cannot afford a mistake in the Jumping arena, and must also be careful not to incur time penalties. The Jumping normally takes place in the arena where the Dressage was held on the first day, and, especially if there are two or more sections, it may be much larger than is necessary to accommodate the Jumping course. In these cases, riders are often tempted into making too much use of the wide open spaces with the result that unnecessary time penalties are added to their scores – and if scores are close, this can affect their final placing.

But for us, all goes according to plan, and we return to watch the final competitors. As the last few jump, the order changes somewhat, and as the leading horse and rider enter the ring there is silence in the stands. A fence down will relegate him to second place, two fences would drop him to fourth. A groan rises as he rattles a fence on the way round, but he is lucky and it does not fall; as he clears the last the cheers can be heard in the nearest town! Finally there comes the prizegiving, and sometimes, as in this case, those who have completed the competition return mounted into the arena with the prize-winners to receive rosettes. As we sit watching the winner receive his trophy, we can reflect that all our hard work and detailed preparation have been worth while, and dream about the future. Our helpers too, without whom we could not have achieved so much, will be happy, and now is the time for a celebration. Most important of all, we now have a Three Day Event horse!

Finally there comes the prizegiving. Bolebec Miler, Anne-Marie Taylor, Chatsworth

131

Part
5

LOOKING AROUND

CHAPTER 15

Sponsorship: the sponsors

The development of sport • Prize money • Paid sportsmen
• Sport becomes business • Sponsors seek a return • Sport offers publicity
• Racing • Dressage and Show Jumping • Eventing • Comparisons with racing
• Expenses • Prize money • Riders need sponsors • What do sponsors need?
• Event sponsors • One Day Horse Trials • Three Day Events • Rider sponsors
• Other sponsors • Sponsors' views on sponsorship • Equipment suppliers

According to the *Oxford English Dictionary*, sport is defined as 'amusement, diversion, fun', and also as 'a pastime or game', and certainly the original conception of sport adhered to these definitions. Later came the promotion and enjoyment of physical fitness, but the essence of sport was participation. Then sport became a spectacle which required officials to control both the sportsmen and the spectators. So sport became entertainment, with spectators paying to watch and sportsmen competing for prizes.

Some sports managed to retain the elements of amusement, diversion and fun, together with the idea of competing for competition's sake; athletics, really the original sport, did so for longer than most. Others found their 'amateur' status threatened, and eventually had to become 'open' like tennis, or, if they clung to their status, saw the formation of a breakaway faction, as happened in the case of rugby football. Some sports became so expensive to pursue that they ended up beyond the reach of individuals, and became big business, Formula 1 Motor Racing being a case in point. As this trend increased, sponsorship arrived on the scene, and although sport had been around for thousands of years before sponsorship was thought of, we now have a situation in which

many sports have become so expensive that they cannot survive in their present form without sponsorship, while sponsorship can only be attracted to a sport that has shown itself to be successful. So what is it that attracts a sponsor? Primarily, the sponsor is in it for money, though that is not to say that he will not prefer to put his money where his interest lies. And if we find a sponsor who injects his money into a sport with no thought of commercial return, then the implication is that he does not need to participate in sports sponsorship but is doing it for his own pleasure.

The main benefit to a sports sponsor lies in the publicity which he or his product receives, and which leads to increased profits. Thus sport becomes an advertising medium, and it is no accident that sponsorship really took off with the advent of television. Television now reaches more homes than newspapers, but the cost of a short piece of prime-time advertising is very high, and in the case of some products – tobacco, for example – the advertisement is subject to regulation, or may be banned altogether. Sponsorship of a televised sport may put the sponsor's name or his product in front of viewers in a way that may have more impact than a half-minute advertisement, and in the case of certain products may be the only way to reach the television audience.

The oldest equestrian sport is racing, which took place in various forms long before it became the sport of kings. But racing has always differed from other equestrian sports in two ways: it has for long been a major, in fact the major, gambling sport; and the big money prizes that originated as stake money put up by competing owners, though now inflated by enormous sums of added money, have always been paid to the owners, who are not usually, in the case of flat racing, participating sportsmen in the same way as athletes or even Show Jumping or Three Day Event riders. In flat racing there are very few amateur jockeys, and in National Hunt they are either restricted to races confined to amateurs or are subject to fairly strict control.

The other main equestrian sports, Dressage, Show Jumping and Eventing, together with polo, originated as forms of 'amusement, diversion and fun' for military officers, and in the international field these three Olympic disciplines continued to be the preserve of the military until the demise of horsed cavalry, and for a decade or so after the end of World War II this remained so.

These three sports then developed in rather different ways and at different paces. Dressage in this country has not even now gained the popular appeal that it has on the Continent. It has nothing like the television exposure of the other two, but has nevertheless managed to attract sponsorship for events and for riders. Show Jumping has proved the most fertile ground for sponsorship, because television coverage is considerable, publicity can also be obtained on the ground, and during an afternoon's televised Jumping at Hickstead, for example, the name of the sponsor is frequently on the screen. The name of the competition with the sponsor's name will appear on the screen at intervals, there may be banners around the arena which the cameras will catch

as they follow the progress of horses round the course, and horses may be seen entering or leaving the arena under an archway which bears the sponsor's name too. For this reason Jumping has proved particularly popular with firms such as tobacco manufacturers, whose advertising is limited by law.

Although the really big prizes of flat racing are not available to the Show Jumpers, it is interesting to note that while the leading 1986/87 season National Hunt money-winner Desert Orchid earned just under £79,000, the leading Show Jumper, Mr and Mrs Tom Bradley's Next Milton, a home-bred horse brought out originally by their daughter, the late Caroline Bradley, and now jumped under the Next team banner, topped £75,000 in 1986 – not far behind. And in the twelve months from June 1986 to May 1987 he won over £93,000. Desert Orchid's total winnings are now approaching £300,000 and in 1988 Next Milton won over £133,000. But whereas the Steeplechasers can aim at the £64,000 of the Grand National with plenty of five-figure prizes on offer during the season, the top Show Jumping prize is £25,000 for Hickstead's Jumping Derby, and there are few prizes over £10,000. The Show Jumpers can, however, compete much more often than the Steeplechasers, and their season is longer; indeed, there is virtually no close season these days and since their winter circuit goes indoors they are less affected by weather.

The winner's prize at the first Badminton in 1949 was £150, and at that time there were plenty of National Hunt steeplechases in which the winner received this sum. In 1988 the Whitbread Trophy at Badminton was worth £6,000 in prize money to the winner, with the money going much further down the line than it does in racing. This represents an increase of 3,900%, and since a steeplechase that gave £150 in 1949 would now be awarding something in the region of £400 to the winner, an increase of 167%, eventing would not seem to have done too badly. The comparison is, however, hardly a fair one, for we should really be comparing Badminton with the Cheltenham Gold Cup (1st prize in 1987: £55,000), for it is the most prestigious Three Day Event in the world and the one that most riders would really love to win. But eventing is not, and hopefully never will be, a medium for gambling, so we are still not really comparing like with like.

But if we consider what it costs to train and produce a top-class Three Day Event horse, and how often he can compete, then the financial reward in terms of prize money is not all that great. Again comparison with racing may be misleading but it is interesting to note that on 4 April 1987 Guy Landau and Lean Ar Aghaidh led for most of the Grand National's $4\frac{1}{2}$ miles, finishing in 3rd place; on 25 April the same combination won the Whitbread Gold Cup over 2.6 miles at Sandown. Admittedly they flew in the face of history – and of the forecasts of the experts – in doing so, for horses that just complete the National do not usually manage even to secure a place in the Whitbread; but could any of the first three horses at Badminton win another Three Day Event three weeks later?

In National Hunt racing the top prize on offer in 1987 was the Grand National's £64,000, and the cost of keeping a horse in training amounted to something in the region of £6,000 a year. In eventing it still costs about the same to compete with a top-class Three Day Eventer, and yet the top prize is only £6,000. How then can a leading rider maintain the several horses that he needs if he is to remain at or near the top? He must seek either an owner or a sponsor, the difference between the two being that whereas the former is in the sport for his own pleasure, the latter may expect a return in commercial terms. What then does a sponsor require in return for his investment in the sport of eventing?

The answer lies in increased sales of his product or services. But is there perhaps more to it than this? Are sponsors attracted to eventing for other reasons too? Is the involvement of Royalty a factor, or the siting of so many Horse Trials in the grounds of 'stately homes'? Are sponsors attracted by the relatively relaxed atmosphere of a sport where no gambling is involved, and where owners and riders are clearly not in it with the prime object of making money? Does the sport provide a suitable ambience in which to entertain customers or staff? Do some sponsors invest their money purely for the good of a sport in which they are interested? Certainly it would appear that the purely commercial returns are limited by the fact that only Badminton and the British Open Championships at Gatcombe Park are televised, plus Burghley when it stages an international championship.

The major sponsors are divided into those who sponsor Horse Trials and those who sponsor riders – a few do both – plus some who give their support in other ways. Into the first category came the Midland Bank, who from 1969 to 1982 provided the prize money for nearly all the One Day Events in the calendar. The debt owed to them during these years of expansion is incalculable, and when they withdrew many forecast the decline of the sport. In fact eventing was now firmly on the map, and it did not prove too difficult to attract sponsors, some national and some local, for individual events, and eventually some of the larger sponsors undertook a series of events. Whilst some Horse Trials were sponsored entirely by one firm that provided the prize money and covered the administrative costs as well, most came to rely on one major sponsor for their prize money, plus a number of individual fence sponsors so that a wide range of local support was obtained.

Amongst the firms that have sponsored a series of events are Croft & Co. Ltd, well known as importers of port for over three hundred years and now importers of sherry, which their involvement with Horse Trials has helped to promote. With a series of sixteen events covering most areas of England, a Novice Championship for young horses at Tetbury in September, and the British Open Championships at Gatcombe Park in August (one of only three events to be televised), their sherries have certainly become well known to the eventing fraternity! Sadly they decided to terminate their sponsorship at the end of the 1987 season, when their sponsorship of Gatcombe was taken over by Barbour (waterproof clothing). *Horse & Hound* sponsors a series of Novice Rider classes with a championship at Great Missenden in September, and Mac-Connal-Mason (Art Galleries) in association with Mercedes-Benz (cross country vehicles) jointly sponsored, until 1988, a series of nine Horse Trials at which points could be earned towards an Accumulator Award worth £3,000 to the winner.

Beehive Car Parks, in association with Spillers (horse feeds) and Pasada (all weather riding surfaces), invest in the future of our teams by sponsoring a series of Junior Classes and Trials, while Strutt and Parker (Estate Agents) sponsor a six-event series and championship for Novice horses in the West of England. Subaru (four-wheel-drive estate cars and cross country vehicles) give prizes in kind for owner riders at a dozen events which qualify for the Owner Riders Championship at Weston Park in October.

Of the eight Three Day Events, the two classified as championships, and the only ones to be televised, are covered by Whitbread and Remy Martin, and both can at least be sure that copious quantities of their respective products, beer and brandy, will be consumed on site! Chatsworth and Bramham, both at Advanced level, and the former an International event, were sponsored respectively by Audi (cars) and the Carphone Group (in-car communications). The Intermediate Three Day Event at Windsor had as its sponsor Beefeater Steak Houses now replaced by Polly Peck, while Osberton and Holker Hall are currently without sponsors.

When it comes to sponsoring riders, there is no shortage of firms willing to look after the established and successful competitor, and there is little doubt that the likes of British National Life Assurance, now in the guise of Citibank Savings (Virginia Leng), S.R. International Communications Group (Lucinda Green), Edinburgh Woollen Mill (Ian Stark), the Mallinson-Denny Group (Nigel Taylor), Beefeater Steak Houses (Robert Lemieux), Merrill Lynch (Mark Todd), and Carphone Group (Rodney Powell and Mary Thomson) all receive value for money in terms of publicity, for all their riders regularly appear in the Top Ten. Indeed, the Carphone Group could hardly believe it when, at the first Three Day Event run under their sponsorship, one of their own riders took first and second places on Carphone horses!

But apart from the sponsors of events and riders, there are other firms whose support takes different forms. Range Rover sponsor Mark Phillips and Karen Straker, but also provide training courses and bursaries for young riders and a scholarship for the Young Rider of the Year; the British Field Sports Society, though not a commercial organisation, provides a training bursary for riders in the East of England. Other firms contribute to the sport by supplying our international teams with their products or by contributing financially to the expenses of sending teams abroad, and their products range from riders' clothing and team uniforms through horse clothing and transport to champagne – presumably in anticipation of success to be celebrated! So what do sponsors, who would not, presumably, be supporting Horse Trials if they did not consider it worth their while to do so, feel are the main benefits to be derived from sponsorship? The magazine *Eventing*, the only periodical devoted exclusively to Horse Trials, ran a survey of sponsors' views, and some of these are interesting.

Graham Thomas of the Carphone Group, formerly sponsors of two Three Day Events, two One Day Horse Trials and a team of four riders and twenty horses, was understandably optimistic after their Bramham success of 1986. Nevertheless, as Chairman of the firm that has probably put more into the sport than any other, his views are worth noting. On the subject of sports sponsorship in general: 'No marketing director worth his salt these days can afford to ignore the advertising opportunities presented by sports sponsorship as a means of putting over his message to the potential market for his company's services and products. More traditional avenues such as national newspaper advertising become daily more expensive and less effective, whilst sports sponsorship presents exciting new ways to promote a message by either backing individual men and women or supporting fixtures.' And on the benefits: 'It is amazing just how loyal Horse Trials people are, and we have been flabbergasted by the amount of business transactions which have come about as a result of our sponsorship efforts over the last two years.'

Edinburgh Woollen Mill are as heavily committed to sports sponsorship as any – athletics, tennis, cricket, squash, and racing all benefit from their support. Not only in Scotland but in England, too, many people are aware of them through their success on the racecourse and in Horse Trials. Ian Stark, Oxford Blue, Sir Wattie and Glenburnie have brought them publicity that can have done the business nothing but good. The views of their Managing Director, David Stevenson, are interesting: 'We are always keen to try to plough back some of our profit into the community from which it came and we feel that sports spon-

sorship is an excellent vehicle for this as not only does it encourage a healthy life style, but it also helps those with a determination to succeed – especially amongst the youth of our society.' It comes as no surprise to learn that Stevenson himself was an Olympic athlete (at pole vaulting).

Neither Carphone nor Edinburgh Woollen Mill provide products or services that come immediately to mind as necessities for the eventing fraternity, though Edinburgh Woollen Mill products probably find their way on to the backs of competitors and spectators alike without their realising it. Strangely enough, the list of major event sponsors for 1988 contained no saddlers, manufacturing, wholesale or retail, no horse feed producers, only one clothing manufacturer (Caldene, who also sponsor Karen Straker), and one producer of veterinary products (Ventipulmin). This last case is interesting, because the manufacturers of a product which cannot be bought except through veterinary surgeons are trying to stimulate competitors into asking for it through their sponsorship of four Horse Trials.

Products likely to appeal directly to riders, owners and organisers are four-wheel-drive and cross country vehicles. Mercedes-Benz promoted their 'G' Series in association with MacConnal-Mason, and in their own words: 'Mercedes-Benz UK Ltd consider the sport of Horse Trials to be an ideal platform to promote this 'G' Series range of cross country vehicles ... The competitors, spectators and organisers are all associated with the farming fraternity which we consider to be the prime market for the 'G' Series.' So much for the commercial aspect. But 'Currently the sport is run on a very friendly informal basis and this attitude has been particularly attractive to many new sponsors.' Daihatsu, sponsors of Brigstock, are another 'natural', and Managing Director Maurice Rourke stressed two aspects of his firm's involvement: 'The atrocious weather conditions at previous Brigstock events have enabled the Daihatsu staff to show just how excellent the Fourtrack really is' (he must be just about the only person to welcome these conditions) and: 'As many of Daihatsu's Fourtrack models are bought by people involved in sport ... it is quite natural that the company should "put something back" into sport by giving an important Horse Trial like Brigstock substantial backing.'

No tobacco firm has as yet descended upon the Horse Trials scene to promote their products, but eventing enthusiasts are obviously considered to be fertile ground for the absorption of drink! Apart from Croft, Remy Martin (cognac) and Piper (champagne) are major supporters. Remy Martin sponsor the Burghley Three Day Event, and feel that: 'The ambience of Three Day Eventing suits existing drinkers of the brand as well as encouraging newcomers', and that: 'The sport, with its courageous riders and horses will benefit.' Piper Champagne, for long involved in racing and sponsors of the Cheltenham Gold Cup, decided to promote their product by spreading it as far round the Horse Trials scene as possible, a move which has paid off in terms of increased sales, and they are now also sponsors of Aston Park and of the revived Locko Park Novice and Intermediate Championships. 'So what have we gained?' asks Justin Llewelyn. 'Most non-drinks companies involved in Horse Trials sponsorship now use us as the champagne in the hospitality areas, and even for this reason alone sales justify the expansion of our original sponsorship involvement. Reflect also upon how many 21st, weddings and Christmas parties will all the people involved in eventing muster between them in the years ahead. So for us is it worthwhile? The answer is a resounding yes.'

A juicy, succulent steak to round off a hard day's riding, grooming, spectating or officiating is a pleasant prospect, and the profile of Beefeater Steak Houses, incidentally part of the Whitbread Group, has certainly been kept in the eyes of the eventing public through their sponsorship of Robert Lemieux. The horsebox, with its awning, the rugs, rider's and grooms' clothing, all in company livery, and even their flag flying in the horse-box park, have been familiar sights at Horse Trials up and down the country, and Robert has certainly done his best to give his sponsors value for money in terms of exposure. Pointing out that it costs between £40,000 and £50,000 to keep a top team of five or six horses on the road for a year, and that as much again is likely to be spent on promotion, administration and hospitality, he stresses that eventing does have one thing in its favour. 'It does not take place in a smoke-filled civic hall. It offers everything that is best in Britain, and captures some of the "spirit" that is so often lost in the hard-nosed commercialism of today.'

The most significant sponsorship news of 1988 was the appointment for the first time of an official sponsor to the British Three Day Event Team. ICI Films, already sponsors of riders John and Jane Thelwall, undertook to sponsor the team for two years, to include the 1988 Olympic Games, the 1989 European Championships at Burghley, and some fourteen international Three Day Events. This sponsorship not only reduces the financial burden of the British Horse Society, but also ensures the best possible team training and preparation.

So on the whole sponsors seem to be happy with their lot, certainly the sport could not exist as it does today without them. But the sport of Horse Trials also seems fortunate enough to be able to attract sponsors who are prepared to put their money into it without too much regard for commercial returns. This is not to say that problems cannot arise for organisers, competitors, or for sponsors themselves – and riders, in particular, have to be clear as to what sponsorship involves on their part.

CHAPTER 16

Sponsorship: the riders

The sponsored and the unsponsored • Acquiring a sponsor
• British Equestrian Promotions • The British Equestrian Federation
• Amateurs and professionals • Military and civilian • 'Shamateurs'
• Show Jumping and the 1972 crisis • The relaxation of Olympic Rules
• Broken-time payments • F.E.I. Rules • B.E.F. Guidelines
• Sponsorship agreements • Advertising • Reclassification • Open Olympics?
• The effects of sponsorship • The sponsor's ideal rider

There are in Britain currently some fifty riders who have entered into sponsorship agreements, and of those in the Top Twenty for 1986 only three were not sponsored. Estimates of what it costs to keep an event horse on the road and competing range from £5,000 to £10,000 according to the simplicity or lavishness of the operation, and what expenses are taken into account. With the season's biggest prize standing at £6,000, not many owners or riders are going to recoup their expenses.

This is not to say that the dedicated one- or two-horse rider whose help comes from his family, and whose transport is a car and trailer or a modest horse-box, cannot be successful enough to make ends meet. It can be done, as Lorna Clarke, perhaps one of the last true amateurs to make it to the top, has shown. Lorna, of course, rose to the top (as Lorna Sutherland) when she won Burghley as long ago as 1967 with the little skewbald Popadom, and has remained there ever since, winning a Bronze Medal at the Gawlor World Championships in 1986; but it was not until that time that she acquired even limited sponsorship. And for every sponsored rider there are literally hundreds who compete in Horse Trials at all levels all over the country. Some manage

to recoup their expenses in prize money, and others do not; but by keeping their expenses to the minimum they are able to enjoy their chosen sport.

But how does the keen young rider with potential set about acquiring a sponsor? It is the chicken-and-egg situation again: most sponsors are looking for a rider with proven ability and success, but how many riders can be successful without sponsorship? Fortunately, it is possible for the young rider to work his way up through Junior and Young Rider classes, in which success brings the publicity that attracts sponsors; and also the sport is lucky in that it attracts a number of sponsors who are prepared to invest their money in a young rider with potential without too much regard for commercial return. Rachel Hunt and MacConnal-Mason provide an example of the first case, and Alex McMeekin and Tetbury Agricultural Merchants the second. Rachel worked her way up through Junior and Young Rider competitions to a 2nd place at Badminton in 1986, Team Gold and Individual Bronze Medals at the Young Riders European Championship, and from there to selection as reserve for the Olympic Team of 1988. Alex McMeekin, still at school in 1987 and studying for 'A' levels, had two Intermediate horses, but T.A.M., a local firm, showed the generosity, foresight and interest in the sport to put their resources behind her.

The successful rider may not have to look far for sponsorship, it may even come to him. Nigel Taylor (9th in the ratings for 1986) was chatting to his vet in the bar of his local pub one evening when a stranger pricked up his ears and introduced himself as the managing director of a firm in the Mallinson-Denny group, one of the country's largest timber importers, and as a result of this chance meeting they became his sponsors. But the ambitious young rider is probably best advised to look for local sponsorship and not to expect too much at the start. There are, however, two organisations, one of which may be concerned in the setting up of a rider's sponsorship deal, and one of which certainly will be.

British Equestrian Promotions was established back in 1973 by the late Bob Dean with the object of handling sponsorship arrangements for equestrian sport, and of ensuring that money put into the sport by commercial firms was used in the best interests of the sport. Later the company, of which equestrian commentator Raymond Brooks-Ward is Managing Director, became involved in the running of shows, notably the Royal International at the Birmingham National Exhibition Centre, the Horse of the Year Show at Wembley, and the Christmas Show at Olympia, but its primary function remains sponsorship, which in the case of Horse Trials was until recently handled by Hugh Thomas, World Championship Bronze Medallist at Burghley in 1974, a member of our 1976 Olympic Team, and now Director of Badminton. B.E.P. is in a position to offer advice to riders seeking sponsorship, and may be able to put sponsor and rider together.

The British Equestrian Federation was formed at about the same time to take over from the British Horse Society and the British Show Jumping Association responsibility for dealing with all international aspects of their respective sports. (Previously there had been no national federation, and the B.H.S. had dealt with the F.E.I. on questions such as the issue of riders' licences.) Since the B.E.F. handles riders' licences, it also deals with the interpretation and implementation of the F.E.I. and Olympic Rules regarding the status of riders, and hence also deals with the question of sponsorship, in order to safeguard the interests of riders and of the sport, and to ensure that riders neither infringe the regulations nor endanger their status as competitors. Its Director General is Major Malcolm Wallace, formerly a successful Horse Trials rider and, until he took up this appointment, *Chef d'Équipe* of our international Three Day Event team.

The question of what is and is not permitted in a rider's sponsorship agreement revolves around the age-old question of amateur or professional status. Since most equestrian sport arose from the desire of officers of the cavalry regiments of the European armies to find 'amusement, diversion and fun', it is not altogether surprising to discover that until the 1950s the F.E.I. definition of an amateur was geared to the status of the military officer. After the 1948 Olympic Games in London, a member of one of the European Three Day Event teams was disqualified because, although his army had seen fit to commission him as an officer in time for him to be eligible to compete in the Games, they were unwise enough to return him to his non-commissioned rank immediately afterwards!

The question of the status of civilians was not at that time too difficult since, especially on the Continent, relatively few of them competed, and it was comparatively easy to define as a professional anyone who made his living out of horses – mainly dealers and instructors. (The fact that cavalry officers were virtually full-time riders was conveniently overlooked on the grounds that they were so obviously 'gentlemen', and that riding was only incidental to their profession and not its essence!)

But as the standards of competition rose, as the expenses of competing soared, and as prize money became an important factor, it became more and more difficult for the part-time rider to reach the top. The clear-cut distinction between the amateur and the professional became blurred, and unfortunately so did most of the rules and regulations, or at any rate their interpretation and enforcement. At the same time the complexities and demands of modern soldiering meant that, with some notable exceptions, the officer competitor at the highest level almost disappeared from the scene, though this took longer to happen in Horse Trials than, for example, in Dressage and Show Jumping.

Thus arrived the so-called 'shamateur', who might be defined as one whose amateur status is questionable but who is nevertheless licensed to compete as an amateur. In some countries little attempt was made to abide by the letter, let alone the spirit, of the F.E.I. or Olympic Rules – and the situation has always been complicated by the fact that each body set different standards by which to judge a competitor's status – and the situation was brought to a head in the early 1970s, when Prince Philip, as President of the F.E.I., called upon member nations to put their houses in order. The B.E.F. had not at that stage been formed, and the finger was in any case mainly pointed at Show Jumping, since this was where the big money prizes, and consequently the major abuses, were to be found.

Feeling obliged to respond to the President's call by setting an example to other nations, the B.S.J.A. promptly designated most of the leading riders professional, a blow from which our Olympic Show Jumping teams are only just recovering. For no other nation followed our admirable example, so while we were deprived of the services in the Olympic Games of riders of the calibre of David Broome, already an Olympic Bronze Medallist, Harvey Smith, Malcolm Pyrah, Derek Ricketts and the late Caroline Bradley, the backbone of the teams that won for Great Britain the President's Cup as well as World and European Championship medals, other nations continued to field riders whose amateur qualifications were considerably flimsier than ours. (One of the leading European riders, and a European Champion, was reported to be conveniently held on the books of a big industrial concern as a car park attendant, while the number of farmers who never did a day's work on the land was growing steadily!)

The Three Day Eventers could stand aside and watch all this with a certain smug satisfaction, for there was not the money to be made out of the sport that there was in Show Jumping. But as the need for sponsorship became apparent, and as firms began to recognise the advantages to them to be gained from it, the question of a rider's status began to be significant. Fortunately, at roughly the same time the International Olympic Committee (I.O.C.), the main stumbling-block in the way of 'open' sport, also began to recognise the need for change. Partly because some nations, while licensing their competitors as amateurs, paid little attention to the rules, and also because it was increasingly apparent that if sportsmen were to achieve the high standards necessary to win Olympic medals, then it was only reasonable that they should receive some form of compensation for the time spent away from their employment, business occupation or profession in doing so, broken-time payments were permitted.

What the I.O.C. in fact did was to throw the responsibility for interpreting its own rules onto the shoulders of the International Federations – in the case of equestrian sports the

F.E.I. Whilst continuing to state (in Olympic Rule 26) that in principle Olympic competitors must not have received any financial rewards or material benefits in connection with their sports participation, in fact 'material advantage' and 'contracts for sponsorship or equipment' were henceforth permissible provided that all arrangements were made through the national federation – the B.E.F. – to whom all payments had to be made. The term 'amateur' disappeared from the Rule Book and all sportsmen were henceforth either 'competitors' or 'professionals', a category which included paid coaches and instructors.

The import of all this is that if a rider is ever likely to compete at an international event in this country or abroad, and does not wish to be classified as a professional, he must be careful not to endanger his status by infringing the rules. Before he can compete at Badminton, Burghley, Chatsworth or Bramham, for example, he must apply through the Horse Trials Office to the B.E.F. for a competitor's licence. If therefore he wishes to enter into a sponsorship agreement he should first of all obtain from the B.E.F. their 'Guidelines on the Status and Eligibility of Competitors Entering International Events'. In principle, unless a sponsor is merely paying for the basic costs of keeping the horse, and is not shown as the horse's owner, the agreement must be approved and signed by the B.E.F., through whom all payments must be made. (The B.E.F. deducts a 2% handling charge before passing the money on to the competitor.)

While most commercial firms sponsoring a rider will expect to be able to derive benefits from advertising the association in one way or another, the rules regarding what is and is not permitted are strict, and the advertising agreement must also be approved and signed by the B.E.F. While the F.E.I. permits the display of a firm's logo on the saddle-cloth, the Horse Trials Committee does not, and unlike

Show Jumpers, commercial names and prefixes are not allowed either. (Even the F.E.I. had to modify the wording of their rule, however: some riders have always viewed rules as there to be circumnavigated, but the ingenuity of one who interpreted the rule restricting the size of a saddle-cloth logo to 100 square centimetres to mean that he could legally enter the arena with a ribbon 1 cm wide and 100 cm long trailing from his saddle-cloth had not been foreseen!)

Since the only Three Day Events barred to professionals are those at the Olympic Games, Regional Games and Young Riders events, it may seem in theory not to matter too much whether a rider acquires professional status unless he has serious ambitions of making the Olympic Team. In practice, however, it might be a step which he came to regret later, and it is one that had best be taken intentionally and not by default. There is now, though, an accepted procedure for a once-only reclassification from professional to competitor, either if the rider no longer pursues the activities that made him a professional in the first place, or if the rules are changed so that his activities now qualify him as a 'competitor'. But the reclassification can only take place once, and if a rider ever again acts as a professional then that will remain his status for life. The I.O.C. is still doing its best to preserve the image of amateur sport, but when the participation in the Olympic Games of millionaire tennis players is allowed, and when two sprinters received $250,000 each for appearing in a race in the month before the 1988 Games, we may be much nearer to 'open' Olympics and the participation of the best in any sport.

Once a rider has acquired a sponsor, with an agreement approved and signed by the B.E.F., are all his worries over? Much depends on the level of sponsorship and what the sponsor expects in return. Whilst the financial burden is eased, it may be replaced by the pressure for results, and this may result in a horse being asked to compete more frequently than is good for him. The five major trophies awarded at the Horse Trials Group Conference at the end of each season, the Tony Collings, the Calcutta Light Horse, the Edy Goldman, the Martin Whitely and the Wide Awake, are all awarded on the basis of points won. But some of these trophies have been in existence for thirty years or more, and it is doubtful if riders or owners have consciously chased the points in order to win them.

But now that *Eventing* publishes each month the Leader Board, showing the top 100 riders and horses, one can hardly blame a sponsor, who may not after all fully appreciate what demands are made on a horse in competition, for checking it monthly to monitor his horse's progress. Fortunately there are plenty of sponsors who are sufficiently enlightened to appreciate that the horse is not a machine, and who genuinely bear the interests of the sport in mind as well as their own commercial motives. On the other hand, sometimes the interests of a sponsor who looks forward to the day when he can entertain his guests at Badminton where his horse is running may put pressure on his rider to gain the necessary qualifications earlier than the interests of the horse would dictate.

Not surprisingly, the views of sponsors on the value of rider sponsorship are less well recorded than the views of those who sponsor events, but the views of riders are perhaps best summarised by Tinks Pottinger, the New Zealand girl who so nearly took the eventing world by storm when she came so close to winning the Gold Medal at the 1986 World Championships at Gawlor, only to have her horse fail the final horse inspection. Talking of her sponsorship by Arpac International, she said, 'I'm absolutely thrilled. It's great not to have to think about the cost of getting to the next event. It means I can concentrate entirely on training the horses for competition.'

So does the model rider drive to the Horse Trial in his palatial horse-box in his sponsor's colours with the name boldly emblazoned on the side? Will he then be joined at the event by his supporting team in a Range Rover, Mercedes or Daihatsu cross country vehicle, kept dry by their Barbour jackets and warm by their Puffas? Will he don his Harry Hall coat before the Dressage, with his horse in its Jabez Cliff bridle, collect his Swaine and Adeney whip for the Show Jumping, and for the Cross Country protect himself with his Ransome back-protector under his Gatehouse Cross Country shirt, and his horse with Woof Boots? Having settled his horse comfortably in its Glentona rug and bandages, and soothed its legs with Hydrophane horse care products, will he then be seen stepping into his Audi Quattro en route for the Beefeater Steak House, having of course already celebrated his success with a magnum or two of Piper Heidseck? Will he remember to call home on the Carphone on the way, and will he finally stagger off to his bed, where sleep will come quickly after generous balloons of Remy Martin VSOP?

Perhaps it is fortunate for the image of the sport, the peace of mind of the sponsors, and the well-being of the horse that our model does not exist!

CHAPTER 17

Behind the scenes

Organisers • Landowners • Course designers • Judges • Fence judges
• Scorers • Commentators • Grooms • Trainers • Selectors
• Chef d'Equipe • Team Vet • Horse Trials Support Group

Behind the successes of our leading riders, and of the events up and down the country, lies a prodigious effort on the part of many whose names never hit the headlines, but without whose contribution the sport could not flourish as it does today. For a few it is their livelihood; for most it is a labour of love, given because of their interest in the sport or as their contribution to a sport from participation in which they themselves have derived pleasure in the past.

Foremost among these come the event organisers, of whom the doyen is surely Lt-Col. Frank Weldon, Director of Badminton from 1965 to 1988. Having pioneered Britain's success in international eventing as a rider during the 1950s and early 1960s, he took over at Badminton at a time when success seemed hard to achieve. Since our victory in the Stockholm Olympics, we had only managed a 4th place in Rome, where Michael Bullen just missed the Bronze Medal, while in Tokyo in 1964 we had come nowhere. In Frank's view, our decline was partly due to the lack of courses of international standard at home, and he set about rectifying the situation.

Under his direction, Badminton has become the world's premier Three Day Event, and the one which, with the exception of the Olympic Games, all international riders most want to win. At the same time he set out to make the competition more attractive to the public, so

that today a small market town springs up each year, and the competition for the best trade stand sites is intense. If the weather is good, up to 170,000 spectators will arrive in some 40,000 cars, hundreds of buses, and over thirty light planes and helicopters. The television outside broadcast unit, with its miles of cable, presents problems of its own. Communications between Cross Country Control and all parts

Lt-Col. Frank Weldon, Director of Badminton 1965–1988.

of the course, together with arrangements for dealing with emergencies involving horses, riders, obstacles or spectators, have to be laid on and rehearsed, for when an emergency happens it is liable to happen quickly and to require instant response. The Director of a major Three Day Event must therefore above all be a first-class administrator.

But it is as a course designer above all that Frank has stamped his name indelibly on the international eventing scene. Pictures of early competitors negotiating the Badminton fences show how flimsy they were in comparison with the massive obstacles of today, which no horse in his right mind is going to 'chance'. The apparent severity of the Badminton courses has not infrequently provoked criticism, but usually before, rather than after, the event. For Frank has developed an uncanny knack of designing a fence which may fill a rider with direst apprehension, yet which, because of its solid and imposing construction, is safely negotiated by most horses. And he has maintained that if the course, which he has designed to the highest international standards, seems severe in relation to the standards of some of the competitors, then it is their qualifications to compete that must be looked at, rather than the course that must be made easier.

The organisers of all our Three Day Events face much the same problems, though perhaps to a lesser degree. At Burghley, Director Bill Henson has introduced innovations, such as Cross Country obstacles that can be viewed from the stands in the Dressage area, to attract the public. The One Day Horse Trial organiser, on the other hand, has a rather different problem. At a major Three Day Event there may be up to 80 starters, the number being governed by the number of Dressage tests that the judges can cope with over two days, and these have to be processed through the competition over four days. The organiser's major headaches may stem from having to make

At Burghley, Bill Henson has introduced innovations to attract the public

satisfactory arrangements for the arrival, parking, feeding, informing, controlling and departure of hordes of spectators. At a One Day Event, which may in fact run over 2 or $2\frac{1}{2}$ days, there may be up to 500 competitors and, unless the venue is exceptionally popular and the weather exceptionally good, insufficient spectators to create much of a problem. The main headache then may be the slotting into the timetable for the three tests these 500 horses, many of whose riders may be riding two or more. In between these two extremes there are well over 100 Horse Trials run all over the country.

If the organiser is the key person in the running of an event, then there would be no event at all without the landowner, and the impact of an event on him (or her) will vary according to the type of land and the status of the event. 7 of the 8 Three Day Events are all held in the grounds of 'stately homes', which have sufficient space and resources to cope with something of this size. One Day Events, too, may be similarly located, but are as often held on farms, racecourses, National Trust property and on land owned by the Army or by a borough council. All require considerable indulgence on the part of the landowner, whoever he may be.

The most important single concern of the organiser must be the Cross Country course, for without a good course neither competitors nor spectators, sponsors nor officials will be happy to return the following year. Many organisers are themselves responsible for the course, while others have the services of a specialist course designer. If Frank Weldon is the doyen of organisers, then Bill Thomson must be the doyen of course designers. After qualification and experience as a vet, he became Secretary to the South Berkshire Hunt, with all the responsibilities for fence repair – and indeed construction – that go with such a post. Then in 1953 Neil Gardner, who had just been appointed Chairman of what was then known as the Combined Training Committee, asked him to design and construct a course for a new One Day Event to be run at his home at Great Auclum. Thus started a career which was to become almost synonymous with the development of Horse Trials in this country. Badminton in its early days, Harewood (forerunner of Burghley), Burghley itself, and literally hundreds of events all over the country have in the last 35 years been influenced by Bill either as the designer and builder of courses, or as the official B.H.S. Steward or the Technical Adviser.

A new breed of course designer and builder is Bill Thomson's successor at Burghley, Philip

Herbert. Having learned the trade from Bill, he now not only designs courses, but also has the mechanical equipment necessary for building them, and he may descend upon a suitable tract of land and transform it into a first-rate Cross Country course. For those events which design and build their own courses, the Horse Trials Committee appoints a Technical Adviser, who may visit the course on several occasions to advise on the general layout and the construction of individual obstacles, and who ensures compliance with the rules.

Two vital aspects of Horse Trials organisation are judging and scoring. At a Three Day Event, the Ground Jury are responsible for the overall running of the competition, and will also judge the Dressage and Jumping tests. At a One Day Event, the Dressage judges must be selected from the national judges lists according to the level of the tests which they are going to judge, and have no other responsibility. It seems odd that at a One Day Event the Dressage judges must be specialists, while at a Three Day Event this task can sometimes be performed by someone whose chief qualification is that he or she was once a Three Day Event rider. Small wonder that the scoring of the Dressage tests at Three Day Events is sometimes cause for comment! Be that as it may, the Dressage judge's task is a lonely one, requiring long hours of intense concentration, and seldom receiving the recognition it deserves.

The Cross Country fence judge's task, on the other hand, may seem simple, but he may have some difficult decisions to make, especially at combination obstacles at Three Day Events, where there are penalty zones. At One Day Events he may double as a radio operator or stopping steward (to stop competitors in the event of a hold-up on the course), and will have to signal for doctor, vet or fence repair team. In the event of a serious accident he may be the only person able to render first aid until the arrival of the doctor.

The fence judges' score sheets are collected at intervals and taken to the scorers, where they join scores from the Dressage and the Show Jumping. The scorers are real 'behind the scenes' people, since they can only perform properly in complete seclusion. But again at a One Day Event they are likely to be harder pressed than at a Three Day Event, since at the former they may be receiving scores for all three tests simultaneously from several sections. Riders expect their scores to appear on the scoreboard within minutes of their completing a test, organisers expect final results for prizegivings within a short time of the last horse finishing the Cross Country, and few have any idea of the complexity of the scorers' task. While for the other tests it may simply be a question of recording information received from elsewhere, in the case of the Dressage, the judges' marks must first be totalled, then divided by the number of judges if there is more than one; the resultant figure must then be subtracted from the maximum marks obtainable to produce penalties, and finally it must be multiplied by a coefficient according to the test being used; and at a Three Day Event there is the further complication of the multiplying factor to ensure the relative influence of the three tests; at the end of all this there emerges the penalty score that actually appears on the scoreboard.

Cross Country and Show Jumping scores may seem relatively simple by comparison, but at a Three Day Event the scorers will have to convert recorded times for each competitor over all phases into time penalties, and at all events master score sheets, showing the penalties incurred by each competitor at each obstacle, must be completed. With the issuing of official result sheets for prizegivings, which may entail decisions as to the relative placings of competitors with equal scores, the chasing up of missing score sheets – Pony Club runners

and even fence judges have been known to leave the course with score sheets in their pockets – and the investigation of competitors' queries by the B.H.S. Steward, there is plenty to ensure that the scorer's job is no sinecure!

Most scorers are appointed by the Horse Trials Office, and at One Day Events will arrive on the preceding day in order to assist with the timings – no easy task where riders have several horses in different sections and classes.

Once the organiser has made all his arrangements, there is no more important person on the day of the event than the commentator; he can make or mar the occasion, whether it be Badminton or a Novice Horse Trial. Perhaps one of the most important lessons in the art of commentary was learned some years ago at Aintree, when the proprietor of the course decided to dispense with the services of the established team of television commentators for the Grand National. The result was chaotic and laughable – or would have been, had it not spoiled for countless thousands of viewers what for many is the sporting spectacle of the year.

A successful commentator today needs many qualities and considerable application. (Gone are the days when a congenial voice, a pair of binoculars and a bottle of gin were enough to sustain him throughout a long day in the control vehicle!) Commentary is a specialist business, and the serious exponent will build up his own ready-reference system so that he can produce the interesting facts about competitors beyond what appears in the programme. His task is not only to keep the public informed about what is going on, but also to assist the course controller, who is responsible for the smooth running of the Cross Country test, and to ensure that sponsors, without whom the event probably could not be held, are given recognition. He will have to 'cover' for gaps in the programme caused by emergencies, and for this he will need a reservoir of information with which he can fill these blank periods.

Most of his day will be spent in describing what is happening out on the course. But while every owner, groom, or other supporter would like a fence-by-fence, even stride-by-stride, commentary on his horse's progress, it can be a little irritating for everyone else if the commentator never pauses for breath. The occasional moment of silence may be welcome, and his most precious attribute may be tact.

To turn from the organisers' to the competitors' needs, although the one- or even two-horse rider may compete without the services of a regular groom – though help from family or friends will almost certainly be enlisted for events – in the larger stables or sponsored teams the grooms have a very important role. The stable management of the event horse is as important as his training, and although both will be very much the rider's concern, the groom has a major part to play, and one which is not confined to the obvious chores of mucking out, grooming or 'strapping', tack cleaning, feeding and watering. All these are important, but the groom can have a significant psychological effect on his charge. A confident, firm, yet quiet groom can over a period of time calm the nervous or excitable horse, while another can reduce the calm animal to a nervous wreck. Horses are quick to assess the disposition of those who are near them, and the mischievous horse who senses that his groom is nervous will have a field day, every day!

At a Horse Trial the groom can take a great load off the rider, by preparing the horse for the three tests, producing him in the correct tack, including studs, and by washing him down and looking after him at the end of the competition. At the top of the tree, grooms may have the added responsibilities of foreign travel. Many are horse-box drivers too, and though most riders travel with their horses,

grooms may have the task of transporting their charges across the Channel and through several European frontiers on their way to an international event. Travel to the Olympic Games and other championships may involve long flights, with the added stress and strain imposed on the horse, and although on such occasions the *Chef d'Equipe* or Team Manager and a vet will probably accompany the horses, the groom can do much to calm his horses and can also detect the first signs of physical conditions such as colic, to which horses are susceptible on very long journeys.

On trips to international Three Day Events the grooms are very much part of the official team, and several have later graduated to becoming successful riders themselves. Constant observation of a top-class rider at work both at home and in competition can be a useful way to learn!

In the chapter on the training of the horse we referred to the necessity of help from the ground, if possible from an instructor. Those young riders who are fortunate enough to graduate, probably by way of the Pony Club, to successful competition in Junior or Young Riders classes may catch the eyes of the selectors, and may then come under the influence of the official trainer to the Junior and Young Riders teams. Gillian Watson was herself a successful Three Day Event rider who won Burghley on Shaitan in 1969, and since taking over responsibility for the training of these teams has guided them to a host of medals. But apart from the Juniors and Young Riders, the concept of a national team trainer has never really caught on in this country. In the U.S.A. Jack Le Goff, former Riding Master of the French Cadre Noir at Saumur, twice winner of the French Three Day Event Championship, and 6th in the Olympic Three Day Event in Rome in 1960, took over the training of the National Team in 1970, since when the team has won, at Olympic Games and World Championships, three Team Gold Medals, a Silver and two Bronze, and three Individual Golds, four Silver and two Bronze. (At the same time another foreign rider, Bertalan de Nemethy of Hungary, was guiding the Show Jumping team to similar success.)

But in this country, each rider tends to have his own trainer, and probably one for Dressage and another for Cross Country and Show Jumping, and without a national training centre the most that has been done is a period of concentration shortly before a major international event. Thus we find that the names of David Hunt, Ferdi Eilberg and Pat Manning crop up as trainers in Dressage to a number of leading riders, while Lady Hugh (Rosemary) Russell, for ever remembered as the Organiser of the Wylye Three Day Event and a familiar sight in wheelchair or Mini-Moke at events at home and abroad, has specialised in Cross Country training. Pat Burgess, emerges as a successful Show Jumping trainer, and Dick Stilwell, himself formerly a successful Show Jumper, has established a reputation as a trainer for both Jumping and Cross Country, and is known for his success with riders of ability who have perhaps lacked the self-confidence necessary to realise their full potential.

Cross-fertilisation takes place, too, from the world of Show Jumping, with the names of John Lanni, Mick Saywell, Ted Edgar, Michael Whitaker and Brian Crago – though he was himself a member of the Australian Gold Medal Team in the Rome Olympics – appearing as trainers to several leading riders. Successful Three Day Event competitors of the past who have achieved success as trainers include Sheila Willcox, winner of Badminton in 1957, 1958 and 1959, Lars Sederholm, the Swedish rider who settled in England in the early 1960s, won the Tony Collings Memorial Trophy for the rider gaining the most points in the season on several occasions, and founded the Waterstock House Training Centre, and

Bertie Hill, member of the all-conquering team of the 1950s and trainer of the winning teams at the Punchestown World Championships in 1967 and the Mexico Olympics in 1968. Judy Bradwell, another Tony Collings Trophy winner, and winner of Burghley with Don Camillo in 1970, divides her time between acting as a member of the Ground Jury at international events, competing with young horses, and instructing young riders. (Tony Collings, incidentally, winner of the second Badminton in 1950, did much to get eventing off the ground in this country and to get a British team to the 1952 Olympics, and had he not been tragically killed in the Comet crash of 1954, would surely have become one of the great trainers.) Another who has quietly built up a record of training riders and producing good horses is the winner of the inaugural Badminton event, John Shedden – he was also runner-up to Tony Collings the following year.

Alison Oliver, whose husband, Alan, after a long and distinguished career as a Show Jumping rider, is now one of our leading course builders, probably did more than anyone else to help the Princess Royal when, as Princess Anne, she started serious competition riding, and went on to win a European Championship and to represent Great Britain in the 1976 Olympic Games. But perhaps no trainer has better reason to be pleased with the results of her efforts than Dorothy (Dot) Wilson, who has guided Virginia Leng to her phenomenal success.

Several contemporary riders play their part in the training of younger competitors through training clinics held at various centres during the summer, but no one does more than Mark Phillips, in conjunction with his sponsors. The winners of Range Rover team bursaries go to Gatcombe Park for a year's training, and he also runs the Gleneagles Hotel training scheme in Scotland, as well as taking training clinics all round the world. Not so long ago only a

Once the selectors have made their difficult choices, it is over to the Chef d'Equipe. Lord Patrick Beresford

Right-hand man of any Chef d'Equipe is the Team Vet. Peter Scott-Dunn

foreigner could gain credence as a trainer in this country, and it is refreshing to see that we can now export our expertise to others.

The trainers having played their part, and the riders having performed to their satisfaction, hopefully the selectors now show interest. Their job is no sinecure, and if all goes well and medals are won, they seldom receive due recognition, while if misfortune strikes and performance falls below expectations they are the first to be blamed. Many hundreds of miles of travel, many a long and often cold or wet day, and many hours of careful deliberation lie behind their eventual selection. Henrietta Knight, formerly an experienced rider and now well known for her success as a trainer of point-to-pointers, chairs the Senior Selection Committee, while Lt-Col. Bill Lithgow, after a long and outstandingly successful period as *Chef d'Equipe* to the senior team, is in charge of Junior selection, with Christopher Schofield, with his long association with all levels of

eventing, guiding the selection of Young Riders.

Once the selectors have made their difficult choices it is over to the *Chef d'Equipe.* (Why we cannot in this country use generally understood terms such as 'Team Manager' or 'Team Captain' remains a mystery to many!) When Maj. Malcolm Wallace had to relinquish the post on becoming Director General of the British Equestrian Federation, his place was taken by Lord Patrick Beresford, whose competitive experience had been acquired mainly on the polo field, but who was quick to savour team success at his first World Championship at Gawlor. Right-hand man of any *Chef d'Equipe* is the Team Vet, and Peter Scott-Dunn, if he does not actually hold the record for participation as an official at the Olympic Games, must come very near it, for he first went with the team to the Rome Olympics in 1960 and has been to every meeting since.

One 'behind the scenes' body that plays an

important part in our international effort is the Horse Trials Support Group. Founded in 1978 with the aim of raising funds to help promising young riders to obtain suitable horses, it now makes grants to enable young riders nominated by the Selection Committee to continue to train and compete until such time as they can obtain commercial sponsorship. But it also has another most important function. In many countries team expenses are funded by the government; in this country, some funds are provided by the Sports Council, and most of the costs of sending a team to the Olympic Games are met by the British Olympic Association; the balance has to be found by the sport concerned, and in the case of equestrian sports the B.E.F. is responsible for this through the British International Equestrian Fund (B.I.E.F.). Each discipline, however, is expected to conduct its own fund-raising activities, and the Horse Trials Support Group does this for Horse Trials, raising the money from membership subscriptions and from special fund-raising efforts. In 1986, for example, the Support Group raised over £50,000 towards the costs of sending the team to the World Championships in Australia, largely owing to the personal effort of Mrs Rosemary Barlow, a member of its Committee. Together with yachting, equestrian teams are the most expensive to transport around the world; at least no one can accuse Horse Trials of not helping themselves!

CHAPTER 18

Great riders past and present

What makes a 'great' rider? • The past • Weldon • Rook • Hill • Willcox
• The Australians, Roycroft and Morgan • Allhusen • Meade • Gordon-Watson
• The present • Green • Leng • Todd • Phillips • Clarke • Stark
• The Americans, Davidson, Plumb • Others • H.R.H. The Princess Royal

The question is often asked, 'What makes a great rider?' If we try to answer it, two further questions usually surface: 'Who are the best riders of today?' and 'How do they compare with the best of yesterday?' In fact, of course, it is difficult if not impossible to answer the last question, since the conditions then and now are so different that we are not really comparing like with like. In the middle 1950s, the Golden Age of British eventing – or perhaps in view of our modern successes we should call it the First Golden Age – the pressures on a top rider were minimal, there were fewer competitions, no sponsors, at least not of riders, and although they certainly took their sport seriously, the element of fun was very much to the fore. Standards were lower, and Cross Country courses very much easier. When a rider brought a horse to the top, it was easier for him to keep it going over an extended period, and there was less need for the 'string' of top-class and up-and-coming horses without which today's successful riders will not for long remain at the top.

Great riders of the past must include the three members of our First Golden Age team – Weldon, Rook and Hill. Frank Weldon won Badminton in 1955 and 1956, having been runner-up twice previously, and he won the Harewood Three Day Event in 1955. Team Gold Medals at the European Championships

in 1953 (Badminton), 1954 (Basle) and 1956 (Windsor) and an Individual Silver at Basle were followed by Team Gold and Individual Bronze at the Stockholm Olympics in 1956. (In those days there was no World Championship.) And all this was achieved on one horse, Kilbarry. But the fact that he did not achieve the highest honours on other horses – though in 1959 he was 5th at Badminton on Samuel Johnson and 9th on Fermoy – was due to his having started eventing at an age at which most riders are considering retirement!

Laurence Rook won Badminton in 1953, and with it the Individual European Championship, and shared in the team successes at Basle and Windsor, all of this on Starlight, with whom he had been so desperately unlucky not to win an individual and probably a team medal at the Helsinki Olympics in 1952. Then on Wild Venture he was 6th in the Stockholm Olympics, helping the team to a Gold Medal at the same time. His achievements as an international rider were recognised on his retirement, and he was appointed the F.E.I. Technical Delegate at three Olympic Games, a European Championship and a Pan-American Games, while at home he became Chairman of the Horse Trials Committee.

Bertie Hill, who later became one of the most successful trainers of Three Day Event riders and horses, came into eventing from racing, and, perhaps because race riders are forever changing horses, achieved success on a variety of mounts. The Team Gold Medal at Badminton's European Championships of 1953 was won on Bambi V, with whom his owner, Margaret Hough, won Badminton the following year. The Individual European Championship was won at Basle on Crispin, owned, together with Wild Venture, by Ted Marsh, and the Team Gold and Individual Bronze at Windsor on his own Countryman, whom H.M. the Queen purchased and for whom they won the Team Gold at Stockholm, despite straddling the Trahkener when the bank on the take-off side gave way.

Sheila Willcox was the first lady rider to make a great impact on the sport, though already Jane Drummond-Hay, now Whiteley, 2nd at Badminton in 1951, and Margaret Hough, the winner in 1954, had given notice that Three Day Events were not for long destined to remain the preserve either of the military or of the dominant sex! Coming 2nd to Frank Weldon and Kilbarry with High and Mighty at Badminton in 1956, Sheila won with the same horse in 1957 and 1958 with record 'plus' scores (in the complicated days of penalties and bonuses), and took the Individual and Team Gold medals at the European Championships in Copenhagen in 1957. Then in 1959, with Airs and Graces, she became the first rider to win Badminton three times. But in spite of having proved herself at international level, she was never able to compete for the highest prize, for it was not until 1964 that lady riders were allowed to compete in the Olympic Three Day Event. She did however achieve the unique distinction of winning all three British Three Day Events of her time by adding victories at Harewood (in 1956) and at Burghley (in 1968), and it is interesting to note that her Burghley winner, Fair and Square, was the sire of Lucinda Green's Badminton winner of 1973, Be Fair. And her victory at Harewood was by

a margin of no less than 89 points!

No list of great riders of the past could omit mention of two riders from 'down under' who must surely be among the greatest natural horsemen of all time. The 1960 Badminton field included five Australian riders with their eyes set on the Rome Olympics. With the likes of Frank Weldon, Bertie Hill, Norman Arthur (now Lt-Gen. Sir Norman Arthur), Michael Bullen and Anneli Drummond-Hay in the Badminton line-up nobody gave the Australians much of a chance, particularly since their leader, Bill Roycroft, had only taken up eventing three years earlier and was at an age when most people would consider retiring.

In the Dressage Anneli Drummond-Hay took a comfortable lead which she maintained through to the final day, when two fences down in the Show Jumping, which in those days cost ten penalties apiece, let Bill Roycroft and Laurie Morgan through to take first and second places, with their team mate Neale Lavis in fourth position. Not a bad exercise in their national sport of 'Pongo bashing'! In Rome, their sixth place after the Dressage did not look too depressing, since this was their weakest link, but they would clearly have to pull something extra out of the bag to win medals. Brilliant clear rounds from Laurie Morgan, Neale Lavis and Brian Crago seemed to have done the trick, since disasters had befallen most of the other teams.

Bill Roycroft had suffered a heavy fall at the notorious concrete drain-pipe obstacle, and though he had remounted and completed the course, he had in fact broken his shoulder and was rushed off to hospital. Then Brian Crago's horse was found to have broken down, and the Australian team seemed to be out of it. Bill therefore discharged himself from hospital, jumped a clear round in the Show Jumping, and the Team Gold and Individual Gold and Silver Medals disappeared to the Antipodes!

The medals may have disappeared 'down

under', but this was by no means the last to be seen of the Australian riders. In 1961 Laurie Morgan returned to Badminton to add the new Whitbread Trophy to his two Olympic Gold Medals, and also won the Foxhunter Steeplechase at Cheltenham. Bill Roycroft not only went on to ride successfully in three more Olympics, but produced two sons and a daughter-in-law who have between them been the mainstay of the Australian team up to and including the 1986 World Championships. Truly a great eventing 'dynasty'.

Although he never won a Three Day Event, one rider whose name cannot be omitted is Major Derek Allhusen, President of the British Horse Society in 1987–88. Having been an Olympic Winter Pentathlete in St Moritz in 1948, he started riding in Horse Trials in the middle 1950s on a mare whose dam he had brought home from Italy after the war and whose sire was no less than Davy Jones, on

whom Anthony Mildmay would probably have won the 1936 Grand National had a rein not broken as they approached the last fence in the lead. Laurien was only 15 hands 2 inches (1.58 m), but their performance at the Harewood Three Day Event in 1956 earned them a place in the team for the European Championships in Copenhagen the following year, where they helped the team to a Gold Medal. Placed 2nd at Badminton and Harewood in 1958 and 4th at Badminton in 1959, Laurien was then retired – and many thought his rider had reached retiring age too!

But six years later, Derek was again at Badminton, now with Lochinvar. With Team Gold and Individual Bronze at the 1967 European Championships, followed by Team Gold and Individual Silver at the Mexico Olympics, surely the time had come to rest on his laurels? Not at all; in 1969 they were back helping the team to win the European Championships again at Haras du Pin. And this was by no means the end of the story, for in the meantime Laurien had given birth to a foal by Happy

Richard Meade's contribution to the team over two decades has been outstanding. Richard Meade, Kilcashel, Burghley

Olympic Games

1964	Tokyo	Barberry	8th
1968	Mexico	Cornishman V	4th & Team Gold
1972	Munich	Laurieston	Ind & Team Gold
1976	Montreal	Jacob Jones	4th

World Championships

1966	Burghley	Barberry	Silver
1970	Punchestown	The Poacher	Team Gold & Ind Silver

European Championships

1967	Punchestown	Barberry	Team Gold
1971	Burghley	The Poacher	Team Gold
1973	Kiev	Wayfarer II	Team Bronze
1981	Horsens	Kilcashel	Team Bronze

C.C.I.

1963	Munich	Barberry	Team Gold
1964	Burghley	Barberry	1st
1970	Badminton	The Poacher	1st
1982	Badminton	Speculator	1st

Monarch, and in 1972 Laurieston was 2nd at Badminton with Richard Meade, and the pair went on to win the Gold Medals at the Munich Olympics.

These Gold Medals were the peak of Richard Meade's long career, which spans a period of twenty-five years in the saddle. Starting in the early 1960s, he first came to prominence when he rode his own Barberry in the Gold Medal team at the Munich C.C.I. in 1963, and in the following year he nearly hit the jackpot early in his career when at the end of the Cross Country at the Tokyo Olympics he was in the lead, only to fall to eighth place when Barberry lapsed in the Show Jumping. But his astonishing list of successes, achieved over so long a period and on so many different horses, is worth tabulating (below left).

This record speaks for itself, and although the number of individual victories has been surpassed by several of his predecessors and successors, his contribution to the team over two decades has been outstanding.

But if a 'great' rider is one who has won a significant number of major international victories over an extended period of time on several different horses, nevertheless there is one rider whose name ought to be mentioned by virtue of an imposing list of successes on one undeniably 'great' horse. Cornishman V, whom Richard Meade rode at incredibly short notice to success in the Mexico Olympics, was surely one of the most popular horses in the history of the sport. With Mary Gordon-Watson in the saddle, he won the 1969 European Championships at Haras du Pin, and Team Gold Medals at Burghley in 1971 and at the Munich Olympics in 1972, and although a Badminton win eluded them, they were 3rd in 1970, and 2nd in 1971, and recorded a host of other successes at home.

And so to the present. While today's top riders have to work harder to reach the top and to stay there, thanks to commercial spon-

To win Badminton six times is no mean feat; to achieve this on six different horses is truly the mark of a great rider: Lucinda Green

sorship most of them have the resources in horses to enable them to do this. But in every case they had to prove their worth before acquiring a sponsor. Lucinda Green, for example, first caught the eye of the Junior Team Selection Committee back in 1971, when as Lucinda Prior-Palmer she won a Team Gold Medal at the Junior European Championships at Wesel, but it was not until 1978 that she was sponsored by Overseas Containers Ltd. Although an individual Olympic medal has so far eluded her (she was 6th and a member of the Silver Medal team in Los Angeles), she won the World title in Luhmuhlen in 1982, and the European Championships twice (at Luhmuhlen again in 1975 and at Burghley in 1977) and contributed to team medals on three other occasions. But her position as a 'great' rider is established above all by a record which may never be broken, though she may yet improve on it herself. To win Badminton six

The first lady rider to win an Olympic Three Day Event medal: Virginia Leng

Day Event at Montreal in 1975. Two years later a very badly broken arm nearly ended her riding career, but she came back to win the Open Championship at Locko Park in 1981, in which year she obtained the sponsorship of the British National Life Assurance Company. Her two great winners, Priceless and Night Cap, both now retired, became household names to followers of eventing. In 1984 she became, with Karen Stives of the U.S.A., the first lady rider to win an Olympic Three Day Event medal, in 1986 her haul included the World Championship, the British Open Championship, and C.C.I.s at Le Touquet, Burghley and Bialy Bor, and in 1987 she took the British Open Championship again, before going on to win her second European Championship. Then in 1988 she rode the relatively inexperienced Master Craftsman into Team Silver and Individual Bronze Medals at the Seoul Olympics.

Mark Todd has put New Zealand firmly on the map in the equestrian world. A product of the Pony Club, Mark's first international experience was a not too happy trip to the notorious World Championships at Lexington in 1978, but this inauspicious start was forgotten when in 1980 he won Badminton at his first attempt with Southern Comfort. To demonstrate that this was no mere fluke, he went on to win the Osberton Three Day Event and to come 2nd at Punchestown in the following year. Back in England in 1984 he came 2nd at Badminton on Charisma, and took the Gold Medal with Charisma at the Los Angeles Olympics. Since then he has been 2nd at Badminton again and won at Rotherfield, Osberton and Luhmuhlen, and in 1987 he became the first rider to finish 1st and 2nd at Burghley. One of the tallest riders, he excels on small horses, and his quiet style and brilliant judgement of a stride have earned the admiration of all who have watched him.

Then in 1988 he established himself as one of the greatest Three Day Event riders of all

times is no mean feat; to achieve this on six different horses is truly the mark of a great rider. Along the way she has picked up many other trophies, including Burghley in 1977 and 1981, Boekelo in 1986 and Punchestown, Chatsworth and Boekelo in 1987.

If Lucinda Green's Badminton record is, so far, unique, Virginia Leng's tally of one Badminton, four Burghleys, an Olympic Bronze Medal, a World and two European Championships, plus numerous other international successes places her right in the forefront of today's riders. Her first major success was the winning of the Junior European Championships at Pompadour back in 1973, and she first hit the headlines when she won the hearts of the Canadians and the pre-Olympic Three

Olympic champion of 1984 and 1988, New Zealander Mark Todd's quiet style and brilliant judgement of a stride have earned the admiration of all who have watched him

time. Having won the British Open Championships at Gatcombe Park, he and the 16 year old Charisma went to Seoul a month later to defend their Olympic title, and became only the second combination in history to achieve this feat.

Capt. Mark Phillips' record of four Badmintons on three different horses comes nearest to emulating Lucinda Green's feat of six wins. He has also helped the team to win Gold Medals at the Munich Olympics, and at two World and European Championships, and he won Burghley in 1973. He does not, however, confine his activities to competing, for, in addition to organising the British Championships at Gatcombe Park, he is much in demand as a trainer both at home and overseas, and in conjunction with his sponsors, Range Rover, he does much to further the ambitions of promising young riders. He is also one of the few international riders to bridge the gap between two disciplines, for he was also in the 1970s a successful member of British Show Jumping teams, winning a Grand Prix and taking part in Nations Cups.

Although her achievements do not match those of Lucinda Green, Virginia Leng, or Mark Todd, Lorna Clarke has made a name for herself as one of the last true amateurs, combining the raising of a family and assistance in running her husband's farms with international successes spanning a period of over twenty years. She will always be remembered for her Burghley win in 1967 on the diminutive skewbald Popadom, and wins followed at Munich (1971) and Boekelo (1972) on Peer Gynt, and again at Burghley in 1978 on Greco. After winning at Luhmuhlen in 1984 with Glentrool, she won Team Gold and Individual Silver at Burghley's 1985 European Championships with Myross, as a result of

Four Badminton's on three different horses: Captain Mark Phillips, C.V.O.

One of the last true amateurs: Lorna Clarke

which they went to the Gawlor World Championships in 1986 where they won the Team Gold and Individual Bronze Medals, and to the Seoul Olympics as reserve in 1988.

Latest recruit to the ranks of great riders is Ian Stark, known to his supporters as 'the Galloping Scotsman'. Unlike most of the others, Ian had no equestrian background, and only took up serious riding in 1982, when he resigned from the Civil Service! Success came quickly to another natural horseman when he was 2nd in his first international Three Day Event at Achselschwang in the following year. Badminton in 1984 confirmed his promise, and he went on to a team Silver Medal in the Los Angeles Olympics. A win at Badminton and Team Gold and Individual Bronze in the World Championships of 1986 were followed by Team Gold and Individual Silver in the European Championships of 1987. Then in 1988 he first achieved the outstanding feat of being 1st and 2nd at Badminton, and then took Team and Individual Silver Medals in the Seoul Olympics.

The success of our riders in international

Three Day Events is principally due to opportunities for competing in this country which are unrivalled anywhere else in the world. The only other country whose riders have consistently been at the top is the U.S.A., but we have more Horse Trials in England, which is roughly the size of Virginia and Maryland combined, than in the whole of the United States. Maybe it is the success of their national training system that consistently produces top-class riders, but for whatever reason, at the sixteen Olympics at which the Three Day Event has been held, the United States has won medals at twelve of them, and since 1966 has produced a double World Champion in Bruce Davidson, who, with his team mate Michael Plumb, must be ranked among the world's best of any time. Apart from his two World titles, he has won virtually every important event in the United States and Canada, the Croft

Bruce Davidson (U.S.A.) must be ranked among the world's best of any time

159

Original Open Championship at Gatcombe in 1986 (Virginia Leng in 2nd place won the British Open), and the Stockholm preview of the 1990 World Equestrian Games in 1987, much of this on J. J. Babu.

Of the other Americans, Michael Plumb has probably been their most consistent team member since he competed in Rome in 1960, and although major individual honours have eluded him, except in his home country where he has been Rider of the Year on ten occasions, he has won five Olympic medals (one Individual Silver and four team medals) and four World medals including an Individual Silver. Torrance Watkins Fleischmann made her name on the little skewbald mare Poltroon, with whom she came 2nd at Burghley in 1979, and Karen Stives (now Reuter) became, with Virginia Leng, the first lady rider to win an Olympic Three Day Event medal.

Any list of great riders is likely to provoke argument on account of those whom it excludes: Richard Walker, for example, Junior European Champion in 1968, youngest ever winner of Badminton in 1969, Team Gold and Individual Silver medals at that year's European Championship, twice a winner of Burghley, four times winner of the British Open Championships, and a winner at Wylye and Falsterbo, and all this on a variety of different horses. Both his record and his quiet style of riding have made him a model for young riders to follow. There is Jane Holderness-Roddam, winner of Badminton in 1968 and 1978 and of Burghley in 1976, and a Team Gold Medal in the Mexico Olympics in spite of two falls during the downpour that threatened to engulf the Cross Country course.

We may think of Jane Starkey, a winner at Antwerp in 1975 and consistently placed in major events; Diana ('Tiny') Clapham, Team Silver Medal at the Los Angeles Olympics; Clarissa Strachan, two European Team medals and Team Gold at the 1986 World Cham-

First at Badminton in 1986, first and second in 1988, Olympic Silver Medallist in 1988: Ian Stark

pionships; Anne-Marie Taylor, who rocketed to the top with her 5th place at Gawlor, and who won Chatsworth in 1986; Mary Thomson, winner and runner-up at Bramham in 1986 and winner at Osberton in 1986 and Windsor in 1987. All these are knocking at the door. But life at the top is tough, and the likes of Rodney Powell, first at Windsor in 1987, and Robert Lemieux, who won Bramham in 1983, and the British Open Championship in 1988, are only too eager to take over.

Finally, no list of great riders, past or present, can exclude mention of H.R.H. the Princess Royal, President of the F.E.I. Granddaughter of one of the greatest patrons of National Hunt racing, daughter of one who has seemed equally at home when taking the salute at her Birthday Parade riding side-saddle or when enjoying a ride at Sandringham or Windsor, daughter and sister of polo players, it is hardly surprising that she shone at her chosen sport of eventing. During her early years, and indeed throughout her time of active competition, she had to endure difficulties that beset no other Horse Trials rider: the intense glare of publicity, the ever-attendant phalanx of photographers, and the perfectly understandable but none the less unwelcome attention of the press – all these made her success that much more commendable.

After a sound grounding in One Day Events, Princess Anne, as she was then, came 5th at Badminton in 1971 on H.M. the Queen's Doublet, and later in the same year, when riding as an individual in the European Championships at Burghley, she won the individual title, a notable achievement by any standards. She holds the coveted Armada Dish awarded for completing Badminton five times, and in 1974 finished on her Dressage score to be placed 4th on her mother's Goodwill. (This must have created some sort of family record, and it is unlikely that ever again will a mother own both the Badminton winner, ridden by her son-in-law, and the 4th placed horse, ridden by her daughter.) In the European Cham-

pionships of 1975 at Luhmuhlen she brought home Team and Individual Silver Medals, and then became the first member of the Royal Family to represent Great Britain in the Olympic Games when she joined the team for Montreal in 1976. As Goodwill took off at the zig-zag over a big ditch, the bank gave way and he fell, concussing his rider, who nevertheless remounted, completed the course, and turned out next day to finish the competition; she and Richard Meade were the only members of the British team to do so.

Since H.R.H. Prince Bernhard of the Netherlands held the appointment in the immediate post-war years, the F.E.I. has been fortunate enough to have as its President someone with a record of international success as a rider (or driver). Prince Bernhard was no mean Show Jumper; H.R.H. Prince Philip excelled at both polo and carriage driving; now the F.E.I. has as President a European Three Day Event Champion.

The President of the F.E.I. excelled at both polo and carriage driving. H.R.H. Prince Philip, Duke of Edinburgh

Now the F.E.I. has as President a European Three Day Event Champion: H.R.H. The Princess Royal

CHAPTER 19

The young entry

The Pony Club ● Aims ● Area competitions ● Championships
● Past winners ● F.E.I. categories ● Vaulting ● Pony Riders ● Juniors
● Young Riders ● Seniors ● The Junior scene ● The Young Rider scene
● Some to watch for the future

The Pony Club was founded in England in 1928, and now has a membership of over 100,000 in twenty-five different countries, which makes it the largest single organisation of riders in the world and one of the largest youth organisations. In the United Kingdom there are now 367 branches, while there are over 1,700 overseas, with a membership which has no official lower age limit, but an upper limit of 17 years for Ordinary Members and 21 for Associates. Its aims are 'to encourage young people to ride and to learn to enjoy all kinds of sport connected with horses and riding; to provide instruction in riding and horse mastership and to instil in members the proper care of their animals; and to promote the highest ideals of sportsmanship, citizenship and loyalty, thereby cultivating strength of character and self-discipline'.

Whilst the majority of members probably do not take part in competitive equestrian sports, the Pony Club organises Inter-Branch competitions, with championships towards the end of the summer school holidays, and the earliest of these competitions to be run was that for Horse Trials in 1949. (Other championship competitions are Dressage, Show Jumping,

Tetrathlon, Mounted Games and Polo.) The Horse Trials Championship is currently held at Weston Park towards the end of August, and is run under B.H.S. Horse Trials rules with certain modifications, contained in Rules for Pony Club Horse Trials.

Apart from the obvious benefits to be derived from a competition which demands considerable dedication, patience and skill from those taking part, it is perhaps no surprise that in recent years Horse Trials have played such an important part in Pony Club activities, since in 1968 Lt-Col. Bill Lithgow, himself a former Three Day Event rider, was appointed Executive Officer, and shortly afterwards became *Chef d'Equipe* of the senior Three Day Event team, guiding it to Olympic, World and European Championship medals.

Many of our successful international riders were introduced to Horse Trials in the Pony Club, and one of the more successful branches at the Horse Trials Championships in the 1950s was the Beaufort Hunt Branch. Richard Meade had by then graduated to a higher level, but with Mark Phillips, Jennie and Jane Bullen (now Loriston-Clarke and Holderness-Roddam respectively) and Michael Tucker as a nucleus of the team there was, in Mark Phillips' own words, 'plenty of competition and plenty of fun too!' In those days the Championships were held at Burghley over a modified course shortly after the senior Three Day Event. 'It was', says Mark, 'a marvellous introduction to the world of senior eventing with much of the atmosphere of the big occasion.'

The list of individual winners of the Championships includes Richard Walker, who won in 1965 and 1966 on Pasha, with whom he went on to win the Junior European Championship and on whom he became the youngest ever winner of Badminton in 1969; Hugh Thomas, Bronze Medallist at the World Championships at Burghley in 1974, runner-up at Badminton in 1976, a member of our Olympic Team in the same year and now a well-known commentator and course designer; Elizabeth Boone, now better known as Liz Purbrick, who won in 1969 – her brother William having won in 1964 – and who won a European Championship Team Gold Medal in 1981; Anne-Marie Taylor, 5th at the World Championships in 1986 and winner of Chatsworth in the same year; Rachel Hunt, 2nd at Badminton and 3rd in the Young Riders European Championships in 1986. Virginia Strawson, Katie Meacham, Madeleine Gurdon and Georgina Anstee are other winners who have gone on to success in senior classes, and Tina Reeve, 2nd at Holker Hall Novice Three Day Event in 1987, won in 1985 and 1986.

Many other successful riders were introduced to eventing in the Pony Club, and recognition was given to the contribution made to the sport by such activities when the F.E.I. added an official category for Pony Riders to those for Juniors and Young Riders. One of the reasons why pony competitions were only recently introduced into the F.E.I. scene lies in the fact that few other countries have a native pony-breeding programme similar to that in this country, with the result that most riders

only start to ride when they are big enough to ride horses. In Germany, however, there was another activity in which children who were keen on horses could become actively engaged. Almost every village in Germany has its riding club or has access to one not far distant, and the first step up the equestrian ladder is through vaulting, where the horse trots and canters quietly round on the lunge while the children vault on and off its back and perform various gymnastic exercises. Inevitably competition develops between local clubs, and so the sport of vaulting expanded, and now vaulting, first seen in this country when teams from Germany gave demonstrations at Olympia some years ago, is now an official F.E.I. discipline.

Thus on the Continent riders tend to start riding horses at an earlier age than in this country, and while the F.E.I. category for Pony Riders runs from 12 to 17, that for Juniors goes from 14 to 18. Then, just to complicate matters, the category of Young Riders starts not at 18 but at 16 and continues to 21. In fact the F.E.I. rules permit a rider of 16 or 17 to take part in competitions for Pony Riders, Juniors and Young Riders in the same year, though he may only take part in one of the relevant championships in the same discipline; he could in theory, though, compete in the championships in three different disciplines in three different categories in one year! At 18 a rider may compete as a Junior, as a Young Rider and as a Senior, though with the same restriction regarding championships.

All this may sound complicated enough, but as far as British riders are concerned the rules are different again, with Juniors ending, sensibly enough, where Young Riders begin, but with Seniors overlapping both by starting at 16. Just to complicate matters a little more, the F.E.I. have in 1987 introduced a further category for children aged 12–14 riding horses, not ponies. The full picture, therefore, looks like this:

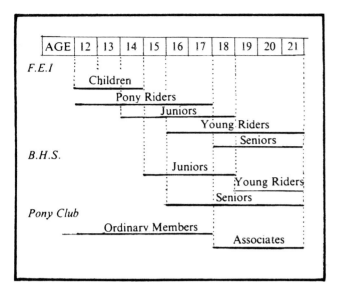

At home, Juniors are able to compete in Pony Club Horse Trials up to the end of their Associate Membership at 21, in B.H.S. Junior classes from 15 to 18, and in Senior classes from 16 onwards. But although successful Pony Club eventers are easily able to cope with B.H.S. Novice courses, until now there have been in the calendar only half a dozen Junior Novice classes, which has meant that these Juniors have had to compete against the top riders bringing out their new young horses in these classes. Also, Junior riders with talent and ambition have had to apply to the Junior Selection Committee for official recognition and the possibility of further training – something that some have been rather hesitant to do.

For some years now the programme of Junior classes has been sponsored by Beehive Car Parks, whose Chairman Graham Hawtree is a familiar figure at most events; his daughter Melanie is herself a product of the system. Starting in 1988, Beehive, in conjunction with Spillers Horse Feeds and Pasada (all weather riding surfaces), sponsored a series of 24 Regional Novice Trials, from which selected riders go on to compete in a new Junior Novice Three Day Event at Tweseldown, as a stepping

stone to the highlight of the Junior season, the British Junior Three Day Event Championship at Windsor in May, won in 1988 by Victoria Osborne and Silver Spoon. In addition there are half a dozen Junior Open Intermediate Trials, and finally each year there is the Junior European Championship, which in 1988 was held at Dijon, France, where the British Team took the Gold Medal, with Kristina Gifford taking the Individual Bronze.

The affairs of Juniors lie in the hands of the Junior Selection Committee, which was chaired for so many years by Lt-Col. 'Babe' Moseley, Assistant Director of Badminton from its inception, and one to whom many of our leading riders of today owe a great debt. He was succeeded by Col. Hubert Allfrey, who continued to guide our Junior teams to international success. Then in 1987 Lt-Col. Bill Lithgow, Executive Officer of the Pony Club, and probably the most successful *Chef d'Equipe* that the Senior team has ever had, brought his vast experience to the Chairmanship of the Junior Selection Committee. The team trainer is Gillian Watson, winner of Burghley in 1969 with Shaitan. The members of the team who have represented Great Britain at an International Three Day Event can be recognised by the Union Jack emblem worn on their coats on a white background.

Young Riders, who if members of the British Team wear their Union Jacks on a blue background, compete as such at home between the ages of 19 and 21, during which time they can still ride in Pony Club events as Associates, and can also compete as Seniors. Their calendar includes two Open Intermediate and two Advanced Trials, and the highlight of their year is the British Young Riders Three Day Event Championship at Bramham at the end of May, won in 1988 by Polly Lyon and Highland Road. In addition they have a class at Advanced level at the British Open Championships at Gatcombe Park in August.

Junior European Champions, 1988, Great Britain.

Bowmanhill Crystal Clear   Alice Clapham
Smithstown Lad   Kristina Gifford
Blackmore Money Spinner   Sophie Newman

The Young Riders, too, have their European Championship, held in 1988 at Zonhoven, Belgium, where the British Team won the Gold Medal, with Polly Lyon, the 1987 European Junior Champion, now becoming the Young Rider Champion. Selection for the team is in the hands of the Committee headed by Christopher Schofield, with Gillian Watson again as trainer, and with Giles Rowsell as *Chef d'Equipe*. Backing up all three Selection Committees as Executive Officer is James Mackie, who has responsibility for all international affairs at the Horse Trials office.

The great advantage of the Junior and Young Rider system is that it brings riders with potential to the notice of the selectors when they might otherwise be overlooked when competing only against Seniors. Having caught the

eyes of the selectors they may then be fortunate enough to come under the aegis of the official trainer, and may then gain international experience at an early age. With this behind them, sponsorship is then not too difficult to obtain, and they will have every opportunity to pursue a successful career in their chosen sport. Our senior teams are thus assured of a supply of up-and-coming riders, and how lucky these riders are compared with those who, though they may have ridden since childhood, have only taken up eventing in their 20s.

Junior European Champion, 1987, Young Rider European Champion, 1988: Polly Lyon and Highland Road

Some of those who have in recent years come up through the system of Junior and Young Rider selection, and who are now making their mark in senior classes are Anne-Marie Taylor, 5th in the World Championships and winner of Chatsworth in 1986; Rachel Hunt, 2nd at Badminton in 1986 and reserve for the Olympic Team in 1988; Katie Parker, British Young Rider Three Day Event Champion of 1987; and Annabel May, 3rd at Burghley in 1988. (Both these last two came from a background of sporting success, for Katie Parker's mother Bridget was a Team Gold Medallist at the Munich Olympics, while Annabel's father, Peter May, captained England's test cricket team, and her mother, as Virginia Gilligan, was herself a successful Three Day Event rider.)

Among those still young enough (in 1988) to ride as Juniors or Young Riders, Polly Lyon, European Junior Champion in 1987, British and European Young Rider Champion of 1988, (and still eligible for Young Rider events in 1989), must surely be a hot tip for senior honours in due course. Others to watch must include Pippa Nolan, European Junior Team Gold Medallist in 1986 and European Young Rider Champion of 1987; William Fox-Pitt, runner-up in the 1987 European Junior Championship and Young Rider Team Gold Medallist in 1988; and Amanda Harwood and Kristina Gifford, daughters of two of our most successful racehorse trainers, both of whom have made their mark on the eventing scene.

Since 1968 the British Team has won the Junior European Championships eleven times, with nine individual champions, while in the Young Rider Championships, initiated in 1981, Team Gold has only eluded us once, and there have been five individual champions. It is doubtful if any other country has a comparable system for producing young riders, and it must bode well for the future of our senior teams.

CHAPTER 20

The international scene and a look at the future

The 1988 Three Day Event season was clearly going to be dominated by the ultimate objective of the Seoul Olympic Games in September, and by the influence that the major earlier events would have on the selection and preparation of teams from the prominent eventing nations. Badminton in late April or early May is usually the first, and probably the most important, Three Day Event of the season, and after its cancellation due to appalling weather conditions in 1987, it assumed even greater importance in 1988.

It began in controversy, when five horses were summarily dismissed at the First Horse Inspection, and continued with understandable confusion in the minds of competitors and spectators as to what the dressage judges were looking for. The Cross Country course was, in Ian Stark's words, 'Big as far as the Lake, and very big thereafter,' but though two World Champions, Lucinda Green and Virginia Leng, and the youngest member of our Olympic squad, Rachel Hunt, came to grief, the going was perfect and eighteen competitors completed the course without penalty, seven of these within the time.

Four more horses were spun at the Final Horse Inspection, including New Zealander Tinks Pottinger's second ride Graphic, on his dressage score at that point. The event ended in triumph for Ian Stark, the first ever rider to be first and second at Badminton (with Sir Wattie and Glenburnie), and though Ginny Leng could not have caught Sir Wattie on either of her horses, it was a considerable feat to take third place with a painful ankle injury as a result of being shot into orbit by Murphy Himself at the Ski Jump on the previous day. With six of the possible Olympic riders finishing in the first ten, the selectors were able to breathe a (qualified) sigh of relief!

But meanwhile across the Atlantic in the United States, the Americans (and the Canadians) looked as though they might well have demolished their Olympic hopes in a series of selection trials that culminated at the Lexington Three Day Event in Kentucky. Had the retirement of team trainer Jack Le Goff after the triumphant 1984 Olympics seen the end of an era? Certainly the new selection committee introduced a new system which seemed to be based on elimination through trials rather than on judgement of form.

The first Advanced One Day Trial in Florida eliminated Kerry Millikin's The Pirate, and broke the limbs of two of Canada's most

167

experienced riders, Phillipe Desourdy and Daphne Cronin. The second trial in North Carolina did little for the Canadians either, but proved a useful workout for Karen Stives and Bruce Davidson, who also dominated the final One Day Event, which resulted in a broken arm for another Olympic hopeful, Matt Firestone. The survivors then faced a Three Day Event at Lexington, scene of the disastrous World Championships of 1978. Here the sorry tale of injuries continued; Kerry Millikin broke a leg, veteran team rider Mike Plumb dislocated a shoulder, and even Bruce Davidson broke a couple of ribs, though this did not prevent him from winning, nor from bringing the veteran J J Babu into second place!

Then to complete the destruction the United States Olympic Committee scored an 'own goal' by directing that selection for the Olympic Games should be based solely on the Lexington results, thus in a single stroke depriving the selection committee of a job and the United States Equestrian Team of several of the remaining possible Olympic candidates. Finally came the news that a competitor was about to sue the selectors because of her omission from the Olympic squad! But whatever their problems, the Americans still had in Bruce Davidson one of the World's greatest riders, as he showed yet again when taking first and second places in the Canadian Three Day Event at Ridgewood, Ontario, ahead of Angela Tucker on General Bugle.

Back in Europe, one with his face wreathed in smiles was New Zealand's Mark Todd, holder of the Olympic title. Having in 1987 been the first rider to be first and second at Burghley, he wisely declined to put the sixteen year old Charisma through as stern a test as Badminton before the Olympics, and with his team mate Tinks Pottinger again showing her class there, the prospect for Olympic medals looked rosy. Meanwhile in France Todd had ridden his second string Bahlua into second

place at Saumur behind David Green, who was riding Lucinda's former European Championship mount Shannagh for Australia.

Then at Punchestown in May Karen Straker won with Corriwack, a victory that, coming after her respectable fifth place at Badminton on Get Smart, earned her a trip to Seoul. Nearer to Seoul itself, the New Zealand two star event at Taupo resulted in the first three finishing on their dressage scores, with Trudy Boyce, Silver medallist at the 1986 World Championships at Gawlor, in second place. At Bielefeld in Germany the French took first and second places, with Mark Todd third and fourth on his less experienced horses. (The obstacles there caused little trouble, but the hills accounted for huge time penalties.) Bialy Bor in Poland gave the home side a boost, with opposition only from USSR and Sweden, while in Breda (Holland) Rachel Hunt was runner-up to Mary Thomson (King Max) who went on to win Bramham on King Cuthbert from Jane Thelwall's King's Jester.

August's main event is the British Open Championship at Gatcombe Park, home of the President of the F.E.I., H.R.H. The Princess Royal, and Captain Mark Phillips, the organiser. The 1988 fixture was inevitably influenced by the proximity of the Olympic Games, with the British team probables either excluded or under orders not to take undue risks. Nominally a One Day Event, the Championships are run over two days and have developed a formula of their own, with the Show Jumping following the Dressage, and the order of starting on the Cross Country being in reverse order of merit, as for the jumping test of a Three Day Event.

Considerable interest centred on a rare happening in top level eventing, the exchange of horses by two of our leading riders. Ever since winning Burghley on Murphy Himself in 1986, Ginny Leng had had some difficulty in channelling this powerful horse's enthusiasm in the required direction, and had finally come to the conclusion that he was a 'man's horse'. What better man than Ian Stark, who happened to have available for exchange the fast improving Griffin, on whom he had won an Advanced section at Gatcombe in 1987. Griffin duly won again for his new rider, while in the 'Galloping Scotsman' Murphy met his match, and coasted home to take third place in the championship. Two riders, two horses, and two sponsors all seemed happy!

The fascination of the Gatcombe formula lies in the fact that as the Cross Country nears its end, the effective Optimum Time for each competitor changes, for he or she is not so much interested in the time laid down as in the speed necessary to retain his position in the light of previous performances, or indeed to move up the order, or to set a target for those who follow. Robert Lemieux, runner-up to Ginny Leng in 1987 with Gamesmaster, produced the fastest round so far on The Poser, though one that meant that Mark Todd, on Charisma's last appearance in this country, would not have to push the sixteen year old too hard to win, which he duly did by ten points, equalling The Poser's time.

Burghley, the second British event of Championship status and one of only two 3-star events in the international calendar, had been voted the international riders' favourite Three Day Event of the 1986 and 1987 seasons. In 1988 it opened as the equestrian teams for the Olympic Games were flying off to Seoul, so the entry was inevitably somewhat below the usual standard. Nevertheless, with Rodney Powell, Rachel Hunt and Jane Thelwall out to show that their omission from the final Olympic squad had been a mistake, with former World Champion Lucinda Green determined to establish Mins Lincoln as a true international prospect, and with a field that included British National Champion Robert Lemieux, Nigel Taylor, Clarissa Strachan, and several younger

riders eager to make their mark, it was clearly not going to be a push-over for anyone.

Lucinda Green led after the dressage, with Robert Lemieux, Paddy Muir, who had been sixth at Badminton, Rodney Powell and Rachel Hunt all not far behind. After the cross country course inspection, the general view was that it was big but fair, with sufficient time-consuming alternatives for the less experienced competitors, though there were reservations about the Jubilee Ditch, a set of rails in front of a wide ditch with a considerable drop at No 6, coming as it did after two imposing fences in the main arena.

But when eight of the first nine competitors failed to complete the course, including such experienced riders as Jane Starkey, Rodney Powell, Claire Mason and Rachel Hunt, spectators, some of whom had not seen a horse for nearly forty-five minutes, began to wonder whether someone had made a miscalculation. But the next six starters all came home with just three refusals on the course between them, and Mark Davies and Normas looked like completing a brilliant round in spite of a fall coming out of the water at the Upper Trout Hatchery, where Mark had managed to avoid contact with the ground until clear of the penalty zone. But at the Double Coffin, a combination that caused only two other penalties during the day, they attempted a route that no one else seriously considered, involving a very awkward take-off from a sloping bank across the corner formed by the first rail and ditch, and the ensuing fall tragically cost the lives of both rider and horse.

Of the dressage leaders, Mins Lincoln came to grief at the Lower Trout Hatchery, The Poser ran out at the Lamb Creep, Paddy Muir went clear but incurred inexplicable time penalties, Rodney Powell retired both his horses, Rachel Hunt fell at the Weir with Aloaf and retired Ballymurphy V (not to be confused with Ballymurphy II, on whom Ruth House completed an apparent clear round, only to be eliminated for jumping out of the Lamb Creep at the wrong place). Then the last to go, Jane Thelwall and King's Jester, incurred the merest fraction of a time penalty to take the lead from Nicola May (McDuff III) and Madeleine Gurdon (Midnight Monarch). On the final day Jane won her first Championship Three Day Event, while the other two changed places.

With one human and two equine fatalities on the cross country, and with 26 out of 55 starters failing to finish, discussion as to the extent to which the course could be held responsible was inevitable. But 20 of the 29 who did complete the course did so without jumping penalties, some by making sensible use of the alternative fences. Nevertheless Burghley, which used to be regarded as a relatively straightforward event of moderate severity, has become more difficult since the FEI designated it, with Badminton, as one of only two 3-star events in the calendar. But as the Burghley fences approach those of Badminton in severity, one of the main differences between the two events asserts its influence; whereas Badminton is relatively flat, Burghley has considerable gradients.

But there was also in 1988 another factor unique to Burghley. After three inviting fences, just as the horse was settling down to the 'relentless gallop' that should have put the Optimum Time within his grasp, he re-entered the main arena where the dressage had been held, and there faced two highly imaginative and beautifully built obstacles which demanded a very considerable effort on his part. Then he left the arena and plunged down the hill to what ought in these circumstances to have been a 'let-up' fence. But instead he met the Jubilee Ditch, an imposing set of rails in front of a wide ditch with a considerable drop. Not only was it a big fence, but unfortunately the bank on the landing side was soft and deep, and six horses fell here and retired,

one was eliminated, and of those who survived, eight were in trouble at the relatively simple Lower Trout Hatchery which they faced next. It is probable that these three testing obstacles, coming so early in the course, contributed to some of the problems encountered later.

The innovations introduced by Burghley's Director Bill Henson have done much in a short time to appeal to competitors, public and sponsors; and with the appointment of Mark Phillips as course designer no doubt a satisfactory formula will emerge for the Cross Country in time for the 1989 European Championships.

And so to the highlight of the year, an Olympic Three Day Event staged in what was perhaps one of the most unlikely venues in the world. The criteria which govern the I.O.C.'s selection of venues for the Olympic Games remains a mystery to most sportsmen; for the equestrian, the choice often results in the placing of a complicated operation such as the organisation of equestrian events in the hands of people with little or no experience of such matters in a site which is far from ideal. Certainly to anyone who took part in the United Nations operations in Korea in the early 'fifties, the idea of holding Olympic Games in Seoul in 1988 would have seemed a fantasy unlikely to be realised. But realised it was, and no expense had been spared to provide adequate facilities for the equestrian events.

13 nations had entered teams for the Three Day Event, with individuals from a further six countries, including at first sight such unlikely participants as Bermuda, Puerto Rico and the Virgin Islands. With the United States team having lost its 'golden look', the favourites were Great Britain and New Zealand, with the Germans, second in the 1988 European Championships, a good each way bet. The transport of horses from all over the world in air-conditioned Boeing 747's enabled teams to arrive fit and ready to run, and the training facilities seemed excellent.

Due to its distance from Seoul, the Cross Country course inspection took place before the First Horse Inspection, after which final team selection had to be made, and the general opinion seemed to be that it was a big course over difficult terrain, and somewhat more testing than at recent Olympics. Horse trials enthusiasts back in England were somewhat dismayed to learn on their breakfast television that Mark Phillips' Cartier had not passed inspection. In fact the Ground Jury (the same that had eliminated five horses at Badminton in May) had referred Cartier, whom they subsequently passed, but they did fail two Canadians, which eliminated their team.

For the British Team, Ian Stark and Sir Wattie and Ginny Leng and Master Craftsman had virtually selected themselves, with the remaining two places to be filled from Mark Phillips and Cartier, who had little recent form since their 6th place in the 1987 European Championships, Lorna Clarke, whose Fearliath Mor was brilliant across country but usually carried forward a hefty penalty from the dressage, and Karen Straker and Get Smart, who earned their place in the squad after brilliant performances at Badminton and Punchestown earlier in the year. Karen's recent form earned her one of these places, and with a question mark over Fearliath Mor's soundness the other went to Cartier.

Cartier's chances of an individual medal were dashed by the torrential downpour that coincided with his entry to the dressage arena, and at the end of the first two days Mark Todd and Charisma, the defending Olympic Champions, led from Germany's Claus Erhorn on Justyn Thyme, on whom Anne-Marie Taylor had been fifth in the 1986 World Championships, with Ginny Leng in third place. The German team found itself in its customary first place after the dressage, but only 27 penalties covered Germany, Great Britain, New Zealand and the United States in that order.

The Ground Jury had modified Hugh Thomas's course in the light of the undulating terrain, as a result of which 17 of the 50 starters went round without jumping penalties, and only 11 failed to finish. The British team suffered an early setback when Cartier was found to be lame on arrival back in the Box before Phase 'D'. Then Karen Straker rode a masterly round as far as the second water obstacle, where she was extremely unlucky to be dumped when Get Smart lost his hind legs on landing – not even Lucinda Green, whose exemplary TV commentary was enlivened by a novel expletive at this point – would have survived that one. That was Get Smart's only mistake, but enough to put a team medal in jeopardy. Ginny Leng was clearly 'going for gold', and how she avoided being shot into orbit when Master Craftsman hit the fourth fence on a steep downward slope we shall never know. Taking all the short routes, she came home clear with 8 time penalties. Then Ian Stark supported her with an even quicker round, and some sort of medal again looked possible.

Meanwhile Andrew Bennie and Margie Knighton had been in trouble for New Zealand, but both Mark Todd and Tinks Pottinger finished the day on their dressage scores to put their team ahead of the British. The US, too, had fallen apart, and it was the Germans whose consistency as a team left them with a 37 point lead over New Zealand.

The final Horse Inspection saw the elimination of three more, including a German and a New Zealander, fortunately in both cases their discard scores. Jumping in reverse order of merit, Andrew Bennie's five fences down spoiled his country's chances, but Karen Straker raised British hopes with a clear round. The Germans, individually 4th, 6th and 9th, duly took the Team Gold in spite of lowering four fences between them, and Ian Stark's clear round put the pressure on Ginny Leng, whose relatively inexperienced horse made two errors, which dropped her from Silver to Bronze but made sure of Silver for the team (and for Ian.)

As Mark Todd and the sixteen year old Charisma entered the arena there were few who were not willing them to win. Memories of Charisma's 20 faults when in the lead at the Stockholm CSI of 1987 must have been in Mark's mind, but with three fences in hand they made just one mistake and so completed an almost unique double. Not quite unique, for at Amsterdam in 1928 and at Los Angeles in 1932 Charles Pahud de Mortanges rode Marcroix to victory for Holland, but no rider has stamped his authority on the sport in quite the same way as Mark Todd, and no horse has captured the imagination of the public to the same extent as Charisma, who now retires.

As to the British team, while there is disappointment that Gold eluded us, two Silvers and a Bronze are cause for celebration, as is the emergence of a new young rider at this level.

This volume opened with the extraordinary story of the Three Day Event at the Berlin Olympics of 1936, when the German teams won all the Gold Medals. It closes with the record of German success at Seoul; Team Gold in Dressage, Three Day Event and Show Jumping, and Individual Gold and Bronze in the Dressage and Show Jumping respectively, a record which is never likely to be equalled, unless it is yet again by the Germans themselves.

So ends another Olympic cycle. What of the future? At home the sport itself appears to be in good shape; eight Three Day Events and over 130 one day Horse Trials in the calendar; the British team holders of the World and European Championships, and with an enviable supply of talented young riders in the pipeline. But there are two dark clouds in the sky.

The decision of Chatsworth's landowners, The Duke and Duchess of Devonshire, to terminate their Three Day Event is a blow, especially in 1989 when only a dozen individual British riders can take part in Burghley's European Championships. But they had generously hosted a major One Day Event for three decades, and it was unfortunate that the inauguration of the Three Day Event saw two unusually wet autumns in its first four years. But its sponsors, Audi, are thought to be keen to remain in the sport, and with the need for an autumn 2-star CCI for horse and rider qualifications it is hoped that a replacement for Chatsworth can be found.

On the sponsorship side, the drastic curtailment of their commitments by the Carphone Group, and the withdrawal of other sponsors, has in part been balanced by the involvement of Barbour and Pedigree Pet Foods. It is also encouraging to note that, in addition to the efforts of British Equestrian Promotions, Horse Trial organisers are themselves making major efforts to attract new sponsorship. Nevertheless, there have recently been several reminders that sponsorship cannot be taken for granted.

On the international scene, although the Koreans have overcome most of the problems connected with the running of equestrian events at a hitherto untried venue in a country with little experience of equestrian sport, these events are already under the searching scrutiny of the I.O.C. They are among the most expensive to run, and attract relatively few of the Olympic nations – 32 out of 169 at Seoul. There are those who favour treating the Olympic equestrian events in the same way as the sports that make up the Winter Olympics, so that the best venue and an experienced organisation can provide the fairest test for horse and rider. And certainly in 1956, when quarantine regulations precluded the holding of the equestrian events in Melbourne, Stockholm provided a successful and enjoyable series of competitions.

But the Olympic Games, in spite of political and commercial overtones, are an international sports festival, and one of the attractions for competitors is the opportunity of meeting the celebrities of other sports and other nations, of watching the top athletes in action, and of experiencing the life of the Olympic Village – even with its often exasperating inconveniences. Riders may miss this if separate Equestrian Games are held. But for the 1990 World Championships for the first time all the equestrian disciplines will meet together when Stockholm hosts the first World Equestrian Games. If these are successful, then this may become the pattern for future World Championships, and even for the Olympics, if the I.O.C. decide to discontinue equestrian events or on occasions when the Games are awarded to a city which does not already have the facilities and experience necessary to run them. This would also enable such excellent facilities as those at Riem, for example, site of the equestrian events at the 1972 Munich Olympics, to be fully used again.

The sport, then, appears to be in good shape, but whatever pressures upon it may build up, and whatever the problems that may arise, we must remember that it has, in common with the other equestrian sports, a unique element – the partnership of rider and horse. Without the horse, it goes without saying, our sport would not exist, and it will only continue to flourish provided that his interests and welfare remain of prime importance. 'If there is any doubt about the meaning of any of the Regulations,' reads the first article of the F.E.I. General Regulations (Article 100), 'they should be interpreted in the sense of ensuring fair conditions for all competitors.' For 'all competitors' let us read . . .

"THE HORSE"

Appendices

APPENDIX A

EQUESTRIAN AUTHORITIES AND USEFUL ADDRESSES

F.E.I.   Fédération Equestre Internationale, Bolligenstrasse 54, CH–3000, Berne 32, Switzerland.

B.E.F.	British Equestrian Federation	
B.H.S.	British Horse Society	
H.T.C.	Horse Trials Committee	
H.T.G.	Horse Trials Group	British Equestrian Centre, Stoneleigh,
	Dressage Committee	Kenilworth, Warwickshire CV8 2LR. Tel.:
	Dressage Group	0203-696697 or 0203-696516 (B.S.J.A.).
B.S.J.A.	British Show Jumping Association	
	The Pony Club	

H.T.S.G.   Horse Trials Support Group, 19 Alexandra Court, Maida Vale, London W9 1SQ. Tel.: 01-286 9935.

B.E.P.   British Equestrian Promotions, 35 Belgrave Square, London SW1X 8QB. Tel.: 01-235 6431/5390.

B.V.A.   British Veterinary Association, 7 Mansfield Street, Portland Place, London W1M 0AT. Tel.: 01-636 6541.

APPENDIX B

METRIC CONVERSION TABLES

1 inch	=	0.025 m	10 cm	=	4 in.
1 foot	=	0.30 m	50 cm	=	1 ft 7 in.
2 ft	=	0.61 m	60 cm	=	1 ft 11 in.
1 yard	=	0.91 m	70 cm	=	2 ft 3 in.
4 ft	=	1.22 m	80 cm	=	2 ft 7 in.
4 ft 3 in.	=	1.30 m	90 cm	=	2 ft 11 in.
4 ft 6 in.	=	1.37 m	1.00 m	=	3 ft 3 in.
4 ft 9 in.	=	1.45 m	1.10 m	=	3 ft 7 in.
5 ft	=	1.52 m	1.20 m	=	3 ft 11 in.
5 ft 3 in.	=	1.60 m	1.30 m	=	4 ft 3 in.
5 ft 6 in.	=	1.68 m	1.40 m	=	4 ft 7 in.
6 ft	=	1.83 m	1.50 m	=	4 ft 11 in.
6 ft 6 in.	=	1.91 m	1.60 m	=	5 ft 3 in.
7 ft	=	2.13 m	1.70 m	=	5 ft 7 in.
8 ft	=	2.44 m	1.80 m	=	5 ft 11 in.
9 ft	=	2.74 m	1.90 m	=	6 ft 3 in.
10 ft	=	3.05 m	2.00 m	=	6 ft 7 in.
15 ft	=	4.57 m	2.25 m	=	7 ft 5 in.
20 ft	=	6.10 m	2.50 m	=	8 ft 2 in.
10 yards	=	9.14 m	2.75 m	=	9 ft
25 yards	=	22.86 m	3.00 m	=	9 ft 10 in.
50 yards	=	45.72 m	4.00 m	=	13 ft 1 in.
100 yards	=	91.44 m	5.00 m	=	16 ft 5 in.
1,000 yards	=	914.40 m	6.00 m	=	19 ft 8 in.
			7.00 m	=	22 ft 11 in.
			8.00 m	=	26 ft 3 in.
			9.00 m	=	29 ft 6 in.
			10.00 m	=	32 ft 10 in.
			25.00 m	=	82 ft
			100.00 m	=	109 yards
			1,000.00 m	=	1,093 yards
			2 km	=	$1\frac{1}{4}$ miles
			3 km	=	1.86 miles
			4 km	=	$2\frac{1}{2}$ miles
			5 km	=	3.1 miles
			6 km	=	$3\frac{3}{4}$ miles
			8 km	=	5 miles
			10 km	=	$6\frac{1}{4}$ miles

APPENDIX C

BRITISH CHAMPIONSHIP THREE DAY EVENT WINNERS 1949–88

BADMINTON

	HORSE	RIDER	OWNER
1949	Golden Willow	John Shedden	Rider
1950	Remus	Capt. T. Collings	Mrs Home Kidston
1951	Vae Victis	Capt. H. Schwarzenbach	Switzerland
1952	Emily Little	Capt. M. A. Q. Darley	Rider
1953	Starlight XV	Maj. A. L. Rook	Mrs J. R. Baker
1954	Bambi V	Margaret Hough	Rider
1955	Kilbarry	Maj. F. W. C. Weldon	Rider
1956	Kilbarry	Maj. F. W. C. Weldon	Rider
1957	High and Mighty	Sheila Willcox	Rider
1958	High and Mighty	Sheila Willcox	Rider
1959	Airs and Graces	Sheila Waddington	Rider
1960	Our Solo	Bill Roycroft	Australia
1961	Salad Days	Laurie Morgan	Australia
1962	Merely a Monarch	Anneli Drummond-Hay	Rider
1963	*Cancelled*		
1964	M' Lord Connolly	Capt. J. R. Templer	Rider
1965	Durlas Eile	Maj. E. A. Boylan	Ireland
1966	*Cancelled*		
1967	Jonathan	Celia Ross-Taylor	Rider
1968	Our Nobby	Jane Bullen	Rider
1969	Pasha	Richard Walker	Rider
1970	The Poacher	Richard Meade	Combined Training Committee
1971	Great Ovation	Lt M. Phillips	Miss F. Phillips
1972	Great Ovation	Lt M. Phillips	Miss F. Phillips
1973	Be Fair	Lucinda Prior-Palmer	Rider
1974	Columbus	Capt. M. Phillips	H.M. the Queen
1975	*Cancelled*		
1976	Wide Awake	Lucinda Prior-Palmer	Mrs V. Phillips
1977	George	Lucinda Prior-Palmer	Mrs H. Straker
1978	Warrior	Jane Holderness-Roddam	Mrs S. Howard and rider
1979	Killaire	Lucinda Prior-Palmer	C. A. Cyzer
1980	Southern Comfort	Mark Todd	New Zealand
1981	Lincoln	Capt. M. Phillips	Range Rover Team
1982	Speculator	Richard Meade	G. Wimpey
1983	Regal Realm	Lucinda Green	S.R. Direct Mail
1984	Beagle Bay	Lucinda Green	S.R. Direct Mail
1985	Priceless	Virginia Holgate	British National Life Assurance
1986	Sir Wattie	Ian Stark	Edinburgh Woollen Mill
1987	*Cancelled*		
1988	Sir Wattie	Ian Stark	Edinburgh Woollen Mill

HAREWOOD

	HORSE	RIDER	OWNER
1953	Neptune	Vivien Machin-Goodall	Rider
1954	Carmena	Penny Molteno	Rider
1955	Kilbarry	Lt-Col. F. W. C. Weldon	Rider
1956	High and Mighty	Sheila Willcox	Rider
1957	Charleville	Ian Dudgeon	Rider
1958	Polarfuchs	Otto Pohlmann	Germany
1959	Burn Trout	Maj. E. H. Schwarzenbach	Switzerland

BURGHLEY

	HORSE	RIDER	OWNER
1961	Merely a Monarch	Anneli Drummond-Hay	Rider
1962	M' Lord Connolly	Capt. J. R. Templer	Rider
1963	St Finbarr	Capt. H. Freeman-Jackson	Ireland
1964	Barberry	Richard Meade	Rider
1965	Victoria Bridge	Capt. J. J. Beale	Rider
1966	Chalan	Capt. Carlos Moratorio	Argentina
1967	Popadom	Lorna Sutherland	Rider
1968	Fair and Square	Sheila Willcox	Rider
1969	Shaitan	Gillian Watson	Mrs Stinton & Mr, Mrs & Miss Smallwood
1970	Don Camillo	Judy Bradwell	R. Smith
1971	Doublet	H.R.H. the Princess Anne	H.M. the Queen
1972	Larkspur	Janet Hodgson	Rider
1973	Maid Marion	Capt. M. Phillips	A. E. & A. G. Hill
1974	Irish Cap	Bruce Davidson	U.S.A.
1975	Carawich	Aly Pattinson	Rider
1976	Warrior	Jane Holderness-Roddam	Mrs S. Howard & rider
1977	George	Lucinda Prior-Palmer	Mrs H. Straker
1978	Greco	Lorna Sutherland	Rider
1979	Davey	Andrew Hoy	Australia
1980	John of Gaunt	Richard Walker	Kent Leather Distributors Ltd
1981	Beagle Bay	Lucinda Green	Overseas Containers Ltd
1982	Ryan's Cross	Richard Walker	John Ambler
1983	Priceless	Virginia Holgate	} British National Life Assurance Ltd
1984	Night Cap	Virginia Holgate	
1985	Priceless	Virginia Holgate	
1986	Murphy Himself	Virginia Leng	
1987	Wilton Fair	Mark Todd (NZ)	Merrill Lynch Europe Ltd & Mrs L. Robinson
1988	King's Jester	Jane Thelwall	Mr & Mrs J. Huntridge

APPENDIX D

BRITISH TEAM SUCCESSES IN INTERNATIONAL CHAMPIONSHIPS 1936–88

OLYMPIC GAMES

1936 Berlin	*Team Bronze* Fanshawe/Bowie Knife Howard-Vyse/Blue Steel Scott/Bob Clive	
1956 Stockholm	*Team Gold* Weldon/Kilbarry Hill/Countryman Rook/Wild Venture	*Bronze:* Maj. F. W. C. Weldon/ Kilbarry
1968 Mexico	*Team Gold* Allhusen/Lochinvar Jones/The Poacher Meade/Cornishman V Bullen/Our Nobby	*Silver:* Maj. D. S. Allhusen/ Lochinvar
1972 Munich	*Team Gold* Meade/Laurieston Gordon-Watson/Cornishman V Parker/Cornish Gold Phillips/Great Ovation	*Gold:* R. J. H. Meade/Laurieston
1984 Los Angeles	*Team Silver* Green/Regal Realm Stark/Oxford Blue Holgate/Priceless Clapham/Windjammer	*Bronze:* Miss V. Holgate/ Priceless
1988 Seoul	*Team Silver* Phillips/Cartier Straker/Get Smart Leng/Master Craftsman Stark/Sir Wattie	*Silver:* I. Stark/Sir Wattie *Bronze:* Mrs V. Leng/Master Craftsman

WORLD CHAMPIONSHIPS

1966 Burghley		*Silver:* R. J. H. Meade/Barberry
1970 Punchestown	*Team Gold*	
	Meade/The Poacher	*Gold:* Miss M. Gordon-Watson/
	Gordon-Watson/Cornishman V	Cornishman V
	Phillips/Chicago	*Silver:* R. J. H. Meade/The Poacher
	Stevens/Benson	
1974 Burghley	*Team Silver*	
	Meade/Wayfarer II	*Bronze:* E. H. Thomas/Playamar
	Parker/Cornish Gold	
	Collins/Smokey VI	
	Phillips/Columbus	
1982 Luhmuhlen	*Team Gold*	
	Green/Regal Realm	*Gold:* Mrs L. Green/Regal Realm
	Meade/Kilcashel	
	Holgate/Priceless	
	Bayliss/Mystic Minstrel	
1986 Gawlor	*Team Gold*	
	Leng/Priceless	*Gold:* Mrs V. Leng/Priceless
	Stark/Oxford Blue	*Bronze:* Mrs L. Clarke/Myross
	Clarke/Myross	
	Strachan/Delphy Dazzle	

EUROPEAN CHAMPIONSHIPS

1953 Badminton	*Team Gold*	
	Hindley/Speculation	*Gold:* Maj. A. L. Rook/Starlight
	Weldon/Kilbarry	
	Hill/Bambi V	
1954 Basle	*Team Gold*	
	Weldon/Kilbarry	*Gold:* A. E. Hill/Crispin
	Hill/Crispin	*Silver:* Maj. F. W. C. Weldon/
	Rook/Starlight	Kilbarry
	Mason/Tramella	*Bronze:* Maj. A. L. Rook/
		Starlight
1955 Windsor	*Team Gold*	
	Weldon/Kilbarry	*Gold:* Maj. F. W. C. Weldon/
	Hill/Countryman	Kilbarry
	Rook/Starlight	*Bronze:* A. E. Hill/Countryman
	Mason/Tramella	

1957 Copenhagen   *Team Gold*
Allhusen/Laurien
Willcox/High and Mighty
Marsh/Wild Venture
Tatham-Warter/Pampas Cat

Gold: Miss S. Willcox/High and Mighty

1959 Harewood   *Team Silver*
Weldon/Samuel Johnson
Allhusen/Laurien
Beale/Fulmer Folly
Willcox/Airs and Graces

Silver: Lt-Col. F. W. C. Weldon/Samuel Johnson
Bronze: Maj. D. S. Allhusen/Laurien

1962 Burghley

Gold: Captain J. R. Templer/M' Lord Connolly
Bronze: Miss J. Wykeham-Musgrave/Ryebrooke

1967 Punchestown   *Team Gold*
Whiteley/The Poacher
Allhusen/Lochinvar
Jones/Foxdor
Meade/Barberry

Silver: Capt. M. F. Whiteley/The Poacher
Bronze: Maj. D. S. Allhusen/Lochinvar

1969 Haras du Pin   *Team Gold*
Allhusen/Lochinvar
Walker/Pasha
Jones/The Poacher
Hely-Hutchinson/Count Jasper

Gold: Miss M. Gordon-Watson/Cornishman V
Silver: R. Walker/Pasha

1971 Burghley   *Team Gold*
Meade/The Poacher
Phillips/Great Ovation
Gordon-Watson/Cornishman V
West/Baccarat

Gold: H.R.H. the Princess Anne/Doublet
Silver: Miss D. West/Baccarat
Bronze: S. Stevens/Classic Chips

1973 Kiev   *Team Bronze*
Meade/Wayfarer II
Prior-Palmer/Be Fair
West/Baccarat
Hodgson/Larkspur

1975 Luhmuhlen	*Team Silver* Prior-Palmer/Be Fair H.R.H. Princess Anne/Goodwill Hatherley/Harley Hodgson/Larkspur	*Gold:* Miss L. Prior-Palmer/Be Fair *Silver:* H.R.H. the Princess Anne/ Goodwill
1977 Burghley	*Team Gold* Prior-Palmer/George Collins/Smokey VI Holderness-Roddam/Warrior Strachan/Merry Sovereign	*Gold:* Miss L. Prior-Palmer/ George
1979 Luhmuhlen	*Team Silver* Hatherley/Monacle II Collins/Gamble Strachan/Merry Sovereign Prior-Palmer/Killaire	*Silver:* Miss R. Bayliss/Gurgle the Greek
1981 Horsens	*Team Gold* Holgate/Priceless Meade/Kilcashel Benson/Gemma Jay Purbrick/Peter the Great	
1983 Frauenfeld	*Team Silver* Green/Regal Realm Holgate/Night Cap II Clarke/Danville Clapham/Windjammer	*Gold:* Miss R. Bayliss/Mystic Minstrel *Silver:* Mrs L. Green/Regal Realm
1985 Burghley	*Team Gold* Holgate/Priceless Clarke/Myross Stark/Oxford Blue Green/Regal Realm	*Gold:* Miss V. Holgate/Priceless *Silver:* Mrs L. Clarke/Myross *Bronze:* I. Stark/Oxford Blue
1987 Luhmuhlen	*Team Gold* Green/Shannagh Hunt/Aloaf Stark/Sir Wattie Leng/Night Cap	*Gold:* Mrs V. Leng/Night Cap *Silver:* I. Stark/Sir Wattie

YOUNG RIDER EUROPEAN CHAMPIONSHIPS

1981 Achselschwang   *Team Gold*
Bywater/The Countryman
Piggott/Asian Princess
Thomas/Divine Intervention
Trevett/Unusual

1982 Fontainebleau   *Team Silver*
Strawson/Minsmore   *Gold:* Miss V. Strawson/Minsmore
Callaway/Bassanio
Piggott/Hong Kong Discoverer
Hunter/Strike-a-Light

1983 Burghley   *Team Gold*
Straker/Running Bear   *Silver:* Miss K. Straker/Running
Schwerdt/Dylan II   Bear
Strawson/Minsmore   *Bronze:* Miss P. Schwerdt/Dylan II
Murdoch/Rugan

1984 Luhmuhlen   *Team Gold*
Hunt/Friday Fox   *Silver:* Miss P. Magill/Headley
Sainsbury/Hassan   Gladiator
Strawson/Sparrow Hawk   *Bronze:* Miss R. Hunt/Friday Fox
Orchard/Coeur de Lion

1985 Le Lion   *Team Gold*   *Gold:* Miss C. Oseman/Another
   D'Angers   Oseman/Another Fred   Fred
Hunt/Friday Fox
Taylor/Justyn Thyme VI
Bevan/Horton Venture

1986 Rotherfield   *Team Gold*
Ashbourne/Hector James   *Gold:* Miss A. Ramus/Spy Story II
Hunt/Friday Fox   *Silver:* Miss V. Ashbourne/
Shield/Crimdon Lucky George   Hector James
Copland/Sweeney   *Bronze:* Miss R. Hunt/Friday Fox

1987 Bialy Bor   *Gold:* Miss P. Nolan/Sir Barnaby

1988 Zonhoven   *Team Gold*   *Gold:* Miss P. Lyon/Highland Road
Fox-Pitt/Steadfast
Macaire/Master Marius
Nolan/Sir Barnaby
Lyon/Highland Road

JUNIOR EUROPEAN CHAMPIONSHIPS

1968 Craon   *Team Silver*   *Gold:* R. Walker/Pasha
                    Borwick/Sermonetto
                    Stevens/Benson
                    Tucker/Clorinda
                    Walker/Pasha

1970 Holstebro   *Team Bronze*
                    Brooke/Olive Oyl
                    Warren/Yogi Bear
                    Raymond/Tawstock Gent
                    Hill/Chicago III

1971 Wesel   *Team Gold*
                    Brake/Say When   *Gold:* C. Brooke/Olive Oyl
                    Brooke/Olive Oyl
                    Prior-Palmer/Be Fair
                    Sivewright/Gameel

1972 Eridge   *Team Gold*
                    Sivewright/Alsedell   *Silver:* A. Hill/Maid Marion
                    Hill/Maid Marion
                    Colquhoun/Belle Grey
                    Brooke/Olive Oyl

1973 Pompadour   *Team Gold*
                    Holgate/Dubonnet   *Gold:* Miss V. Holgate/Dubonnet
                    Bailey/Red Amber   *Silver:* Miss S. Bailey/Red Amber
                    Scrimgeour/Lysander
                    Brooke/Olive Oyl

1974 Rome   *Gold:* Miss S. Kerr/Peer Gynt
                                                Silver: Miss J. Winter/Stainless Steel

1975 Cirencester   *Team Gold*
                    Salmond/Orpheus   *Gold:* Miss V. Salmond/Orpheus
                    Saffell/Double Brandy   *Silver:* Miss D. Saffell/
                    Winter/Stainless Steel   Double Brandy
                    Pointer/Royal Slam   *Bronze:* Miss J. Winter/
                                                          Stainless Steel

1976 Siekkrug   *Team Gold*
Saffell/Double Brandy   *Silver:* Miss D. Saffell/
Bouet/Sea Lord V   Double Brandy
Jack/Burnt Oak   *Bronze:* Miss S. Bouet/Sea Lord V
Saunders/Cymbal

1979 Punchestown   *Team Silver*
Tilly/Tom Temp   *Gold:* Miss N. May/
May/Commodore IV   Commodore IV
Calloway/Bassanio
Ensten/Carbrooke Charles

1980 Achselschwang   *Team Gold*
Strawson/Greek Herb   *Silver:* Miss C. Needham/ Solo
Needham/Solo
Brooke/Super Star IV
May/Commodore IV

1981 St Fargeau   *Team Silver*
Strawson/Greek Herb
Dudgeon/Tom Faggus
Schwerdt/Dylan II
Sandall/Moss II

1982 Rotherfield   *Team Gold*
Straker/Running Bear   *Gold:* Miss K. Straker/Running
Taylor/Gin & Orange   Bear
Gracey/Rustic Rambler
Bevan/Horton Venture

1983 Rome   *Team Gold*
Brown/Fleetwater Opposition   *Gold:* Miss H. Brown/Fleetwater
Williams/Spiritos   Opposition
Macaire/Latin Tempo
Hunt/Friday Fox

1984 Poland   *Team Silver*
Gurdon/The Done Thing   *Silver:* Miss M. Gurdon/The Done
Gooderham/Rustic Moon   Thing
Search/Capricorn VI
Parker/Master Chester

1985 Rotherfield

Team Gold
Ramus/Spy Story II
Hoeg/Norton Boy
Bateson/Scalphunter
Chambers/Talisman SC

Bronze: Miss A. Ramus/
Spy Story II

1986 Walldorf

Team Bronze
Martin/Krugerrand
Cope/Juicy Lucy
Nolan/Airborne II
Hazlem/Gang Star

Silver: Miss P. Martin/
Krugerrand

1987 Rome

Team Gold
Bowley/Fair Share
Gifford/Song and Danceman
Lyon/Highland Road
Morris/Jack O'Lantern

Gold: Miss P. Lyon/Highland Road
Silver: W. Fox-Pitt/Steadfast

1988 Dijon

Team Gold
Clapham/Bowmanhill Crystal
Clear
Gifford/Smithstown Lad
Newman/Blackmore Money
Spinner

Bronze: Miss K. Gifford/
Smithstown Lad

PICTURE ACKNOWLEDGEMENTS

All photographs by Brian E Hill ABIPP/EVENTING MAGAZINE except:
Desmond O'Neill: Page 29
Peter Doresa/EVENTER: Pages 56/57, 58, 60/63, 65/67, 74, 75, 77
Dr J. M. Lloyd Parry: Page 165

The Publishers have made every attempt to contact the owners of the photographs appearing in this book. In the few instances where they have been unsuccessful they invite the copyright holders to contact them direct.

Design and illustrations by Victor Shreeve

INDEX

Italics refer to colour illustrations